Revival!
A people saturated with God

Revival!
A people saturated with God

Brian H. Edwards

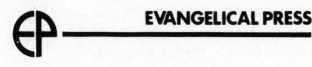

EVANGELICAL PRESS

EVANGELICAL PRESS
12 Wooler Street, Darlington, Co. Durham, DL1 1RQ, England

British Library Cataloguing in Publication Data
Edwards, Brian
    Revival!
    1. Christian church. Revivals
    I. Title
    269.24

ISBN 0 85234 273 X

Unless otherwise indicated, Scripture quotations in this publication are
from the Holy Bible, New International Version. Copyright © 1973, 1978,
1984 International Bible Society. Published by Hodder & Stoughton.

Printed in Great Britain by The Bath Press, Avon

To Stephen, Fiona and Andrew
with the prayer that their generation might
experience a people saturated with God.

Contents

Acknowledgements

I must express my sincere thanks to all who have made this book possible. Many have encouraged me to keep going, and in particular I am grateful to those who have so freely shared with me their own experiences of revival. The Evangelical Library in London has, once again, proved an invaluable resource, and the continued support for my writing of my own church, Hook Evangelical Church in Surbiton, has made it all possible. Special thanks must go to Jenny Wigginton, who invested many word-processing hours so willingly and efficiently, and to my wife, Barbara, who never wavers in support and in valuable criticism of my manuscripts. If our joint labours light a small flame for revival in the country, we shall all be more than rewarded.

Introduction

Howel Harris gave an account of the preaching of Daniel Rowland in Wales during March 1743: 'O! such power as generally attends the labours of brother Rowland, in particular, is indeed uncommon and almost incredible until one sees it himself. Their singing and praying is indeed full of God! O! how did my soul burn with sacred love when I was among them! They fall almost as dead by the power of the Word, and continue weeping for joy, having found the Messiah; some mourning under a sense of their vileness, and some in the pangs of the new birth! I am now in Pembrokeshire where Rowland has been preaching; he has been wonderfully attended with blessings in these borders also. The power at the conclusion of his sermons, was such that multitudes continued weeping and crying out for the Saviour and could not possibly forbear.'[1]

In 1858 John Girardeau was leading an evening service at his church in Charleston, North Carolina, when 'He received a sensation as if a bolt of electricity had struck his head and diffused itself through his whole body. For a little while he stood speechless under the strange physical feeling. Then he said: "The Holy Spirit has come; we will begin preaching tomorrow evening." He closed the service with a hymn, dismissed the congregation, and came down from the pulpit; but no one left the house. The whole congregation had quietly resumed its seat. Instantly he realized the situation. The Holy Spirit had not only come to him, He had also taken possession of the hearts of the people. Immediately he began exhorting them to accept the Gospel. They began to sob, softly, like the falling of rain; then, with deeper emotion, to weep bitterly, or to rejoice loudly, according to their circumstances. It was midnight before he could dismiss his congregation. A noted evangelist from the North, who was present, said, between his sobs, to an officer of the church: "I never saw it on this fashion." The meeting went on night and day for eight weeks.'[2]

During 1905 the pastor of Charlotte Chapel in Edinburgh visited Wales and when he related the story of God's great work in Wales to his own congregation a movement of the Spirit began there also. The following year a fresh wave of new life came to the church: 'It was at a late prayer meeting, held in the evening at 9.30, that the fire of God fell. There was nothing, humanly speaking, to account for what happened. Quite suddenly, upon one and another came an overwhelming sense of the reality and awfulness of His presence and of eternal things. Life, death, and eternity seemed suddenly laid bare. Prayer and weeping began, and gained in intensity every moment. As on the day of laying the foundation of the second temple, "the people could not discern the noise of the shouts of joy from the noise of the weeping of the people" (Ezra 3:13). One was overwhelmed before the sudden bursting of the bounds. Could it be real? We looked up and asked for clear directions, and all we knew of guidance was, "Do nothing." Friends who were gathered sang on their knees. Each seemed to sing, and each seemed to pray, oblivious of one another. Then the prayer broke out again, waves and waves of prayer; and the midnight hour was reached. The hours had passed like minutes. It is useless being a spectator looking on, or praying for it, in order to catch its spirit and breath. It is necessary to be in it, praying in it, part of it, caught by the same power, swept by the same wind. One who was present says: "I cannot tell you what Christ was to me last night. My heart was full to overflowing. If ever my Lord was near to me, it was last night."'[3]

A similar description is found of a church meeting in Malawi in 1910: 'An elder began to pray, confessing before all the sin of having cherished a spirit of revenge for an evil done him. Then another began to pray, and another and another, till two or three were praying together in a quiet voice, weeping and confessing, each one unconscious of the other. Suddenly there came the sound of "a rushing wind". It was the thrilling sound of two thousand five hundred people praying audibly, no man apparently conscious of the other. I could think of no better image to describe the noise than the rushing of wind through the trees. We were listening to the same sound as filled that upper room at Pentecost. Not noisy or discordant, it filled us with a great awe.'[4]

Duncan Campbell described a meeting in the Isle of Lewis, Scotland, during 1949: 'The lad rose to his feet and in his prayer made reference to the fourth chapter of Revelation, which he had been reading that morning: "O God, I seem to be gazing through the open door. I see the Lamb in the midst of the Throne, with the keys of death and of hell at his girdle." He began to sob; then lifting his eyes toward heaven, cried: "O God, there is power there, let it loose!" With the force of a hurricane the Spirit of God swept into the building and the floodgates of heaven opened. The church resembled a battlefield. On one side many were prostrated over the seats weeping and sighing; on the other side some were affected by throwing their arms in the air in a rigid posture. God had come.'[5]

Wales, North Carolina, Malawi and Scotland, from 1743 to 1949 — and yet a common theme runs through each account. Here is something unusual and powerful; it is God at work, but not in his normal way. Here are outpourings of the Holy Spirit that cannot be dismissed by talk of culture, psychological pressure or empty enthusiasm. We are reading the serious yet exciting stories of God in revival when the only response possible is an awesome: 'God has come.'

Introduction

Why this book?

A book must be judged on its intention, and I will need to justify adding yet another to the list of those already on revival. Generally speaking, books on this subject can be divided into two groups. There are those that deal with specific revivals in history; these are our most valuable source material, and the Christian churches owe a great debt to those who have carefully sifted history so that we can read accounts of what God has accomplished when he has come down to his church with unusual power. But secondly there are the books that analyse the whole subject of revival. Sometimes they are clinical and dry, even though they may be helpfully accurate. This group is more for the specialist, and what they rarely do is to create a heart-longing for God to do it again; perhaps a passing, wistful thought, or a few occasional prayers, but not a heart-longing.

It is the creation of this heart-longing that is the intention of this book. A few decades ago prayer and talk amongst evangelicals on the subject of revival were both commonplace. In more recent years the word 'revival' has been moved down as a poor relation to the vogue words, 'restoration' and 'renewal'. That is simply a matter of fact, however you wish to interpret it. What is perhaps most worrying is that many today confuse revival with 'a touch from the Spirit' (which we must never despise), and with Christian enthusiasm or extravagance. There are even those who believe they have something better than revival; but this betrays a poor knowledge of the history of God at work in his church. There can be nothing better on earth than a true Holy Spirit revival and, sadly, it is doubtful whether in the United Kingdom today anyone is experiencing such a thing. This book intends to show what true revival is.

As a nation we have reached a very low ebb spiritually and therefore morally, and the church has very little effect on the lives of the great majority; they hardly know we exist. To cover our weakness and ineffectiveness we have taken a number of alternative routes. Many hide behind the façade of excitement and activity, keeping congregations high on promises and pretence. In addition, for two decades now we have been arranging ever more elaborate missions and conferences; they are very impressive, and the sheer weight of work and preparation takes our minds off the reality of our lack of success and the absence of the presence of God.

Spurgeon, the great preacher of the last century, told the story of a small church in the United States that decided to halt its decline in numbers by purchasing an impressive chandelier for the sanctuary. The first Sunday it was in place, the church building was packed with local people; the second Sunday only the regular few gathered. Everyone had seen the chandelier and it was not worth a second visit!

Twenty years ago *The Daily Telegraph* commented that evangelicals were known for their 'showmanship and uplifting entertainment', and, sadly, we still are. Even where numbers are increasing we have little cause for satisfaction. We are hardly reducing the millions who are careless of God; the spiritual life of our churches is generally low and the quality of our righteousness is rarely an embarrassment to the world. Of course, we have some large Sunday morning congregations dotted around the country where the pew fodder sits gazing round the hundreds and concluding that Christianity in the U.K. is doing well. But let them slip out into the sunshine for a few minutes and watch the thousands of families crawling round the M.25 in search of their chosen exit to a day's happiness;

in the light of this the congregation will look far less impressive at the next glance.

On the other hand, another escape route has been to immerse ourselves in the social needs of the nation. Of course, our care for issues of poverty, homelessness, abortion, embryology, pornography and keeping Sunday special is to be commended, but the danger is that these things can keep us busily away from the real issue of seeking God. One exasperated editorial commented upon the meeting of the World Council of Churches in Canada in 1983. Having inconsistently voted down a motion demanding the immediate withdrawal of Russian troops from Afghanistan, the Council then overwhelmingly carried a motion condemning America's involvement in Central America. The editorial concluded: 'The clerics who attend these protracted jamborees — mercifully only held every seven years — seem more concerned to woo the Third World than prepare fallen humanity to face the next.' We can smile smugly, but how much evangelical social involvement is a cover for our failure to prepare this fallen society for the world to come?

Alternatively, to cover our powerlessness we enter the world of marketing and management. Christian leaders are constantly badgered by books and conferences that will help them to increase their leadership skills, their management control and the size of their churches. All this is not necessarily wrong; in fact it will almost always guarantee some degree of growth, but still we are avoiding the real issue: where is God?

For all our excessive noise, extravagant claims and efficient administration, the world around us is not aware that we exist. God is not felt among his people. And the tragedy is that, by and large, we don't seem to care. And even some of those who do care have come to the despondent conclusion that nothing can change it: these are days of hard work and small returns and there we must let the matter rest.

Others read the handbooks that tell us around seven per cent of the population of the United Kingdom are evangelical Christians. That sounds, and is, an impressive figure, and so we sit comfortably thinking that all is not so bad. Unfortunately the figure is optimistic nonsense! Where is the factory, workshop, office, classroom, college, or street where seven out of every hundred people are evangelical Christians? I live in a borough of 132,000 inhabitants and I think I know most of the evangelical fellowships and churches among all the denominations; I also have an idea of the numbers that will be found worshipping among them each Sunday and it is hard to get much above one and a half per cent! And this is the so-called 'Bible-belt' of the south-east! I have discussed these statistics with Christians living in other towns, particularly in the north, where little more than a handful of believers meet week by week, and it would be difficult to muster one per cent of the population in the evangelical community. I know of one missionary who, during the 1970s, visited every home in a particular town in the north-east with a population of 80,000. He found only six evangelical Christian families; that is 0.015% ! How the figure of seven per cent was ever arrived at I do not know, but if it is accurate, then most evangelical Christians in the United Kingdom are unrecognizable during the week and keep well out of the way of Christian fellowship on Sunday — and for that reason alone the church would desperately need reviving! It is time we lived in the real world and not the world of over-optimistic statistics.

But this book is certainly not written to depress the discouraged. On the contrary, it is written for those who are honest enough, whatever their evangelical label, to admit that we are making little impact on our nation and that God is not seen and felt to be among us. When the psalmist realized this and faced up to reality, he decided upon a definite course of action; he looked back to what God had done in the past:

'I thought about the former days,
    the years of long ago;
I remembered my songs in the night.
    My heart mused and my spirit enquired...
Then I thought, "To this I will appeal:
    the years of the right hand of the Most High."
I will remember the deeds of the Lord;
    yes, I will remember your miracles of long ago.
I will meditate on all your works
    and consider all your mighty deeds'

(Ps. 77:5-6, 10-12).

At a time like this there are two things that Christians ought to be doing. First, we should be studying our Bibles to find out what God has to say on the subject of revival and, second, we should be searching into our history to discover what God has done in the past. I believe the result of those two things must drive us to prayer.

My plan is a simple one. From both Scripture and history I want to introduce revival to those who may never have read much on the subject. I have not set out to write a classic analysis of revival; that has been ably done already, from the many detailed accounts available, to the wide sweeps of John Gillies' *Historical Collections of Accounts of Revival* (1754) and William Sprague's *Lectures on Revivals of Religion* (1832). There are the more modern assessments by Edwin Orr, who stands unequalled in the vast treasure he has left us of what God has been doing in the world. The heart-cry of Martyn Lloyd-Jones in the book of his sermons on *Revival*, as well as the biblical challenge of Arthur Wallis in *In the Day of Thy Power*, should be read by all who have an interest in the subject. All these and more, though very different from each other, are vital contributions to the literature of the churches today.

But not everyone has the time or even the motivation to view either the detail or the panorama. Few Christians in our churches have read even one small book on the subject of revival, and that *must* be changed if God is to hear a cry for him to 'do it again'. One of the facts we shall learn about revival is that it is contagious: the story of a revival there often excites people to long for it here. But a contagion does not spread without contact! In this book I want to help you 'touch' the heart of true revival. It will be impossible to cover, or even refer to, all the accounts of revival in the history of the church — even if anyone knew them all! We must be content here to be introduced to the broad canvas of revival, from the well-known and well-documented eighteenth-century 'Awakening' to those little-known and more localized events that are none the less real. I have chosen revivals widely separated from each other historically, geographically and culturally.

The reader will soon become aware that the same revivals are referred to again and again to illustrate various themes. This is deliberate. In the first place, regular reference will fix the revival in our minds, whereas a passing 'one-off' reference would probably be forgotten at once. But it is also my purpose to show those features that are common to revivals, wherever they occur; merely to pick out the unusual or the occasional will hardly prove a point. By constant reference to a limited number of revivals we can show that if you were to take half a dozen revivals across the world and history at random, you would find certain features common to them all. It is these common factors that not only prove a revival is from God, but should give us reason to long for God to bring revival in our time.

Sadly, the story of revival in our books rarely begins much before the eighteenth century. This gives a distorted view of the history of the church because it implies that there were no revivals before that time. But this is certainly not the case. A movement of God began in the fourteenth century and ran right through to the seventeenth. Those 300 years were the most dramatic in the history of Europe. They marked a widespread return to New Testament Christianity and the authority of Scripture which we refer to as 'the Reformation'. A reformation is only different from revival if it is imposed by the 'authorities', and against the wishes of the people; in which case it is therefore not a 'people's movement'. But the Reformation of the sixteenth century *was* a people's movement. Through its notable leaders, the whole of Europe was stirred.

But even before the Reformation, as far back as the twelfth century, Peter Waldo of Lyons sent out his preachers, across France, Flanders, Germany, Poland, Bohemia, Austria and Hungary. As a result of this gospel preaching, the Waldensians (a people in the Piedmont valleys whose history and faith goes back to apostolic days), spread at such a rate that they covered vast areas of the continent. Two by two the preachers travelled central and eastern Europe and then beyond, until hundreds of thousands shifted their allegiance from the formal and dead church of the day to Christ himself. So far-flung was the Waldensian movement that it is said the missionaries could travel from Cologne in Germany to Florence in Italy, a distance of nearly 600 miles as the crow flies, and stay every night at the home of one of the brethren.[6] One historian has called the sending out of these 'Poor men of Lyons', 'the most remarkable missionary movement that has ever occured'. By 1592, when Henry IV of France made a treaty with the churches in the Piedmont valleys, it was stated that the Protestants outnumbered the Catholics in the proportion of one hundred to one. That must be called revival. But how many evangelicals have ever heard of it?

In England at the end of the fourteenth century, John Wycliffe led a team of Bible translators, and his 'Poor Preachers', or

Lollards, went throughout the country with their handwritten copies of the Bible in English. So successful were they that over a century later one of the greatest opponents of evangelicalism, Sir Thomas More, was compelled to admit: 'You cannot meet two men on the road but one of them is a Wycliffite.' Allowing for some exaggeration to show his alarm and disgust, this complaint reveals a revival of true Christianity among the people. The eager hands that received William Tyndale's printed New Testament in English in 1526 were part of a new wave of revival. Over the next ten years the Bible, at that time a book outlawed by the authorities, was smuggled across the country, sold by the thousands, and reached poor and rich alike. At last even King Henry VIII, having filled his prisons with Christians, despaired of stemming the tide and gave the Bible his royal licence!

If only we had more detailed records, it might well be found that the revival during the early part of the Reformation was as great as that 300 years later. At least no evangelicals were burnt at the stake in the time of Whitefield and Wesley. Our difficulty is that although we have access to many contemporary records of the early Reformation period, they are almost entirely official documents and personal letters of the leaders. What we do not have in detail is the account of the movement of the Spirit in the lives of thousands of ordinary people. None of them kept records; few of them could even write and the age of diary-keeping was still some 200 years away. For this reason it is hard to be excited about the Reformation revival because colour is missing from the picture. But to think of the Reformation only as a reformation of theology is a great mistake. All over Europe God was stirring the people, and vast numbers were brought to a joyful salvation. Men like Wycliffe in England, Jan Hus in Bohemia (Czechoslovakia) and Gerhard Groote in Holland were undoubtedly leaders of a revival among the people. In the long history of the church, revival is not as rare as we may imagine, and the vantage-point of eternity may show that there has never been a time in the story of the church when, somewhere in the world, God has not been powerfully at work by his Spirit in a supernormal way. But because the detail is missing, most of our illustrations have to be confined to the past 200 years.

I have set out to bring you into contact with revival. And to do this, I have chosen one great story of revival in the Bible and illustrated its themes by small flash-cards of history. In this way we can admire some of the detail and some of the panorama at once, and it will not take us long. In a few chapters we can grasp what God teaches us about revival in his Word, which is always the wisest place to start, and at the same time see how he has done it again and again through the story of the church.

Throughout this book I have quoted, often at some length, from the records of revivals which occurred long ago, and the language of past centuries may occasionally jar on the modern reader. Never mind, keep going! The language you and I speak and write today will sound strange in a hundred years! I have not attempted to update the language of an eighteenth-century Jonathan Edwards.

I have chosen a very simple way of covering the subject of revival. In three main sections we will look at the events *before* revival, the events *during* revival, and the immediate and lasting results *after* revival; though this third part contains some material that might as accurately be included in the second.

I hope that this introduction to God's great and remarkable work in the past will begin to create in us a holy dissatisfaction with our present condition, and a longing for things to be different — but different in God's way. I make no pretence that this book breaks new ground; I am content to reap from other men's fields. I have been ransacking history to discover where God has been at work in revival. Of course, he is at work apart from revival, and we must not despise whatever he is doing, but our subject here is revival. There is a whole generation growing up who are strangers to revival even by report, and when the word 'revival' is mentioned, they will have a very inadequate idea of what we really mean. I want to go a little way to change that. If we are to be moved by the stories of spiritual revival, we must read about them and know what revival really is. Perhaps the greatest problem with this subject today is that few Christians have ever read anything about revival. Consequently, when half a dozen people are converted, or we have a crowded meeting, or we hear a powerful sermon, or even plan a mission, we think we have revival.

To encourage Christians to pray for revival when they don't know what it is would be like inviting me to take a holiday on Mars. The idea leaves me completely cold! I have no interest in such an invitation because the little that I think I know about Mars does not attract me to the idea of a holiday there. To convince me, you will have to demonstrate that Mars is the most wonderful place where anyone could spend a holiday, that it far exceeds anything I could possibly have experienced in my normal holidays here on earth, and that I must go there at all costs. Only when I am convinced will I sign up! It is the purpose of this book to do that with revival. I want to show you that it is the most wonderful thing that can happen to the church on earth, that it far exceeds the very best that we think we have in this country today, and that we must go for it at all costs.

Towards the end of the book I have included five short word-pictures of revival. They are all of revivals that have taken place this century, three in Britain and two abroad. Each is compiled from an eyewitness account and all but one are by people who are still living. I have not edited the accounts to bring them into line with the rest of the book, nor have I added to them from my own reading elsewhere about those revivals. They stand as personal and eyewitness impressions of what happens when God saturates his people with his presence. These cameos of revival may help to offset one particular weakness in this book. It is written by someone who has never personally been involved in community revival. In reading about and talking to those who have, I am well aware that some of the things I write of have to be experienced to be understood fully. This does not make the retelling of them irrelevant, any more than sermons on heaven are irrelevant, but it does remind us that a true Holy Spirit revival is far more wonderful than anything a printer's page can convey.

One correspondent from the Khassi Hills in India in 1905 commented: 'The great things of the Revival cannot be recorded, men can only describe the commonplace events. It is necessary to come into touch with the Spirit's power in order to see and feel what the work is; many scenes are too holy, too sacred to be even described, and yet God wants us to make known His power, and so glorify His name. Those who write, do so in the hope that even an imperfect account may be blessed by God to rouse the interest and expectations of men and get them to feel their need of, and to plead for a similar blessing.'[7]

It is not my intention to defend revival from its critics. Revival does not need a defence; it needs to be experienced. Nor is it my intention to explain some of those aspects of revival that remain strange and mysterious — the unusual things or 'phenomena' of revival. Some things are clearly wrong because they are contrary to Scripture, and since God never acts in contradiction to his Word, we can safely say they are wrong, whatever else may seem to be right. Other things are excessive, and some are just strange because they are unusual. Occasionally it is hard to make a judgement at all because too much time separates us from the event and we have insufficient evidence. One thing is certain: we must not despise a genuine work of God and refuse it the title of revival just because some things were encouraged of which we, by our tradition, would strongly disapprove. It is equally important to make it clear that for excitable people, who love to be thrilled by the unusual and the spectacular, there will be no true revival as long as they are seeking those things. Revival comes when Christians are longing for God, and God alone.

I may not be mistaken in thinking that there is a breeze of change blowing gently today. I detect a gathering renewal of interest in the subject of revival, even where you might least expect it. Of course, some have never lost their longing or crying for revival, though it has been hard for them to maintain their desire in the face of what has been going on recently. Over the past two decades there has been a lot of noise and zeal and enthusiasm, often a lot of heat without much light; as one canny Highlander expressed it in prayer: 'Lord it must hae grieved yer hairt tae see sae much o'the steam blowin' oot thro' the whistle that should hae gang tae the piston.' On the other hand, there has also been far too much sterile correctness. And those who think they stand between the two have not had much to boast about either! If you put us all together, whatever hue and cry we have made as evangelicals, we have not made much impact upon this nation. But there is a growing momentum among those who believe there is a better way forward.

Any interest in spiritual revival must be a reflection of the state of the church. It must be healthy when we begin to realize where we are, and compare it with where we ought to be and could be. If we are beginning, or in the case of some are continuing, to long for something better, then that must be a good thing. The purpose of this book is not to be controversial but encouraging. There are many differences amongst evangelicals today, but a longing for revival is a great leveller. And a longing for revival with a knowledge of scriptural example and historical precedent could prove to be a great force for uniting those who are unnecessarily divided. The best thing for the church today would be for us to stop trying to outdo one another with our claims, and to admit that we are *all* lacking the felt presence and the power of God, and then to leave our secondary differences aside and together cry to God for revival.

Count Nikolaus Ludwig of Zinzendorf recounted the events of that incredible morning in the life of the Herrnhut community in Saxony on Wednesday, 13 August 1727. It was a day when God came down and left the members 'hardly knowing whether they belong to earth or had already gone to heaven'. What preceded it? Zinzendorf tells us that the congregation which had been bitterly divided and quarrelsome on such issues as baptism, church government and prophecy, 'were all dissatisfied with themselves. They had quit judging each other because they had become convinced, each one, of his lack of worth in the sight of God...'⁸ A true understanding of revival will inevitably lead to this, and whatever else follows — in their case earnest and serious prayer — it must be good for the church and the glory of God.

Therefore the intention of this book is to inform the mind and inflame the heart. If, at the end, we are a little more knowledgeable about the subject, and a little wiser about what we are asking for, and what dangers we should be on guard against, then only a small part of its purpose will have been served. On the other hand, if the book serves to awaken a holy dissatisfaction with where we are, create an agony of longing for God to come and prompt us to pray that God will be glorified in revival, then the intention will have been adequately fulfilled.

> 'Restore us again, O God our Saviour,
>   and put away your displeasure towards us.
> Will you be angry with us for ever?
>   Will you prolong your anger through all generations?
> Will you not revive us again,
>   that your people may rejoice in you?
> Show us your unfailing love, O Lord,
>   and grant us your salvation'
>
>   (Ps. 85:4-7).

Introduction

What is revival?

Edwin Orr, one of our greatest authorities on the subject of revival, reported having seen two churches in a town in America both advertising revival meetings. One displayed a board saying, 'Revival here every Monday night,' whilst the other promised: 'Revival here every night except Monday'! If nothing else, that reminds us how loosely the word has been used. In America it has often been used in place of the word 'mission' or 'campaign'. It is something a church arranges, men organize, and God may or may not bless it. But on this side of the Atlantic the word 'revival' has been displaced by words like 'renewal' and 'restoration'. Many who use these words see them as a modern equivalent of 'revival'. Of course, people are entitled to give words the meanings that they want to — that is how language changes over the years — but unless we are careful in our definitions, effective communication becomes impossible. For my part I am quite happy for Christians to use 'renewal' and 'restoration' in whatever way they wish. This book is about something far, far bigger; and if you stay with me, you will see what I mean. Because of our modern-day meanings, 'renewal', 'restoration' and 'reformation' should never be used as synonyms for 'revival'. 'Revival' swallows up all other words as the shark swallows the shrimp. So, historically, what does the word 'revival' refer to?

The church historian James Buchanan defined revival as 'the imparting of life to those who are dead, and the imparting of health to those who are dying'. But that does not take us far enough. Jonathan Edwards, who saw revival in his church in America 250 years ago, explained it as 'God's major means of extending his kingdom', and more recently Edwin Orr defined these outpourings of the Spirit as a 'movement of the Holy Spirit bringing about a revival of New Testament Christianity in the church of Christ and its related community'. One thing is clear: almost as soon as you try to *define* the word revival, you find yourself *describing* what a revival is. This at least shows that revival is nothing theoretical. It is certainly not a theological idea for academics and historians to play with; revival is intensely practical and it always has cata-strophic results for the church. Duncan Campbell, who was himself involved in revival this century, described it simply as 'a community saturated with God', and I am not sure that we shall ever get closer to the heart of it than that.

Let Duncan Campbell speak a little more on this. He is describ-ing revival as he witnessed it in the Western Isles of Scotland between 1949 and 1952: 'In writing of the movement, I would like first to state what I mean by revival as witnessed in the Hebrides. I do not mean a time of religious entertainment, with crowds gather-ing to enjoy an evening of bright gospel singing; I do not mean sensational or spectacular advertising — in a God-sent revival you do not need to spend money on advertising. I do not mean high-pressure methods to get men to an inquiry room — in revival every service is an inquiry room; the road and hill side become sacred spots to many when the winds of God blow. Revival is a going of God among his people, and an awareness of God laying hold of the community. Here we see the difference between a successful campaign and revival; in the former we may see many brought to a saving knowledge of the truth, and the church or mission experi-ence a time of quickening, but so far as the town or district is concerned no real change is visible; the world goes on its way and the dance and picture-shows are still crowded: but in revival the fear of God lays hold upon the community, moving men and women, who until then had no concern for spiritual things, to seek after God.'[9]

Charles Haddon Spurgeon experienced a continuous revival in his church in London for many years in the middle of last century and he was convinced that 'A true revival is to be looked for in the church of God.' In other words, revival begins with the church and spills over into the world. Those who look for revival just as a short-cut to get unbelieving masses into the church must think again. It always begins by getting Christians right first, and, as we shall see, this can be very painful. In December 1866 Spurgeon explained in his magazine *The Sword and the Trowel* what revival is: 'To be revived is a blessing which can only be enjoyed by those who have some degree of life. Those who have no spiritual life are not, and cannot be, in the strictest sense of the term subjects of a revival...A true revival is to be looked for in the Church of God.'[10]

Preaching at the Keswick Convention in 1922, Douglas Brown, who was used in a revival the year before, rightly maintained: 'Revival is a church word; it has to do with God's people. You cannot revive the world; the world is dead in trespasses and sins; you cannot revive a corpse. But you can revitalize where there is life...'[11]

Evan Roberts made the same claim in Wales in 1904: 'My mission is first to the churches. When the churches are aroused to their duty, men of the world will be swept into the Kingdom. A whole church on its knees is irresistible.'[12] Revival always brings the church to its knees. Rhys Bevan Jones, who preached in Wales throughout 1904, declared that if ever there was a slogan for that revival it was this: 'Bend the church, and save the people.'[13]

It is also true that we should never refer to a revival as 'a revival of religion'. There have been many 'revivals of religion' both within Christianity and in other world faiths. The Tractarian Movement of 150 years ago was a 'revival of religion' in the loosest possible sense. But it was not a spiritual awakening, merely the re-establishing of high church ritual and ceremony. A true revival begins always with those who are believers in New Testament Christianity and, as Edwin Orr wisely reminds us, 'more particularly those who had enjoyed the New Testament experience of conversion and regeneration'.[14] Revival is therefore an evangelical experience; it is an 'evangelical awakening'.

In searching for a biblical definition and description of revival it is commonplace to use the account in Acts chapter 2. However, we must not forget that in some ways the story of the Holy Spirit coming to the early Christians at Pentecost is unique. This is not to say that it has nothing to teach on the subject; on the contrary, there has never been a community so saturated with God as those 120 Christians in the upper room. But the uniqueness of that story is that they did not start where the church finds itself today. Pentecost was not a reviving of what was dying, nor a cleansing of what had become polluted by the world. The disciples were not commanded to wait in Jerusalem until they received repentance or forgiveness or revival. There was only one thing the Christians had to wait for, and that was power to carry out their Lord's command to go and witness to the world (Acts 1:8). Revival is not primarily to give the church power, though it certainly does this, but to give it life. There is a world of difference. In one sense the church had no history before Pentecost. In Acts 2 the church was not restored to where it ought to have been and from where it had fallen, but it was the starting-point of the new covenant church. So the story of Acts will certainly describe the effects of a community 'saturated with God', but it cannot tell us all we need to know on the subject.

I turn instead, to the Old Testament for our example of revival. And I do this on the basis that the same Holy Spirit was at work then as now. Though Pentecost saw an outpouring of the Spirit in a new way, we cannot doubt that men of faith in the Old Testament had also received the gift of the Spirit and could experience true faith, repentance, assurance and new birth. Without this it would be impossible to explain the spiritual strength, faith and power of many whose stories make up a large part of our Old Testament.

The example I have chosen is the revival that took place during the reign of Hezekiah, King of Judah. His story is well told in three places in the Old Testament: 2 Kings 18-20; 2 Chronicles 29-32 and Isaiah 36-39. In 2 Chronicles 29:36 we have a description of the revival: 'Hezekiah and all the people rejoiced at what God had brought about for his people, because it was done so quickly.' That marks it as a revival. Many definitions and descriptions of revival have been offered but I would elaborate it like this: a true Holy Spirit revival is a remarkable increase in the spiritual life of a large number of God's people, accompanied by an awesome awareness of the presence of God, intensity of prayer and praise, a deep conviction of sin with a passionate longing for holiness and unusual effectiveness in evangelism, leading to the salvation of many unbelievers.

Revival is remarkable, large, effective and, above all, it is something that *God* brings about. It is quite impossible for man to create revival. Though men may prepare and pray for it, revival is the work of the sovereign God, not primarily for the benefit of his people, but for his own honour and glory. Commenting upon Acts 2:1, 'when the day of Pentecost came,' Arthur Wallis claims: 'Every genuine revival is clearly stamped with the hallmark of divine sovereignty, and in no way is this more clearly seen than in the time factor. The moment for that first outpouring of the Spirit was not determined by the believers in the upper room but by God, who had foreshadowed it centuries before in those wonderful types of the Old Testament.'[15]

Looking back on revival you can only claim it was something God had brought about. If there is any other explanation for it then it is not a revival. To quote Duncan Campbell once more, 'Revival is a community saturated with God.' There is no better way to explain or describe it.

This suddenness is a typical feature of revival. What happened in the time of Hezekiah was 'done so quickly' and the same was true 700 years later when, on the day of Pentecost, 'Suddenly a sound like the blowing of a violent wind came from heaven and filled the whole house… '(Acts 2:2). No matter how long people have been praying for it or expecting it, when it comes it is always a surprise.

When God came to the north of Korea in January 1907 it was on the Monday following a particularly formal and weary Sunday; the missionaries and national Christians longed for revival, but it hardly seemed that this would or could be the time.[16]

In 1859 God moved in a powerful way across Great Britain. At Broughshane, a village four miles from Ballymena in Northern Ireland, it was May when the revival began; the Presbyterian minister in the village, Archibald Robinson, records that 'We had been praying for and expecting some such precious blessing, but were taken by surprise, so sudden, powerful, and extraordinary were the manifestations of the Spirit's presence.'[17]

In revival things happen suddenly and unexpectedly. Meetings are lengthened, crowds gather, and sermons have to be preached, not because it is all arranged in advance, but because God is at work. People will arrive without warning for a meeting, moved by an unseen hand. Isaiah described such a time when God did 'awesome things that we did not expect, you came down and the mountains trembled before you' (Isa. 64:3). In revival God takes over; it is his sovereign work. At Herrnhut in 1727, Zinzendorf acknowledged, 'Hitherto *we* had been the leaders and helpers. Now the Holy Spirit himself took full control of everything and everybody.'[18] Revivals are never publicized in advance; they cannot be, because God chooses the time. A revival that is proclaimed in advance and arranged ahead of time is not a true revival. Again and again in the story of the church we discover that revival surprises the people of God; this is exactly what happened in the time of Hezekiah.

However, there is little that is new in revival. All the elements we discover in revival, whether in the Bible or in the story of the church, are present in the normal life of the church. The church prays, repents, worships and evangelizes. It ceases to be the church without these things, but in revival they are heightened and intensified. I refer to the 'normal life of the church' deliberately. Revival is not normal any more than spiritual decline and backsliding are normal. These are opposite ends of the normal life of the church. Revival is supernormal and backsliding is subnormal. So we rarely find new things in revival. Where there are unusual things, I would call them the phenomena of revival. The main difference between the normal life of the church and revival is that in revival you find the old things with new life. The church should always pray and preach, Christians should always long for holiness and seek for-giveness and witness to their faith. These are the main ingredients in revival but they are nothing new. What is new is the *way* the Christians pray and preach, seek after holiness and forgiveness and witness to their faith. In revival there is remarkable life and power that cannot be explained adequately in any human terms. Christians do everything at a different level in revival.

God expects his people to be doing constantly those things that, in revival, he will take up and use in a quite unexpected way; but we must never imagine that we can create a revival simply by imitating those elements that accompany revival. We cannot manufacture revival any more than a schoolboy can make a masterpiece by copying a Constable. On the other hand, we can react too strongly against the theology of man-made revival, and have sometimes done so, and there is a reason for this. There were great revivals in America in the eighteenth and nineteenth centuries and then they began to fade. The American characteristic was to stir up the enthusiasm and keep it going; that is the American temperament. The Englishman lets the fire go out, shovels a spade of earth on top, and settles down for the long wait before the next spontaneous ignition! But the American does not; he decides that he is going to keep this good thing going. And who can blame him for that desire? Before we are critical of the man-made approach to revival, we should at least admire it, because it is the right spirit, even if it is quite the wrong theology and practice! What happens is that some try to relight the fire themselves; their theology tells them they can. This is quite contrary to Scripture; revival is something *God* brings about.

An American evangelist in the nineteenth century, Charles Finney, firmly believed that revivals could be produced by following a set of rules. He followed his own rules and was very effective. There was a great movement and many lives were changed, but how far it was a true revival is a subject the historians still argue about. That story by Edwin Orr of the two church notice-boards sums up the sad efforts of men. Of course, it betrays a wrong understanding of true revival, but we can over-react. We can come to the conclusion that we can do nothing for revival but pray. But I want to stress that there is more that we can do, namely that we must prepare the way by demonstrating to God that we are serious in wanting revival. Generally speaking, God will not do anything for those who will not do anything. He says simply, 'You do not have, because you do not ask' (James 4:2). And we shall never seriously want revival unless we know what it is. Hence this book!

Some things seem to be essential if we are to demonstrate our seriousness for God; there are preparations that we can make, but we must be careful to distinguish between the things that are essential in our preparation for revival, and the things that almost always accompany revival. For example, it cannot be doubted that both prayer and singing accompany almost all revivals, but whereas prayer is an indispensable pre-condition of God meeting with his people, singing is not. Historically the church has prayed its way to the outpouring of God's Holy Spirit, but it can never sing its way into revival. Sometimes the days and conditions are too serious for over-much singing, and crying is the only way. However, when God comes, singing is inevitable.

Lloyd-Jones makes the same point when he comments about the characteristics of revival preparation: 'There is no time for singing, it is time for thinking, for preaching, for conviction. It is a time for proclaiming the message of God and his wrath upon evil, and all our foolish aberrations. The time for singing will come later. Let the great revival come, let the windows of heaven be opened, let us see men and women by the thousands brought into the Kingdom of God, and then it will be time to sing.'[19]

Peterus Octavianus, from the Indonesian Missionary Fellowship, who was greatly used by God in the revival in Borneo in 1973, did not preach an easy message. It was claimed that he had no time for frills or gimmicks, and he made it clear that 'Revivals do not begin happily with everyone having a good time. They start with a broken and contrite heart.' One contemporary report reminded its readers that the church in Borneo did not need 'an upsurge of bright gatherings or an emotional binge, but repentance, confession and the forsaking of sin'.[20]

This subject is therefore a serious one. It may be the most serious that any Christian could be reading about in these days. There is something that God can do which few of us have ever seen. We may have felt his touch and experienced a little of his presence, but there is more — much more. In the beginning, 'Mist came up from the earth and watered the whole surface of the ground' (Gen. 2:6, NIV footnote). But the results were very different when 'the floodgates of the heavens were opened'! (Gen. 7:11). Nothing should fully satisfy us on earth until our community is 'saturated with God'.

2.
Before revival

Before revival

The state of the church and the nation

We are introduced to Hezekiah as a young man of twenty-five around the year 716 B. C. We know nothing about his earlier years except that his father was Ahaz and his mother was Abijah, but we do know the life of his father Ahaz, because it is well recorded for us. He was a godless man and so was the age in which he lived. You will get a flavour of it simply by reading 2 Kings 17:40-41: 'They would not listen, however, but persisted in their former practices. Even while these people were worshipping the Lord, they were serving their idols. To this day their children and grandchildren continue to do as their fathers did.'

There had been a steady decline for many generations, and in the time of Hezekiah's father things seem to have hit bottom: 'Ahaz...walked in the ways of the kings of Israel and also made cast idols for worshipping the Baals. He burned sacrifices in the Valley of Ben Hinnom and sacrificed his sons in the fire, following the detestable ways of the nations that the Lord had driven out before the Israelites. He offered sacrifices and burned incense at the high places, on the hilltops and under every spreading tree...King Ahaz became even more unfaithful to the Lord. He offered sacrifices to the gods of Damascus, who had defeated him; for he thought, "Since the gods of the kings of Aram have helped them, I will sacrifice to them so that they will help me."...Ahaz gathered together the furnishings from the temple of God and took them away. He shut the doors of the Lord's temple and set up altars at every street corner in Jerusalem. In every town in Judah he built high places to burn sacrifices to other gods and provoked the Lord, the God of his fathers, to anger...Ahaz rested with his fathers and was buried in the city of Jerusalem, but he was not placed in the tombs of the kings of Israel. And Hezekiah his son succeeded him as king' (2 Chron. 28:1-4, 22-27).

It was a generation of godless rejection of the Word of God. That was the situation Hezekiah inherited. Religious life was at a low ebb, the temple was closed and true worship was gone. The greatest sins that could be committed by Judah were being committed, including the child-sacrifice, to the god Moloch, of some of Hezekiah's brothers. As a result, Judah had suffered humiliating defeats by Aram, Israel, Edom and the Philistines. The fortunes of Judah were at a desperately low ebb. The prophet Isaiah was on the stage of Judah at this time, and he had no doubt at all about the condition of the nation:

> 'Ah, sinful nation,
>   a people loaded with guilt,
> a brood of evildoers,
>   children given to corruption!
> They have forsaken the Lord;
>   they have spurned the Holy One of Israel
>   and turned their backs on him...
> From the sole of your foot to the top of your head
>   there is no soundness —
> only wounds and bruises
>   and open sores,
> not cleansed or bandaged
>   or soothed with oil.
> Your country is desolate...'

(Isa. 1:4, 6, 7).

Isaiah has much to say to the nations around Judah, but much more to say to Judah herself. We have a habit, when dealing with the Old

Testament prophets, of comparing the state of Judah and Israel with the conditions in our own nation, but that is to miss the mark entirely. In the days of the prophets, Judah represented the people belonging to God, the church. It is the prophets' messages to the surrounding nations that are appropriate to our own secular society. We have a strange inconsistency in the way we gladly take the *promises* of the prophets to Israel and Judah and apply them to the church, and then take the *judgements* of the prophets and apply them to the world! That is neither biblical nor honest. In fact, to be accurate, we should apply the preaching of the prophets to Judah to the true church of Christ today, and their ministry to Israel to the apostate, though professing Christian church. It is their message to the nations that we can apply to the unbelieving world around us. If this is done, we are forced to accept the larger part of Isaiah's preaching for the state of the church today. That is where it hurts.

In Isaiah 62 the prophet declares that he would go on preaching until the city that is now indistinguishable from the surrounding nations becomes 'a crown of splendour in the Lord's hand' (v.3) and her righteousness becomes so attractive that the nations long for it (v.2), and until 'her righteousness shines out like the dawn, her salvation like a blazing torch' (v.1). Tragically the city was unholy and deserted (v.12). Whilst the prophet may well have preached chapter 62 some time after the revival years of Hezekiah, when a fresh revival was needed, certainly the same conditions were true in the time of the new king.

There will be no hope for revival until the evangelical churches of our nation recognize and admit that Isaiah is preaching to us. Outwardly there may be many good things in the churches today, but beneath it all there is the rottenness of worldliness, carelessness, a lack of deep commitment and a triviality about holy things. Our churches are divided and quarrelsome; our leaders are proud of their reputations and hard-working to build their own empires. Generally speaking, Christians think and behave like the world and are afraid to act differently. And, as we noted earlier, in spite of our pretence to the contrary, we are hardly making any impact upon our society, and our churches are not growing vigorously by regular, life-changing conversions. Of course, some churches are growing and some sinners are being converted, but by and large we have become expert at simply shuffling the pack as dissatisfied or grumbling Christians move from church to church. Revival is not when the churches exchange members, but when the Holy Spirit changes lives. Revival is needed, not because of the state of the world, but because of the state of the church. Only when we realize this can there be any hope of God sending us revival. When God came to the Congo (Zaïre) in 1953 it was two months before large numbers of people were being saved. But those two months were a painful time for the church!

Today we are good at analysing the nation around us. We can catalogue the sins of Edom and Moab, Syria and Assyria, Egypt and Babylon; we even know what is wrong with Israel, that apostate church that hardly knows what it believes. But God's finger points at Judah. Isaiah was preaching in the days of Hezekiah's great-grandfather, grandfather and father, and Hezekiah was listening when it came to his own turn. He might have found it all rather depressing as Isaiah tore the church apart, but the king soon realized that the prophet had not come to blow bubbles, but to burst them! We fool ourselves into thinking that our churches shine like the dawn and blaze like a torch, whilst in reality many of them are in almost total eclipse. The world has effectively snuffed out our light. Our Lord never knocks at the door of the unbeliever's life, but he does plead with his people. 'Come now, let us reason together' (Isa. 1:18) is God's invitation to his people. 'Behold, I stand at the door, and knock' (Rev. 3:20, AV) is never spoken to the soul dead in sin, but to the local church that should be alive for God, but is distastefully lukewarm. Most of our churches are like Laodicea.

Before God came down in power at Cambuslang and Kilsyth in Scotland in 1742, spiritual life was at a very low ebb. Two faithful ministers were preaching, William McCulloch at Cambuslang and James Robe at Kilsyth, but for years they had seen very little fruit for their hard work. Neither man was greatly gifted in public speaking, and McCullock was nicknamed an 'ale-minister', because when it came to the sermon many in the congregation would leave to quench their thirst in the ale-house next door! Robe described conditions in the church as 'a formal round of professional duties...and as to the multitude they were visibly profane'.[1]

Prior to the revival in Wales in 1859 the same problem existed: 'The means of grace had become more or less a formality, made unattractive to the world by the coldness even of its orthodoxy; sinful practices were rampant and carried on openly without any sense of shame; the church was spiritually "asleep", oblivious of its mission to the world, and satisfied with its lukewarmness. The prayer meetings were not burdened for the souls of the unconverted, and preaching was theoretical, oratorical and "popular" in the worst sense.'[2]

At the Association meetings of the Calvinistic Methodist churches during the 1840s and '50s, the subjects for discussion reveal the state of the churches: 'The inefficiency of the ministry, and the low state of religion'; 'Worldliness in its relation to religion'; 'The ungodliness of the present generation'; 'The hardness of the times', and so on.[3] Prior to 1733 Jonathan Edwards complained of 'a time of extraordinary dullness in religion' in his North American town of Northampton.[4] More than 200 years later, the Free Church Presbytery of the Isle of Lewis, off the west coast of Scotland, expressed its concern, 'not only in the chaotic conditions of international politics and domestic economics and morality, but also, and especially, in the lack of spiritual power from Gospel Ordinances'.[5] That was the most urgent problem for the Free Church Presbytery — not the state of the nation, but the condition of the churches.

Sadly, this is all too descriptive of our own day. For all our noise and claims, the mission societies are desperate for new workers and more funds, we have to plead for attendance at the prayer meeting, and an increasing pattern of gathering with the Lord's people just once on a Sunday is developing in this nation. Sermons are, in the main, either heavily dull or flippantly irrelevant, leading one modern writer to dismiss preaching as 'an ocean of verbiage'. Few unbelievers are being converted, and the Word of God does not seem to be changing the lives of God's people. If the living are not alive, what hope is there for the dead?

An alarming description of one church in the Assam district of India prior to the revival of 1905 led to urgent prayer by the missionaries: 'Nearly all the members, men and women, were given to drinking, some smoked ganja. They quarrelled, they fought, they lived immoral lives, and shielded each other so that the missionary would not find these things out. It was almost impossible to get them to attend more than one service on the Sabbath day, and the weekly service was very badly attended. The missionary often felt ready to give them up altogether, it seemed a hopeless church.'[6]

This is not so far from our situation as a first reading might lead us to consider. The way many Christians in our churches behave and dress would have been unthinkable two decades ago. We have lowered our stand on the use of tobacco and alcohol under the pretence of 'freedom', and many of our members are hooked on the equally mind-and-soul-destroying drug of television. Professing Christians watch close on the national average of five hours viewing time each day and rush to the prayer meeting or Sunday service with a mind filled with impressions of the worst this world has on offer. We squabble and gossip and divide and are careless of those who are sitting beside us in urgent need of friendship and help. We go through our evangelical duties as coldly and routinely as a well-trained regiment of soldiers.

It is no use one section of the evangelical church delighting in the fact that this is all a description of the 'other side'; I have worshipped in churches across the evangelical spectrum and it is largely true of us all. I have attended churches with activity, enthusiasm and gifts to make even the angels envious, yet which had to appeal for more people to join the prayer meeting! I have attended churches with plenty of music and movement and churches with solemn stillness. Yet none of them exhibits the awareness of the presence of God. There will be no revival all the time we analyse the state of the nation and merely lament the terrible sins of the world around us. After all, we should have learnt in 2,000 years that sin is what is to be expected of an unbelieving world. And there will be no revival all the time we lay the blame exclusively on the other wing of evangelicalism. God comes to a people who admit their own sin and cry for forgiveness for their own coldness and unholiness.

The problem with our nation is not the government, or the education system, or the economic conditions, and it is not that dead and lifeless institutional religion that believes everything or nothing. The real problem lies with the evangelical churches who claim to have the truth and think they are rich in spiritual gifts and life, and yet are cold, complacent and unattractive to the watching world. I am afraid this means most of us today. Covering our tracks with big bonanzas and impressive projects will never convince a godless world of the reality of our God, though the world may certainly admire our expertise at showmanship. We can gather large numbers of Christians together for giant conferences, monster banner-waving marches and technically brilliant satellite-relayed missions. All these may have their place and value, but the danger is that they fool us into thinking that there are a lot of us and that we are making a strong impact upon society. In reality we are thinly scattered among a godless nation and we are hardly making a scratch on its surface.

It is always risky to try to identify a fundamental problem in society, but I will hazard the risk of stating that there is one great tragedy among people today, and the fault lies with the church. The book of Ecclesiastes in the Bible is the story of Solomon's backsliding. A wise king with absolute power and unlimited wealth, the envy of the world around him, allowed his heart to be turned away from God. According to Ecclesiastes 2:4-9 he tried everything as a substitute for God and yet he discovered that his life was empty and meaningless. The more he left God out, the more miserable he became. Our Western society has everything it needs and yet half our National Health Service hospital beds are taken up by mental health patients. The Samaritans tell us that suicide is rising at an alarming rate (more than one young person commits self-murder every day in this country) and alcohol-related problems cost the nation twenty-six billion pounds each year. At work, at home, and even at our sport, we are not a happy people. Why is this?

Man was originally created in the image of God and in friendship with God, and the first recorded conversation between man and his Creator concerned matters of morality and eternity: 'You must not eat from the tree of the knowledge of good and evil, for when you eat of it you will surely die.' This is because, as Solomon soon came to realize, God had 'set eternity in the hearts of men' (Eccles. 3:11). This gift is part of the uniqueness of man. Unlike the animal world around him, man is aware of eternity. For this reason there are very few real atheists in the world because atheism is a hard religion to believe in; it runs contrary to that voice within man that cries out to him that there is a God and an eternity and a judgement to come. It is this gift that accounts for the fact that wherever we find man, we find him worshipping; he must worship because he has 'eternity in his heart'.

The tragedy of modern man is that he has, with great effort and by careful practice, squeezed this sense of God and eternity out of his mind. An age of mind-blowing scientific achievement, colossal consumer choice and a soft luxury beyond imagination a few decades ago has all helped modern, Western man to convince himself that there is no eternity to worry about. And our generation has achieved this far more successfully than have billions of roubles spent in anti-God propaganda in the Eastern bloc! The greatest tragedy of man today is that he has lost the sense of eternity in his heart and mind. C. S. Lewis once criticized Rudyard Kipling and his age for lacking 'a doctrine of ends' and concluded: 'He has a reverent, pagan, agnosticism about all ultimates.' That may be another way of making my criticism of today's generation: we have a pagan agnosticism about eternity.

During his ministry on earth, Christ spent much of his time turning the minds of his hearers to eternity. Many of his parables were about heaven and hell, like the vivid story of the rich man and Lazarus. Other parables spoke of the suddenness of death, like the rich fool and his barn. The parable of the tenant farmers taught about rewards and punishments, and the parable of the talents pointed to a day of judgement. And the list can go on. The terrifying thing about modern man is that he no longer feels afraid, or feels anything, about eternity. To tell him that Christ came into the world to save sinners invites the question: 'To save sinners from what?' And when we reply, 'From judgement and hell,' the response is invariably, 'Oh, is that all? I thought you had something important to say.' To describe hell as a Christless eternity is an irrelevancy to modern man. He lives all right without Christ now, so why not in eternity? Man has lost his uniqueness today; he has lost a mind filled with a sense of eternity. And, contrary to what we are often told, there is not a world out there just waiting to respond to our good news if only we will get onto the streets and tell people. Any face-to-face evangelist or faithful door-to-door visitor will tell you that people simply do not want to know. Eternity is not in their minds.

And when society no longer thinks about eternity, it almost goes without saying that it is because the church no longer thinks that way either. Our lives as Christians, and our worship when we are together, impress the world with our love of this life. There is little about us to convince the world that we are motivated for eternity rather than for time. People do not touch eternity in our meetings, they rarely hear of it in our conversation and they certainly do not see it as the priority of our lives. Of course, it glances off our gospel here and there, but we are not passionate about heaven and hell or the second coming of Christ, and we have lost a sense of accountability to God.

One thing revival does, and it always does it, is to reawaken, in both Christians and the community around, a sense of the reality of eternal issues. One observer described the eighteenth century as 'Stomach well alive, soul extinct'. How did that change? God sent a revival that swept across the nation until hundreds of thousands knew that God was real. When 40,000 people gathered on Kennington Common in London in the mid-eighteenth century, they had not come to watch the West Indies play the MCC; they had come to hear George Whitefield preach the gospel of eternal things. In 1737, when Whitefield was only twenty-two years old, he was preaching to crowded churches in London and thousands were turned away because there was no room; he had not yet begun preaching in the open air. At this time he said of the congregations, 'They were all attention, and heard like people hearing for eternity.'[7] Interestingly, this is exactly the same description that Alexander Webster used five years later during the revival at Cambuslang in Scotland: 'They hear as for eternity...'[8] When God comes in revival, whole communities are aware that there is a God and that eternal issues really matter. Not everyone will believe, but everyone will be made to think.

In 1859 when God swept Ulster with revival, the October meeting at the Maze racecourse attracted less than 500 race-goers instead of the usual 10,000. Clearly some people were being made to think seriously about eternity. Here is a description given by a minister in Comber, a small town in County Down, just nine miles from Belfast: 'The whole town and neighbourhood were roused. Many did not retire to rest the first night at all, and for several days great numbers were unable to attend their usual vocations, but gave themselves almost unceasingly to the study of the Scriptures, singing and prayer: and for the first month, with about three exceptions, I did not get to bed till morning, such was the anxiety of the people for pastoral instruction and consolation.'[9]

In Wales in 1904, whole towns were stirred, and everybody was talking about God and eternity. The *North Wales Guardian* for 20 January 1905 carried the following reports: 'In consequence of the revival the annual eisteddfod arranged to be held on Friday Jan 27th at Llansantffraid near Oswestry has been postponed. The secretaries who have widely advertised the postponement, discovered that the usual eisteddfod enthusiasts were devoting themselves to the revival gatherings, and that choirs have been unable to obtain accommodation for practice. At a Football Association meeting at Chirk, when the draw for a charity cup was made, it was deemed useless to fix a match at Rhos, as the Black Park Club secretary announced that in a recent match — Rhos-v. Black Park — the gate receipts only amounted to 9s.'[10]

It was not that people considered either the eisteddfod or football as sinful, but their minds and lives were gripped with something far more important. In revival God puts eternity back into men's minds, not just as individuals, but as whole communities. Another newspaper in Wales reported 'a pervading and overwhelming solemnity, convincing even the most stoical that eternal realities had come into intimate contact with the men and women present'.[11]

Duncan Campbell recalls the same thing happening on the Isle of Lewis in 1949: 'News of what was happening in Barvas spread faster than the speed of gossip...Within a matter of days the whole neighbourhood was powerfully awakened to eternal realities. Work was largely set aside as people became concerned about their own salvation, or the salvation of friends and neighbours. In homes, barns and loom-sheds, by the roadside or the peatstack, men could be found calling upon God...'[12]

The population of New England in the eighteenth century was probably around 340,000, and it is estimated that the revival there brought up to 50,000 to salvation. If fifteen per cent of the population are converted in a short time, almost everyone has to think about eternity! When revival spread from Lowestoft in 1921 right up to the Scottish fishing ports whole communities were changed. One newspaper reported that in a small town of 1,500 inhabitants, no fewer than 600 professed faith in Christ; the paper also commented that gambling disappeared and tobacco was destroyed.[13] So powerfully did God work in a revival in Birmingham in 1834 that the bars and beer-shops were left 'vocal with lonely grumblers'.[14] A community cannot avoid thinking about eternity when things like this take place.

When Hezekiah came to the throne he did not begin by analysing the disastrous effects of the rampaging Assyrian army; he called to the Levites to 'Consecrate yourselves now and consecrate the temple of the Lord' (2 Chron. 29:5). He knew exactly where the problem of the nation really lay. If we start here, we have hope for revival. But we must start *now*. Whole books can be written analysing what is wrong with the church today, but there is hardly a need for this. We must simply admit that we are not an eternity-minded people. We live like the world we are supposed to be saving: for the things of time rather than for the things of eternity. Our priorities are world-related rather than heaven-directed; our treasure is on earth. Revival always begins by putting eternity back into the minds of the Christians, and only when the church takes eternity seriously can we expect the world to do so.

Before revival

The men God uses

Revival commences with those who in bad times remain good, in godless days remain Christian, in careless years remain constant and who have eternity in their hearts. Revival begins with those who stand firm, like Hezekiah, in an age of godless rejection, in an age when the people do what is right in their own eyes. It begins with the man who stands for that which is true and right and good; but it also requires a man who can see what the state of the church and the nation really is. It would have been too easy for Hezekiah to have persuaded himself that things were not all that bad; after all, religion was still practised and things could have been worse. But Hezekiah knew how low the spiritual life of the nation had sunk. Revival requires not only a man who remains faithful and is aware of reality, but one who cares. Hezekiah cared. He was only twenty-five when he came to the throne, but clearly the state of affairs had been bothering him for a long time, and he made up his mind to do something.

God frequently uses particular men in revival; we need not be afraid of this because it is God's way. He is not only the God of the end, which in this case is revival, but the means to that end, which is so often committed Christian leaders. This was always God's way in the Bible. At every major junction of Jewish Bible history God prepared particular men, and occasionally women, to lead his people: men like Abraham, Joseph, Moses, Joshua, Gideon, Samuel, David, Daniel, Nehemiah and the many prophets — to list a few at random. Christ chose his disciples and sent them out to establish churches in the power of his Holy Spirit. The story of the first-century church is woven around the lives of men like Peter and John, Philip and Stephen, Paul and Silas, Barnabas and Mark. God has chosen, with few exceptions, to build his church by preparing particular men.

Some of the names in the story of revival are well known. 250 years ago, there were men like John and Charles Wesley, George Whitefield, Howel Harris and Daniel Rowland in Britain, and Nikolaus Ludwig von Zinzendorf in Saxony and Hans Hauge in Norway. Across the Atlantic there were Jonathan Edwards in New England and David Brainerd among the North American Indians. At the beginning of the nineteenth century God used Asahel Nettleton in America and later Dwight L. Moody. Back home in Britain, in 1859 he prepared Humphrey Jones and David Morgan in Wales, James McQuilkin in Ulster, Charles Haddon Spurgeon in England and, a little earlier, William Chalmers Burns, Robert Murray M'Cheyne and Brownlow North in Scotland. And at the beginning of this century he prepared men like Evan Roberts and Rhys Bevan Jones in Wales, Douglas Brown in England and Jock Troup and Duncan Campbell in Scotland. Further afield, he pre- pared John Sung in China, Bakht Singh in India and Peterus Octavianus in Borneo. All these, and others, we shall meet as the story progresses. The point is that God has almost always used particular men to lead his work. That is his method; and if it is, it is not wrong for Christians to be praying for God to prepare his men for leadership in revival. We need to pray for God to give us such men today.

In 2 Chronicles 29 we are introduced to Hezekiah, the king in Jerusalem. Hezekiah is one of the very few kings in history that have been at the centre of a revival. There are two others, if you refer to Josiah as leading a revival rather than merely a reformation, and if you consider the work of God in the life of the king in Nineveh, at the time of Jonah, a revival. As we have already seen, we are introduced to Hezekiah as a young man of twenty-five, and we know nothing about his earlier years except who his parents were. That was not a very hopeful start! We know the life of his father Ahaz because it is well recorded for us: he was a godless man. And we have already seen something of the age in which he lived. But we need to look at the quality of Hezekiah's life, because revival is always a personal thing, and no one is used in revival who is not himself revived first. That is very important to understand. Those whom God uses in leadership in revival are always men who have met with God in a powerfully personal way and have a burning passion for the glory of God and a life of holiness. It is not possible for the Holy Spirit to come in great power upon his people without creating a longing for right and pure living. Anything that claims to be a work of the Holy Spirit but does not bring about a desire to be holy must be suspect.

The man God uses may have little attraction physically. At Corinth there were those who despised the apostle Paul; they admitted that his letters were powerful, but, they said, 'In person he is unimpressive and his speaking amounts to nothing' (2 Cor. 10:10). They sneered at both the person and the preaching of Paul, even though he preached with 'a demonstration of the Spirit's power' (1 Cor. 2:4). It is a rare thing in Scripture for us to be offered a physical description of God's leaders; the reason for this is that it plays little or no part in the use to which God puts a man. We do not know anything about Hezekiah's appearance, but it would not have been that for which God chose him because God does not look on the outward appearance.

Silas Told, who was converted through the powerful preaching of John Wesley and became one of Wesley's earliest teachers and prison visitors, describes his first sight of Wesley at a crowded meeting at five o'clock in the morning at the Foundry: 'I had a curiosity to see his person, which, when I beheld, I much despised. The enemy of souls suggested that he was some farmer's son, who, not able to support himself, was making a penny in this low manner.'[15]

David Brainerd, who travelled hundreds of miles in wild and dangerous frontier territory to preach to the North American Indians in the 1740s, was a sickly tuberculosis sufferer.

Similarly, the first sight Rajamani had of Bakht Singh, the leader of the revival in South India in the early 1940s, was very disappointing. He was expecting a strong, smart and well-dressed converted Sikh; instead, 'Here was a lean, unimpressive young man with neither moustache nor beard, and not dressed up like a great preacher in tie and collar and shoes either, but barefoot and simply clad. I felt sure that, just as I had been disappointed in so many preachers before, so I would now be disappointed in this man also.'[16]

The men whom God has used in revival have come from no stereotyped background. At Herrnhut in Saxony the two men who worked together in a revival that fell on the community in 1727 were a rich count, Zinzendorf, and a modest carpenter, Christian David. The Wesley brothers and George Whitefield were educated men from the university when God used them in the eighteenth century, but others, like Billy Bray, the Cornish miner 150 years ago, or Jock Troup in England and Scotland in this century, who was trained as a cooper, had barely enough education. John Sung was a brilliant scientist when he joined the Bethel Band in China. When God poured out his Spirit at Pentecost, you could hardly have found a more mixed group of men, and the two most widely used men in the book of Acts were a fisherman and a university graduate. Hezekiah instructed the priests and the Levites who should have been instructing him.

In revival God will frequently use those who are unqualified in the eyes of men. Although Evan Roberts became a significant leader during the 1904-5 revival in Wales, this was not apparent at first. Early in 1904 one local newspaper contrasted what was happening in Wales with the work of God in the eighteenth century. Canon Wynne Jones addressed the Montgomeryshire Clerical Association on the revival and the paper commented: 'There was the peculiarity about the movement that, unlike the great revival in John Wesley's day, it did not appear to have any visible head to direct and organize it. Evan Roberts himself was represented as too unassuming to claim anything like leadership...'[17]

Whilst we may admire or honour the men God used in revival, we must beware of falling into the danger of giving some particular authority to their practices, preferences or principles, as if the fact that God used them validates all they did. Rhys Bevan Jones maintained a very different approach from Evan Roberts, laying far greater emphasis upon preaching, and yet both were greatly used by God in Wales in 1904. William Haslam was surprised, when preaching in Scotland, to hear the rustling of the pages of Bibles as the congregation followed his references carefully; he was not used to this in Cornwall and actually discouraged it by not giving full references; he felt it hindered the flow of the sermon. On the other hand, Bakht Singh in India urged the people to bring a Bible and even made them display their copies for all to see! William Haslam and Duncan Campbell had little problem with women preaching during revival times, whilst for others such a thing was quite out of place — to put it mildly!

We shall never settle these issues just on the ground of whether or not God used such practices. Scripture is to be our guide. There is sufficient diversity between revivals to warn us that when men become our authority, however great and godly the men may be, we shall be like a ship with a brilliant captain yet lacking wheel, rudder and anchor. We have our leaders today, but rarely do they have the mark of God's Spirit upon them. They have become leaders by denominational progression or by their force of character, or by their organizing ability and their capacity for hard work. Someone has said that what the church needs today is heaven-anointed men, not human-appointed machines. More quaintly Timothy Edwards, the father of the great eighteenth-century American pastor Jonathan Edwards, once said, 'Ministers must needs have the Spirit upon them in order to the receiving of the people.'

However, revival will rarely begin only by the faithfulness of a few good and godly men; there will almost always be others who join in the longing and praying and preparing for revival. This is especially seen in the part that prayer plays in bringing down the Spirit in power. Rarely will revival come as a result of one man's praying. God stirs a few here and there to pray until, as is sometimes the case, thousands or tens of thousands are assaulting heaven with the insistent demand that God should come among his people. Before the revival in America in 1857, a city missionary, Jeremiah Lanphier, called a prayer meeting in Fulton Street, in downtown New York. Within six months 10,000 business men were praying for revival, and within two years it is claimed that 2,000,000 converts were added to the churches. In 1856 Mrs Colville in Ulster influenced a young man towards Christ who, after his conversion, gathered a few friends for prayer; the Ulster revival of 1859 led to the conversion of an estimated 100,000 people. So, in understanding the way God used Dwight L. Moody in America or James McQuilkin in Ulster, we must never forget the contribution of hundreds of lesser-known, or unknown, warriors for the gospel. As we look at the men God uses, their lives will speak for many more. And these lives will show us those ingredients that should be present in us, whoever we are, if we long for God to come and saturate the community with himself.

In 1858, a minister of Aberdare in Wales wrote of the urgent need for revival and made suggestions as to how a revival might come. His suggestions included 'a pure ministry — apostolic preaching...the awakening must start in the pulpit...the church must be in full sympathy with the ministry'.[18] This last is a vital point. In emphasizing the importance of the leaders, it cannot be stressed too much that others must be in harmony and unity with the leadership. Preparing for revival is not the work of the leaders alone.

Before revival

An experience of God

When Hezekiah 'did what was right in the eyes of the Lord', his actions are compared to those of his father David (2 Chron. 29:2). Hezekiah stood in the direct line of the great King David, not merely as his physical descendant, but as his spiritual heir. As David longed for God, so did Hezekiah. The revival started there, in the soul of a man who longed for God. Hezekiah's determination to 'make a covenant with the Lord' was no idle promise. It expressed something of his relationship with God — a relationship that ran deep and firm. Hezekiah knew God personally, just as David had done, and he was determined that nothing would come in the way of his love for the covenant-keeping God.

In 2 Kings 18:5-6 we are told simply that Hezekiah 'trusted in the Lord...held fast to the Lord and did not cease to follow him'. The secret of Hezekiah's later ministry began here. This holding fast speaks of a deep and personal relationship with God, not merely a grim and determined obedience. It was in this trust, holding fast and following, that the king learnt in his soul something of the character of God. And Hezekiah was constant. I know he was later disobedient, but even then he returned to the Lord. He was an obedient child and 'The Lord was with him' (v.7). The Lord is always with such a man even if it does not appear like that. Even when the temple is closed and the priests are idle and nothing is happening, the Lord is always with those who love him and hold fast to him. The name Hezekiah means 'whom Jehovah strengthens'.

When the early disciples looked for a man to make up the place left by Judas Iscariot, they set the qualification as 'one of the men who have been with us the whole time the Lord Jesus went in and out among us, beginning from John's baptism to the time when Jesus was taken up from us. For one of these must become a witness with us of his resurrection' (Acts 1:21-22). This qualification was not only so that the new apostle would be a good apologist, having clear convictions about the life, death and resurrection of Christ, but so that he would be a man who had experienced the living and risen Christ. And the purpose of Pentecost was not only to give power to the apostles' preaching, but to give reality to their experience. By the opening of Acts, the disciples had no doubt that Christ was risen from the dead, but still they needed a powerful experience of being 'filled with the Spirit' (Acts 2:4). God wanted to use men who were utterly convinced, both by their theology and their experience, that Christ was a living, powerful and personal Saviour.

Men whom God uses in revival have always been men who maintained a close walk with God and longed for a holy life. It was Robert Murray M'Cheyne who, so greatly used by God in Dundee in 1839, had prayed from his heart, 'Lord, make me as holy as a saved sinner can be.'[19] The evidence of his sincerity in this prayer is seen in the fact that people would be moved to tears just by seeing him in the pulpit or walking down the corridor of the church. Brainerd spent whole nights in prayer, so did Wesley and White-field, and this was before revival came. They were men who knew what they wanted and were determined to get it.

There has always been personal revival before public revival in those whom God uses. This personal revival may take many forms, but it always has the same effect: to convince of the greatness and glory of God.

David Brainerd makes the following entry in his diary, dated 12 July 1739: 'As I was walking in a dark, thick grove, *unspeakable glory* seemed to open to the view and apprehension of my soul. I do not mean any external brightness, for I saw no such thing, nor do I intend any imagination of any body of light somewhere in the third heaven or anything of that nature, but it was a new inward apprehension or view that I had of God, such as I never had before, nor anything which had the lest semblance of it. I stood still, wondered and admired! I knew that I never had seen before anything comparable to it for excellency and beauty, it was widely different from all the conceptions that ever I had of God or things Divine. I had no particular apprehension of any one Person in the Trinity, either the Father, the Son, or the Holy Ghost, but it appeared to be *Divine Glory*. My soul *rejoiced with joy unspeakable* to see such a God, such a glorious Divine Being, and I was inwardly pleased and satisfied that He should be *God over all* for ever and ever. My soul was so captivated and delighted with the excellency, loveliness, greatness, and other perfections of God, that I was even swallowed up in Him…'[20] I have quoted from Brainerd's diary at length, not because we must demand the same experience, but to emphasize that personal revival is always a renewing of our appreciation of God.

Jonathan Edwards, who was like a father to Brainerd, describes similar experiences of his own. Writing of an occasion in 1737 when he rode to a wood in order to be alone to think and pray he concludes: 'I had a view that for me was extraordinary, of the glory of the Son of God as Mediator between God and man, and His wonderful, great, full, pure and sweet grace and love, and meek and gentle condescension. This grace that appeared so calm and sweet, appeared also great above the heavens. The person of Christ appeared ineffably excellent with an excellency great enough to swallow up all thought and conception — which continued, as near as I can judge, about an hour …'[21]

Four years before Brainerd's experience, Howel Harris, who was so powerfully used in the Awakening across Wales, described how, on 18 June 1735, he met with God. It was so real that he referred to it often throughout his life: 'I felt suddenly my heart melting within me like wax before the fire with love to God my Saviour; and also felt not only love, peace, etc. but longing to be dissolved, and to be with Christ; then was a cry in my inmost soul, which I was totally unacquainted with before, Abba Father! Abba Father! I could not help calling God my Father; I knew that I was his child, and that He loved me, and heard me. My soul being filled and satiated, crying, "'Tis enough, I am satisfied. Give me strength, and I will follow thee through fire and water." I could say I was happy indeed! There was in me a well of water, springing up to everlasting life, Jn. 4:14. The love of God was shed abroad in my heart by the Holy Ghost, Rom. 5:5.'[22]

It is this deep and personal knowledge of God, that captivates the whole soul with the glories of God's character, that is lacking among Christian leaders today. We don't even understand the language, let alone share the experience.

Before the outbreak of the China-Japan war in 1937, Dr John Sung travelled all through China and beyond into Java, Singapore, Malaysia, Burma and Thailand, and God used him powerfully in revival; but he had 'a profound spiritual experience which changed the direction of his life and led him to give himself and his rich talents to God for the salvation of his people'.[23]

At the time of his call to return to the work of an evangelist, Duncan Campbell experienced such an overwhelming sense of the love of God that he wondered if he could bear it. This, together with an awesome awareness of the reality of hell, left him no option but to obey the command of God.[24]

For others, personal revival came in a less dramatic way, sometimes over a period of time, even years, but always, step by step, they are led into a closer walk with God and a deeper understanding of God. But this is not achieved through any set formula, and it has no doctrinal label that can be tied to it. This is one of our problems today: people experience God and immediately label it and then demand that others receive the same; but that is a human attempt to shackle God and confine him to a set experience. God comes in a thousand different ways to his people, and to put a label on these experiences or to demand that others follow the same kind of pattern is completely false. True revival is dangerously uninhibited.

It was never experiences that these men were looking for. In all the lives of those used significantly in revival, they did not go for impressive gifts or exciting signs. We shall always miss the mark when we long for another man's experience. Leaders in revivals have wanted God and holiness and have done everything in their power to gain both. Of all the great names associated with revival, very few spent time involving themselves with 'spiritual gifts'. I do not recall reading of one leader who pleaded with God for these things. They were looking for something much bigger. Sometimes such things happened in their lives and ministry, but this was incidental. On the contrary, when Humphrey Jones took to 'prophesying' in 1859, his ministry and leadership in the revival in Wales came to a sad and abrupt end; and the weakest part of Evan Roberts' ministry in Wales in 1904 was his encouragement of certain 'gifts' that occasionally spoiled his meetings. Hezekiah began by longing for God and holiness; when later in his life he became proud and boastfully showed off his kingdom to the Babylonian envoys, the revival was at an end (2 Chron. 32:24-31).

A study of the lives of men God used in Bible times reveals the same thing. Time after time we can identify the experience of God that changed their life: Abraham at Mamre (Gen. 15), Jacob at Luz (Gen. 28), Moses in the Midian desert (Exod. 3), Joshua outside Jericho (Josh. 5), Gideon under the oak in Ophrah (Judg. 6), Samuel in the tabernacle (1 Sam. 3), Isaiah in the temple (Isa. 6), and so we could continue. Always the revelation of God in their lives convinced them of the Creator's holiness and sovereign power. No one is ever used in revival whose experience of God is no more than a coldly impersonal theology. Revival leaders are men with hearts on fire. It is as if God has invaded their lives in every part and taken them captive; they are men who love God, trust in him, hold fast to him and never cease to follow him. Their ministry is not a job, still less an interest or hobby; rather it is an all-consuming passion. And they fear above everything losing the sense of the presence of God. Most of the great men of revival had a strong hold on theology, but never at the expense of a vivid and life-changing relationship with God.

C. H. Spurgeon, who saw almost continuous revival in his church for many years, could claim that barely fifteen minutes went by without his turning his thoughts towards God. Preaching at the Keswick Convention in 1922, a year after revival in Lowestoft, Douglas Brown declared, 'Revival begins with a vision, and the vision begins with a new sense of Jesus Christ. Revival does not begin in a theology, but in a theophany. It begins in a revelation of Jesus Christ Himself and a sense of the nearness of the Master.'[25] There is a heart-beat in this somewhat loose wording of Douglas Brown. He did not deny the importance of theology, far from it, nor did he pretend by 'theophany' to have seen God; he was making the point strongly that revival begins with men who have a deep, firm and life-changing experience of God. Today, men who have no interest apart from God are considered out of touch and boring — but these are the men God is looking for.

Yet these men were always concerned that God should have the honour for anything he chose to do through them. Deep experiences of God did not allow them to boast of themselves, any more than Paul did in the New Testament. The apostle experienced things he felt it unwise even to write down (2 Cor.12:4), and the only boasting he allowed was of those things that showed up his weakness.

In 1737 George Whitefield was on his way to Georgia when he prayed, 'God, give me a deep humility, a well-guided zeal, a burning love and a single eye, and then let men or devils do their worst!' Five years later he could still record in his diary: 'I spent most part of my time in secret prayer...Pray that I may be very little in my own eyes, and not rob my dear Master of any part of his glory.'[26]

During the first two months of 1859, David Morgan did not preach beyond Cardiganshire, but a meeting at inappropriately named Devil's Bridge on New Year's Day was typical of what was to follow all over Wales that year. An old minister described it, together with David Morgan's response on the way home from the meeting: 'The evening service was terrible. So near was the revivalist to his God, that his face shone like that of an angel, so that none could gaze steadfastly at him. Many of the hearers swooned. On the way home I dared not break the silence for miles. Towards midnight I ventured to say, "Didn't we have blessed meetings, Mr Morgan?" "Yes," he replied; and after a pause, added, "The Lord would give us great things, if He could only trust us." "What do you mean?" I asked. "If He could trust us not to steal the glory for ourselves." Then the midnight air rang with his cry, at the top of his voice, "Not unto us, O Lord, not unto us, but unto *Thy* name give glory".'[27]

When three ministers of the United Free Church of Scotland visited the scenes of revival in Scotland in 1921 they reported: 'The men whose names come to the front would be the last to take credit. They are honest, earnest, modest young men, with a humble idea of their own ability.'[28] Those are the qualities that God is looking for in the men he will use in revival. Unfortunately 'a humble idea of their own ability' is not what we seem to encourage in young Christians, or our leaders, in these days of self-assertive leadership training. It was said of Asahel Nettleton, whom God used in revival in America in the early eighteenth century: 'This favoured servant of Christ came, with no trumpet sounded before him, in the meekness of his master, and the Lord was with him in very deed.'[29] If praise was directed towards him, or if he suspected too much confidence was placed in him, Nettleton would often simply disappear from the scene, much to the annoyance of those waiting for his ministry! Douglas Brown described revival as 'the humbling of self before the...majesty of that consciously present Jesus'.[30]

God brings revival not for the enjoyment of his people, but for the glory of his name; and he will not share that glory with men: 'Surely his salvation is near those who fear him, that his glory may dwell in our land' (Ps. 85:9). The moment men boast of their achievements the glory will depart. 2 Chronicles 32:25 is the most tragic comment upon Hezekiah: 'But Hezekiah's heart was proud and he did not respond to the kindness shown him; therefore the Lord's wrath was on him and on Judah and Jerusalem.' It was at this time he boastfully showed off his treasures and power to the Babylonian envoys (2 Kings 20:12-13) and the revival was at an end. The men God uses in revival have a firmer hold upon another world than upon this one, and their love for Christ far outweighs the treasure of men. Whatever faults there may be in their character, whatever frailty in their lives, a passion for Christ is dominant.

Perhaps Howel Harris expressed this as clearly as any when he wrote in his diary, 'I must have the Saviour, indeed, for he is my all; all that others have in the world, and in religion, and in themselves, I have in Thee; pleasures, riches, safety, honour, life, righteousness, holiness, wisdom, bliss, joy, gaiety, and happiness...And if a child longs for his father; a traveller for the end of his journey; a workman to finish his work; a prisoner for his liberty; an heir for the full possession of his estate; so, in all these respects, I can't help longing to go home.'[31]

God is looking for men and women who love him like that and whom he can therefore trust with revival.

Before revival

Holiness
of life

It is impossible to read the story of Hezekiah without being impressed with his longing for everything to be done in line with the holy character of God. The revival that swept through the nation and brought cleansing from the house of God outwards had actually begun in the heart of the king. God looks for men who will be willing to surrender anything and everything so long as their life can be kept clean. This is an essential part of personal revival.

The men God chiefly used in the Bible, and who stand as an example to us today, were men whose experience of God led them into a passionate desire to be holy. They were men with a sensitive conscience. Joseph learned holiness in the face of fierce temptation (Gen. 39:6-10), and, to the average Christian today, Daniel might seem to have been unnecessarily precise in his insistence upon keeping his distance from the contamination of Babylon (Dan. 1:8). But without exception those whom God uses in revival are men and women who fear God and sin, and nothing else! They take seriously the command: 'Be holy as I am holy, says the Lord.' The New Testament is full of commands to be holy, and without doubt unholiness by our Christian leaders is a major reason why we have so little spiritual success today. We turn Christianity into a thing of fun, and seem to be afraid of appearing different from the world. In fact we forget that God would rather a man be over-precise in true holiness than enjoy himself and sin. Christians boast of being worldly-wise, and of not being in 'bondage' to this or that regulation. Of course, there is a Pharisaic self-righteousness that is not holiness at all, but where are our leaders who are prepared to break every habit, cancel their magazine or newspaper, sell their television, burn their novels, down-market their car, house and holiday, and strive for purity of mind and heart above everything? In short, where are our leaders who will walk in humility and holiness with God, and take seriously the words of Scripture? The New Testament is full of urgent commands and warnings concerning personal holiness:

> 'Be...innocent as doves...' (Matt. 10:16)
> 'Be innocent about what is evil' (Rom. 16:19).
> 'In regard to evil be infants' (1 Cor. 14:20).
> 'Touch no unclean thing' (2 Cor. 6:17).
> 'There must not even be a hint of...it is shameful even to mention...' (Eph. 5:3,12).
> 'Whatever is pure...think about such things' (Phil. 4:8).
> 'Set your minds on things above...' (Col. 3:2).
> 'Keep oneself from being polluted by the world' (James 1:27).
> 'Hating even the clothing stained by sinful flesh' (Jude 23).

And those who wrote these instructions lived what they preached. The New Testament writers were men whom God could use, simply because their view of the holiness of God, and their love for Christ, compelled them to live as clean and holy men in a godless world.

Zinzendorf prayed, as a child of four years, 'Dear Saviour do thou be mine, and I will be thine.'[32] And it was that spirit of total commitment that stayed with him and led to the outpouring of God's Spirit at Herrnhut in 1727. Wesley declared in 1734: 'My one aim in life is to secure personal holiness, for without being holy myself I cannot promote real holiness in others.'[33] This was four years *before* his conversion! But although he might later express himself more to the glory of God, yet the thrust of his concern was always the same. David Brainerd recalls the time when he was among the Indians in North America and, the night before a pagan festival, he went to the woods to be alone with God. His experience during that night reveals the kind of men God can trust in revival: 'All things here below vanished, and there appeared to be nothing of any considerable importance to me but holiness of heart and life, and the conversion of the heathen to God. All my cares, fears, and desires, which might be said to be of a worldly nature disappeared, and were, in my esteem, of little more importance than a puff of wind. I exceedingly longed that God would get to himself a name among the heathen, and I appealed to him, with the greatest freedom, that he knew I "preferred him above my chief joy".'[34]

The North Wales Guardian on 14 April 1905 reported the assessment of Evan Roberts made by the vicar of Rhos, Rev. T. Pritchard: 'He believes him to be true to the backbone, and understands the man's nature thoroughly. Above all he is faithful to God and his conscience; he cannot be bought or bribed; his strength is his character sanctified by communion with the invisible.'[35] That was high praise by a wise and cautious leader.

Duncan Campbell describes his own experience of surrendering fully to Christ. He was shot from his horse and seriously wounded in one of the last cavalry charges of the Great War; while a Canadian trooper was carrying him on horse-back to the casualty clearing station, Campbell reviewed his life and saw how empty it had been, even as a Christian. He prayed M'Cheyne's prayer: 'Lord, make me as holy as a saved sinner can be.' At that moment the Spirit seemed to come into his life in such power and he experienced the presence of God in such reality that he felt he was going straight to heaven. From then on he was a man with eternity in his mind.[36]

After twenty-six years of apparently successful ministry in a large London Baptist church, Douglas Brown became acutely aware that something was missing from his life: 'Christ laid his hand on a proud minister, and told him that he had not gone far enough, that there were reservations in his surrender... He nearly broke my heart while I was preaching.' Throughout November and December of 1920 an intense struggle went on; it carried on through to January of the following year. Then in February 1921 Douglas Brown was wrestling in prayer when he felt able to yield his life fully to God. 'Then something happened. I found myself in the loving embrace of

Christ for ever and ever; and all power and all joy and all blessedness
rolled in like a deluge…God had waited four months for a man like
me; and I said: "Lord Jesus, I know what you want; you want me to
go into mission work. I love thee more than I dislike that."'[37] In the
same month, whilst Douglas Brown was conducting a mission in
Lowestoft in Suffolk, God began a revival that spread all over East
Anglia and up into the fishing ports of Scotland.

The men God uses in revival all have a burning conviction that
God will not hold back from giving 'good things' to his people and
so they have a bold impertinence to ask and expect good things from
him. But they are equally sure that these are only given to 'those
whose walk is blameless' (Ps. 84:11). They know that sin will
quench the Holy Spirit, and their passion for God is equalled only
by their fear of offending him. These are not men who take God
lightly. Their understanding of the holy character of their Creator is
awful in its scope.

Hezekiah prayed, 'O Lord Almighty, God of Israel, enthroned
between the cherubim, you alone are God over all the kingdoms of
the earth. You have made heaven and earth…' (Isa. 37:16). Bold he
could be, but not over-familiar. Hezekiah did not see God as a 'Big
Daddy', but an awesome, holy, heaven-enthroned and sovereign
Creator. Like the psalmist, he knew that God could be angry 'against
the prayers of your people' (Ps. 80:4). The prophet Isaiah had
certainly warned him that if he did not put away evil and 'learn to
do right' then God would not listen, 'even if you offer many prayers'
(Isa. 1:15-17). Men used in revival have a great opinion of God and
are touch-sensitive to sin, long before the revival comes.

Together with our prayerlessness, it is probably the unholiness
of the lives of Christian leaders today that convinces God we are not
really serious about revival. God's concern is well expressed
through his prophet Ezekiel, some 600 years before Christ: 'The
people of the land practise extortion and commit robbery; they
oppress the poor and needy and ill-treat the alien, denying them
justice. I looked for a man among them who would build up the wall
and stand before me in the gap on behalf of the land so that I would
not have to destroy it, but I found none. So I will pour out my wrath
on them and consume them with my fiery anger, bringing down on
their own heads all they have done, declares the Sovereign Lord'
(Ezek. 22:29-31). That is a powerful challenge to us all.

Before revival

Obedience to the Word of God

Not only are the leaders in revival men with a deep experience of God and a passion for holiness, but, as we should expect, they are men who are obedient to the Word of God. In 2 Chronicles 29:2 we are told that Hezekiah 'did what was right in the eyes of the Lord'. But how did he know what was right in the eyes of the Lord? The answer is that he was reading the law of Moses: 'He held fast to the Lord and did not cease to follow him; he kept the commands the Lord had given Moses' (2 Kings 18:6). The commandments of Moses mattered to Hezekiah; he wanted to know what the Word of the Lord had to say. Here was a diligent man searching out the Word of God, and there is evidence for this because Hezekiah is mentioned in the book of Proverbs. In Proverbs 25:1 we have the beginning of a new section; these are proverbs of Solomon that seem to have been lost for a while and had been rediscovered: 'These are more proverbs of Solomon, copied by the men of Hezekiah King of Judah.' If you look down the next few verses in Proverbs 25 you will notice how often the word 'king' is referred to. The proverb that caught Hezekiah's attention, and which he ordered to be copied out, were not the proverbs that referred to his military commanders, or the proverbs that told the people in the fields how best to organize their vineyards. He was not concerned chiefly to copy proverbs that told his educators how they should be teaching the nation. He was primarily concerned for proverbs that spoke of the life of a king. In other words Hezekiah was concerned to know what God's Word had to say to *him*. That is where revival begins.

All who have been used by God in spiritual revival were diligent in the study of Scripture and the application of the Scripture to their own lives. God uses men and women who submit to his authority. He does not begin revival with those who have no interest in his Word. When we look at the course of revivals, and those things that inevitably accompany them, we will see this again. However, it is the preparation we are concerned with here, and in particular the preparation of the people God uses. He will not trust revival to those who will not trust his Word. It has to be stated as a point of historical fact that revival never begins with the 'liberal' wing of the church; that is, those who deny the full authority and accuracy of Scripture. I am not aware of any exception to this. Of course, those who are critical of Scripture may subsequently be swept into revival and receive full blessing from it, but always their attitude to the Word of God will change. Revival is an *evangelical* awakening.

A significant comment is made by an observer of the revival in China from 1927-39, himself a national. Gih Tsu-wen reported that the revival was hardest and slowest in those schools and institutions where 'modernism' was taught; the poison had to be taken out of their system before students could be converted. Long before revival broke out under the preaching of George Whitefield, he records his own relationship to Scripture, and in doing so he could be speaking for all leaders in revival: 'I began to read the Holy Scriptures upon my knees, laying aside all other books and praying over, if possible, every line and word. This proved meat indeed and drink indeed to my soul. I daily received fresh light and power from above. I got more true knowledge from reading the Book of God in one month than I could *ever* have acquired from *all* the writings of men.'[38]

You will notice that Hezekiah *did* 'what was right in the eyes of the Lord'. He kept the Lord's commands. Perhaps one of the greatest problems of the church in its current scene is summarized by Ezekiel 200 years after Hezekiah: 'As for you, son of man, your countrymen are talking together about you by the walls and at the doors of the houses, saying to each other, "Come and hear the message that has come from the Lord." My people come to you, as they usually do, and sit before you to listen to your words, but they do not put them into practice. With their mouths they express devotion, but their hearts are greedy for unjust gain' (Ezek. 33:30-31).

Dr Tozer has said, 'Christians don't tell lies; they sing them in their hymns,' and one of the great tragedies today is that we come and listen to the Word, and we may invite others also to 'Come and listen to the Word of God', but we do not do what the Word of God tells us. The men God uses in revival were always men who did not merely pay lip-service to the authority of Scripture. They had a fear of being disobedient.

This was the key factor in the reformation under Josiah. The people rediscovered Scripture and obeyed it (2 Chron. 34). Similarly Nehemiah celebrated the completion of the rebuilding of the city walls in Jerusalem on return from exile with a half-day of Bible reading followed by exposition (Neh. 8).

A statement of the centrality of Scripture in the life of the church is presented as the first recorded words of the disciples in the assembled church in the Acts of the Apostles: 'Brothers, the Scripture had to be fulfilled' (1:16). And this is no accident. In fact the first action taken by the disciples that can properly be called church organization was the direct result of the application of Scripture. The Scriptures were used in preaching (2:17), in the prayer meeting (4:25) and in policy-making (15:15). The attitude of the early Christians towards the authority of Scripture is beyond debate. They had no doubt at all that the Holy Spirit had spoken through the mouth of the prophets in the Old Testament and the words were to be accepted without question. But if the Holy Spirit spoke through the prophets, he also spoke concerning the church, and action must be taken when the Scriptures demanded it. Never, in the book of Acts, did the church call a council or conference to discuss the nature of biblical inspiration. For these Christians, what the Scripture said, God said, and there could be only one proper response from the church: 'Therefore it is necessary...' (1:21). Obedient action must follow.

This total acceptance of Scripture as the Word of God, and

instant obedience to its commands, has characterized those whom God uses in revival. There is no escaping this fact. The reforms that took place under the leadership of both Hezekiah and, more than half a century later, Josiah, were all stimulated by a love for the Word of God and obedience to it. A study of the lives of the leaders in revival will reveal the same thing. If we long for revival, we must begin here. Jonathan Goforth was greatly used in China and elsewhere in revival from 1908 onwards. Looking back at those years he had this to say: 'We wish to affirm, too, that we can entertain no hope of a mighty, globe-encircling Holy Spirit revival without there being first a back-to-the-Bible movement.'[39] Goforth certainly practised what he believed, for in nineteen years he read through his Chinese New Testament fifty-five times!

The reason for this essential acceptance of Scripture is that in revival God uses his Word to change and correct his people, and there is always a renewed love and acceptance of Scripture. God will not trust leadership into the hands of those who deny the very weapon he is going to use more effectively than any other.

During the eighteenth-century Awakening in New England, Jonathan Edwards remarked on the new attitude to Scripture among the people: '[They] often speak of religious things as seeming new to them; that…the Bible is a new book: they find new chapters, new psalms, new histories, because they see them in a new light…' And speaking of one convert who had been listening to the gospel for nearly seventy years, Edwards continued: 'Reading in the New Testament concerning Christ's sufferings for sinners, she seemed to be astonished at what she read, as what was real and very wonderful, but quite new to her…'[40]

Martyn Lloyd-Jones experienced revival in his church in Aberavon during the 1930s. In 1931 135 were added to the church by conversion. But Lloyd-Jones was marked out during his time in Wales, and throughout his later ministry, as a preacher who took his authority exclusively from the Bible. During his ministry in London from 1938 until his retirement thirty years later he could hold between 1,500 and 2,000 at his evening congregation, and his preaching had as its greatest appeal a firm, uncompromising confidence in the authority of Scripture and the necessity of obedience to it.

Eighty years before Lloyd-Jones arrived in London, Brownlow North was converted, in November 1854, from a life of idle pleasure and godless indifference; but once saved, his powerful and urgent preaching stirred Scotland and Ulster by the revival year of 1859. For him, the Bible was his infallible guide to be believed and obeyed without question or hesitation. He wasted no time even to debate with those who denied Scripture; Brownlow North simply preached it. To enquirers he would advise, 'Go home and read your Bible,' and shortly before his final illness he declared to a friend: 'There is nothing for any of us but the Bible.'[41]

Charles Haddon Spurgeon preached to 6,000-8,000 people every Sunday night at the Metropolitan Tabernacle during the nineteenth century and his church experienced continuous revival for many years, with sixty new members each month being added to the membership. Spurgeon claimed no other authority than the Word of God and when he saw the Bible being downgraded by those in positions of church leadership, he exposed their actions fearlessly. The personal attacks that his courage attracted probably shortened his life.

Long before Lloyd-Jones or North or Spurgeon, Peter Waldo in the twelfth century, John Wycliffe in the fourteenth, Edwards, Whitefield and Wesley in the eighteenth, and a host of others, who were all leaders in times of revival, were fully committed to the authority of the Bible. And they were equally committed to obedience to it. They did not preach what they did not believe, and they did not believe what they did not obey.

Before revival

Determined courage

It required great courage and self-discipline to go for the thing Hezekiah most longed for. The king was determined, and you can hear it in his words to the Levites: 'Now I intend to make a covenant with the Lord, the God of Israel, so that his fierce anger will turn away from us' (2 Chron. 29:10). That is the kind of man God will hear; whatever else others might do, Hezekiah had made up his mind that nothing would deflect him from this great purpose. And he was aware also that his sin and that of the church deserved the anger of God. Humanly speaking, he took a great risk in setting out to transform the people; they might not want it, or be ready for it. Assassination was by no means unknown to the kings of Israel and Judah. If revival came, it would not mean an easy ride for the king; hard work and holiness are never divorced, but Hezekiah was determined.

Whitefield was not afraid of hard work. He preached at his Tabernacle in London every day (except Saturday) at 6.00 a.m. and 6.00 p.m. In addition he preached three or four times each Sunday and on many more occasions throughout the week, at weddings, funerals and in home meetings. He also kept up a wide correspondence. He spoke of being 'continually hurried and [I] scarce have time to eat bread'. The men God uses are prepared for hard work and discomfort. David Brainerd travelled through 3,000 miles of dangerous frontier territory, mostly alone and whilst suffering from tuberculosis, to preach to the North American Indians, and God blessed him with revival. John Wesley travelled 5,000 miles each year on horseback and preached, on average, three sermons a day; he wrote more than 250 books, edited over 450 publications and could quote from the Greek New Testament as easily as from his English version. God rarely uses in leadership in revival those who are afraid of hard work because he would not be able to trust them with the commitment that revival demands. The apostle Paul listed in his letter to the Corinthians his hard work and suffering for the gospel (2 Cor. 11:23-28). God came to Ethiopia in such power when the missionaries were expelled that the church grew from forty-eight to 10,000 between 1937 and 1943. We are told, 'The leaders were and are common, ordinary men with an uncommon, extraordinary faith in Christ.'[42] They were men willing to suffer repeated imprisonment, flogging and many cruelties, and yet stand firm to the gospel. God prepared courageous men, ready and willing to give up everything in order to be available to God. It is this 'extraordinary faith in Christ' that marks out leaders in revival.

They were also determined men. Before the 1904 revival in Wales, Evan Roberts was challenged by a church elder never to miss the fellowship meeting. 'Remember to be faithful,' the elder warned him. 'What if the Spirit descended and you [are] absent? Remember Thomas! What a loss he had!' Roberts tells us that from that moment he determined: 'I will have the Spirit. And through all weather, and in spite of difficulties, I went to the meetings…Prayer meetings Monday evening at the chapel; prayer meeting Tuesday evening at Pisgah (Sunday School branch); Church meeting Wednesday evening; Band of Hope Thursday; Bible class Friday evening. I could sit up all night to read or talk about revivals. It was the Spirit that moved me to think about revivals.'[43] Roberts was determined to get revival from God and he saw no cost and no discipline as being too great in order to achieve that.

When God came to Lewis off the west coast of Scotland in 1949, a local minister, James Murray MacKay, had prayed with his church officers for four months that God would pour out his Spirit in revival. They were determined to keep on until God heard them. The men God uses in revival are those who are wholly committed to him, passionately longing for God, and determined never to give up until God has his way with them. They may not be gifted in the eyes of the world, but they have a gift from God that may have no name in Scripture and therefore is little spoken about today — a gift of diligent and courageous determination.

Anything will distract us from the determined search for revival in these days. Sometimes it is the fear of being misunderstood, or that our fellow-leaders will not share the vision, or that the church will not follow. So a passing acknowledgement of the need for revival is followed by a rush into better structures and better man-management, more hectic activity and harder work. We will adopt anything rather than make a serious covenant with the Lord to give neither him nor ourselves any rest until his anger is turned away from us.

None of this must imply that the men God uses are incapable of error. Hezekiah was a great figure on the pages of Old Testament history, but Scripture does not hesitate to describe his frailty. In the fourteenth year of his reign, after all the work of God among the people, the king wavered in his confidence in God and stripped the temple to pay off the invading armies of Assyria (2 Kings 18:13-16). Later his pride, as we have seen, led him to betray the nation to the Babylonian ambassadors (2 Kings 20:12-18). There are very few who come away from God's searchlight wholly clean in the Bible records. Every man has his blemishes. The squabbles between Whitefield and Wesley and between Harris and Rowland over points of doctrine, though important points, hardly do justice to the men. Humphrey Jones returned from America determined to 'set Wales alight', and by God's hand he did, until his foolish 'prophesyings' put him out of usefulness to God. Howel Harris could be intolerant and arrogant, and Evan Roberts could be headstrong and unwise. And so we could go on. God does not demand that a man should be perfect in every part, but he does expect him to long for God above everything. And the fact that God uses a man at a particular time, and in a remarkable way, does not give authority or infallibility to all that he does or believes. One of the facts of revival is that God takes up and uses men whose theology, at some points, is certainly wrong. John Wesley was wrong in preaching against the doctrine of election, and in his views of 'sinless perfection'; similarly Charles Finney, in eighteenth-century America, was in error when he thought that revivals could be guaranteed if only man created the right conditions. But we cannot doubt that God used such men in spite of themselves. We shall return to this again when we look at the errors and excesses that sometimes accompany revival.

However, this cannot be taken to excuse poor theology or overlook personal unholiness. When Paul rejoiced that the gospel was preached even by men who did so 'out of envy and rivalry' (Phil. 1:15), he was not excusing the sinful motives of these preachers, but he did have a higher view of the sovereignty of God than of the sinfulness of man. God reads the heart, and unless we fear God and sin above all else, we cannot expect his Spirit in revival. There can be no point in seeking revival for the church, and its benefit for the nation, until we are prepared and longing for revival in our own lives. And if God has used leaders to prepare the way for his Spirit in the past, where are these leaders today? Where are the men who are humble and broken before God, men who are longing for God beyond all else, and men who ache with a longing for God to get glory to himself and saturate the community with his presence? And where are the men with courage and determination to lead the church forward and never to give up the vision of what God can do? 'Revival', claimed Douglas Brown, 'begins with a vision.'[44]

Before revival

Urgent prayer

This courageous determination in the life of the men God uses in revival is seen also in their boldness in prayer. They are never flippant and careless before God, nor are they over-familiar or presumptuous; but they are bold. The confidence and insistence of Hezekiah with God is seen in his prayer when Sennacherib, King of Assyria, threatened the city. Hezekiah was aware of the sovereign power of God, and on this ground he took his stand; he expected God to act, and even demanded it: 'Hezekiah prayed to the Lord: 'O Lord, God of Israel, enthroned between the cherubim, you alone are God over all the kingdoms of the earth. You have made heaven and earth. Give ear, O Lord, and hear; open your eyes, O Lord, and see; listen to the words Sennacherib has sent to insult the living God…Now, O Lord our God, deliver us from his hand, so that all kingdoms on earth may know that you alone, O Lord, are God' (2 Kings 19:15-16,19).

He may have learnt this confident way of praying from Isaiah who, when pleading for revival, acknowledged the same sovereign God and was insistent on gaining a response:

'Yet, O Lord, you are our Father.
   We are the clay, you are the potter;
   we are all the work of your hand...
Our holy and glorious temple, where our fathers praised you,
   has been burned with fire,
   and all that we treasured lies in ruins.
After all this, O Lord, will you hold yourself back?
   Will you keep silent and punish us beyond measure?'
                                                    (Isa. 64:8,11-12).

One of the most powerful prayers recorded in the Bible comes from
the lips of Daniel, who confessed his sin without reservation (Dan.
9:1-16) and then boldly urged God to respond: 'Now, our God, hear
the prayers and petitions of your servant. For your sake, O Lord,
look with favour on your desolate sanctuary. Give ear, O God, and
hear; open your eyes and see the desolation of the city that bears
your name. We do not make requests of you because we are
righteous, but because of your great mercy. O Lord, listen! O Lord,
forgive! O Lord, hear and act! For your sake, O my God, do not
delay, because your city and your people bear your Name' (Dan.
9:17-19).

All the ingredients of great and confident praying are found in
that cry of Daniel: an honest confession of sin and a total lack of
confidence in himself are contrasted with Daniel's conviction that
God must respond to defend his great name and honour.

Not surprisingly, the same pattern is found in the story of the
young church in the book of Acts. In spite of fierce opposition, the
Christians expected their Sovereign Lord to act for them: 'You
spoke by the Holy Spirit through the mouth of your servant David:
"Why do the nations rage and the peoples plot in vain?"... Now,
Lord, consider their threats and enable your servants to speak your
word with great boldness. Stretch out your hand to heal and perform
miraculous signs and wonders through the name of your holy
servant Jesus' (Acts 4:25, 29-30). For the early church prayer was
not an option but a necessity. They were 'devoted' to it (Acts 2:42),
and the definite article, '*the* prayer', in the Greek of Acts 1:14; 2:42
and 6:4 implies a commitment to corporate prayer.

You cannot read far into the story of a revival without discov-
ering that not only is prayer part of the inevitable result of an
outpouring of the Spirit, but, from a human standpoint, it is also the

single most significant cause. 'In the first month of the first year of
his reign, [Hezekiah] opened the doors of the temple of the Lord and
repaired them' (2 Chron. 29:3). The fact that this was the first
recorded action of his reign shows that he made it a priority.
Opening the doors of the temple was his way of re-establishing his
relationship with God, and that of the people, because the Holy
Place was in the temple, and it was there that the high priest brought
the prayers of the nation before God. Hezekiah started here because
he was aware that this was the root of the people's trouble: 'Our
fathers were unfaithful; they did evil in the eyes of the Lord our God
and forsook him. They turned their faces away from the Lord's
dwelling-place and turned their backs on him' (v.6). That was their
sin — prayerlessness. And Hezekiah started at that point. We
cannot overstress this. What Hezekiah did in that action of reopening the temple was to bring himself back into a true and prayerful
relationship with God. Those whom God uses in revival are men
and women of prayer. That is their great priority. And this is true of
a community also. If we really want God in revival, we must ask for
it. Our fundamental problem today may be a simple one: 'You do
not have because you do not ask.' And when we do ask it is half-
hearted and insincere, 'because you ask with wrong motives'
(James 4:2-3). We want revival to improve our reputation, vindi-
cate our theology, add to our denomination, or just to encourage or
excite us. In other words we want revival for our sake, not God's.

When the Holy Spirit saturated the 120 on the Day of Pentecost,
they had been in desperate prayer. And I use that word 'desperate'
carefully. Our Lord left them alone for what must have seemed an
eternity; they were terrified of the Jews and Romans, and on this
particular occasion were locked in the upper room. That was the
position God wanted them in. He wanted them at an end of their own
devices and without any confidence in themselves. They must have
been praying in desperation. This was the moment God came.
Generally among the churches in our country today we have not
reached that point. As we noted in the introduction, we have masked
our failure by extravagant claims and glittering showmanship. Only
when we realize and admit our true condition will we long for
revival. Praying for revival is not enough: we must long for it, and
long for it intensely. We have our revival prayer meetings, but we
are neither confident in God's willingness to answer, nor desperate
for the answer.

In describing how revival comes we can never overlook the part that urgent prayer and confident expectation play. There must be, especially among the leaders, the determination that God will come, that he must come. William Bramwell was typical of this. A powerful Wesleyan preacher towards the end of the eighteenth century and the first twenty years of the nineteenth, Bramwell was on the Dewsbury preaching circuit and longing for God to come in revival. He had been praying fervently for this when God gave him the assurance that the revival, which actually broke out in 1792, would come. Here is his own description: 'As I was praying in my room, I received an answer from God in a particular way, and had the revival discovered to me in its manner and effects. I had no more doubt. All my grief was gone; I could say, "The Lord will come; I know he will come, and that suddenly."'[45]

Duncan Campbell maintained: 'Desire for revival is one thing; confident anticipation that our desire will be fulfilled is another.'[46] God frequently brings his people to the point of desperation before he sends revival; only then will they learn that 'Without me you can do nothing.'

Before Thomas Charles was used in revival in Bala, North Wales, in December 1791, he had expressed his view that 'Unless we are favoured with frequent revivals, and a strong, powerful work of the Spirit of God, we shall in great degree, degenerate, and have only a name to live: religion will soon lose its vigour; the ministry will hardly retain its lustre and glory; and iniquity will, of consequence, abound.'[47]

In 1739 David Brainerd wrestled with God all night for his North American Indians: 'I exceedingly longed that God would get to Himself a name among the heathen...Indeed, I had no notion of joy for this world. I cared not where or how I lived, or what hardships I went through, so that I could but gain souls to Christ. I continued in this frame all evening and all the night. When I was asleep I dreamt of these things, and when I waked (as I frequently did), the first thing I thought of was this great work of pleading for God against Satan.'[48] The next morning he returned to his Indians with 'a strong hope that God would bear the burdens and come down and do some marvellous work among the heathen'. The following day their wild dancing was transformed first into repentance for sin and then joy in salvation.

John Wesley records a meeting in Fetter Lane when, with his

brother Charles and George Whitefield, 'About three in the morning, as we were continuing instant in prayer, the power of God came
mightily upon us, insomuch that many cried out for exceeding joy,
and many fell to the ground.'[49] George Whitefield drew up a list in
his diary of those actions by which he would judge himself each
day. There were fifteen items, and the first three concerned his
prayer life. The first one read: 'Have I been fervent in private
prayer?'; and the second was: 'Have I used stated hours of
prayer?'[50] Whitefield's diary shows that his 'stated hours of prayer'
were in the morning, at midday and at night. And he kept to these
times, as a minimum, with strict discipline. Jonathan Edwards
argued that it is through intimacy with heaven that men are made
great blessings in the world. And his carefully disciplined prayer
life gave his congregation in Northampton, New England, an
example of this. Nearly a century after Edwards first saw revival in
New England, Daniel Baker was greatly used by God on the same
continent. After his settlement as pastor of the Independent Church
in Savannah in 1828 he spent a day 'in fasting, humiliation, and
prayer'. The site he chose for this was a brick tomb in a Negro
cemetery, but it became a Bethel! His cold congregation was
revived, his ministry was transformed and, until his death in 1857,
Baker saw the continuous hand of God on his ministry with
hundreds converted.

It is said of David Morgan that for ten years before 1858 he
never prayed in public without praying for revival.[51] In 1904 Joseph
Jenkins in Cardiganshire in Wales prayed for the careless young
people of his church, sometimes praying until he lost all sense of
time. Jenkins had read Andrew Murray's *With Christ in the School
of Prayer* and he was convicted of not discharging his duty as a
minister. He set himself to pray as never before, until God came
down.[52] Commenting upon that revival in Wales in 1904, R. B.
Jones looked back to the latter years of the previous century. From
1897 many younger ministers were meeting together to pray for
revival: 'This fellowship intensified their hunger, bringing it at last
to a pitch near to desperation.'[53] One minister recalled that on a
Saturday evening when his sermon preparation was finished, he
spent time in prayer and 'There would come upon him such a power
as would crush [him] to tears and agonizing praying.'

Almost every Christian leader today laments a lack of personal
prayer, but very few are determined to do anything about it. We are

not sufficiently concerned to make a radical alteration in our diaries and get down to the 'unproductive' and unnoticed battle of assaulting heaven. We would all prefer to be compared with Hezekiah rather than his father Ahaz, but it was the latter who 'shut the doors of the Lord's temple', and in our lack of prayer we have done just that. When Hezekiah received news of a national emergency, he went straight to God (2 Kings 19:14-19), but, faced with an emergency among the churches, we prefer to tackle the problem ourselves.

But prayer cannot be left only to the leaders. Churches must pray also. Joel 2:15-17 is a vital passage for us to come to terms with:

'Blow the trumpet in Zion,
  declare a holy fast,
  call a sacred assembly.
Gather the people,
  consecrate the assembly;
bring together the elders,
  gather the children,
  those nursing at the breast.
Let the bridegroom leave his room
  and the bride her chamber.
Let the priests, who minister before the Lord,
  weep between the temple porch and the altar.
Let them say, 'Spare your people, O Lord.
  Do not make your inheritance an object of scorn,
  a byword among the nations.
Why should they say among the peoples,
  "Where is their God?"'

Here is a community of the people of God called to pray for revival, and it clearly involved a radical alteration of their regular programme. The first hint of revival is frequently a stirring in the life of prayer in the church. However, it is frequently the example of the leaders that brings about this burden for prayer in the church. Hezekiah set the example for the people by his own commitment to God in prayer. When Paul urged Timothy to prayer (1 Tim. 2:1), it was in the context of a letter to a Christian leader.

Zinzendorf was the leader of a Moravian community on his

estate in Saxony. The twenty-seven-year-old count was discouraged at the lack of spiritual life among the nine girls in his Bible class, so he prayed, and his praying was contagious; it led directly to the revival that began on 13 August 1727: 'Truly the great Moravian revival of 1727, which reached its climax on August 13, was preceded and followed by most extraordinary praying. The spirit of grace and supplications manifested itself in the early part of the year...What a spectacle! A gifted, wealthy, young German nobleman on his knees, agonizing in prayer for the conversion of some little schoolgirls! Later on we read that the Count poured forth his soul in a heart-affecting prayer, accompanied with a flood of tears; this prayer produced an extraordinary effect, and was the beginning of the subsequent operation of the life-giving and energetic Spirit of God...Not only Count Zinzendorf, but many other brethren also began to pray as never before...A number of brethren covenanted together of their own accord, engaging to meet often on the Hutberg, to pour out their hearts in prayer and hymns. On the 5th of August the Count spent the whole night in watching, in company of about twelve or fourteen brethren. At midnight there was held on the Hutberg a large meeting for the purpose of prayer at which great emotion prevailed.'[54]

The revival that came to England in 1859, and particularly to the preaching of Charles Haddon Spurgeon, can be traced back six years to the prayers of his London congregation. Spurgeon himself commented: 'When I came to New Park Street Chapel it was but a mere handful of people to whom I first preached, yet I could never forget how earnestly they prayed. Sometimes they seemed to plead as though they could really see the Angel of the Covenant present with them, and as if they must have a blessing from him. More than once we were all so awe-struck with the solemnity of the meeting that we sat silent for some moments while the Lord's Power appeared to overshadow us; and all I could do on such occasions was to pronounce the benediction, and say "Dear friends, we have had the Spirit of God here very manifestly tonight; let us go home and take care not to lose His gracious influence." Then down came the blessing; the house was filled with hearers, and many souls were saved.'[55]

It is not always clear when prayer meetings are part of the revival itself or are preceding it. But the distinction does not matter too much. Prayer is both the cause and result of the coming of the

Spirit in revival. In 1857 revival had come to America and, once again, it was a direct result of prayer. The name of the evangelist Dwight L. Moody is well known, but few are familiar with Jeremiah Lanphier, the New York businessman who became a city mission-ary. 'He had not been a city missionary long before he sent out an advertisement for a noon-day prayer meeting to be held on Wednes-days in the Dutch Church at the corner of Fulton Street in downtown New York. This man went to the room that he had hired. Five, ten, fifteen, twenty, twenty-five minutes went by, and no one turned up, until after he had waited half an hour, six others came one after the other. They prayed, and the next week there were twenty, and the famous Fulton Street prayer meeting had begun. The first week in October it was decided to hold the meeting daily instead of weekly, and within six months 10,000 businessmen were meeting every day to pray for revival. Within two years a million converts had been added to the American churches.'[56]

The same pattern is found before the 1859 revival in Ulster. James McQuilkin had been converted in 1856 at his home town of Ballymena by the witness of an English lady, and before long he had led three friends to Christ. The four of them agreed to meet every week for prayer and Bible Study. They chose the old schoolhouse near Kells and during the winter of 1857-58 each of them gathered an armful of peat and made his way to the schoolhouse every Friday evening. The peat fire warmed their bodies and their prayers called down fire from heaven. Two more joined them, including an old man named Marshall, but it was not until New Year's Day 1858 that they saw their first conversion. By the end of that year the prayer meeting had grown to fifty. They prayed 'for an outpouring of the Holy Spirit upon ourselves and upon the surrounding country. This was the one great object and burden of our prayers. We held right to the one thing and did not run off to anything else.' The prayer group was ridiculed for praying in this way 'but we kept right on praying until the power came'. It did come, and by the close of the following year 100,000 people had been converted in Ulster.[57]

You will notice that urgency and determination about the prayer meetings in Ulster: 'We held right to the one thing and did not run off to anything else.' Today few have learnt this. We pray occasion-ally for revival but not consistently; we pray casually for it, but not urgently. Surely this is what Paul meant by urging his readers to 'pray continually' (1 Thess. 5:17). He did not mean that we should

pray without a break, but that we should never give up. If revival is
to come, some Christians, somewhere, must pray continually and
never 'run off to anything else'. There are few prayer meetings for
revival today even though there may be an increase in prayers for
revival. In these days of busy agendas, prayer for an outpouring of
the Holy Spirit has to take its place alongside prayer for Mrs Jones'
back-ache and for sunshine on the Sunday School outing. Not many
Christians today know what to pray for when it is suggested they
pray for revival. More than 100 years ago Brownlow North, who
was greatly used in revival both in Scotland and Ireland, complained to the General Assembly of the Presbyterian Church of
Scotland: 'I believe there is one thing for which God is very angry
with our land, and for which His Holy Spirit is so little among us,
viz. the neglect of united prayer, the appointed means of bringing
down the Holy Spirit.'[58]

In Wales, the 1859 revival was preceded by earnest prayer in the
churches. William Griffiths of Llanharan urged his people to pray
and reported: 'When the stated Sabbath arrived, we were blessed
with remarkable earnestness at the throne of grace for the descent
of the Holy Spirit to revive the church and convert the world. Ever
since that memorable Sabbath, the prayer meetings presented a new
aspect — they gradually increased in warmth and number during
the following months. This continued to February (1859)…when it
pleased Jehovah to pour down His Spirit from on high, as on the day
of Pentecost.'[59]

A meeting of the Congregational Churches of Monmouthshire
on 14 June had urged upon the churches the need for prayer for
revival: 'The Conference unanimously recommended … That the
first Sabbath of next August should be set aside to hold prayer
meetings throughout all the churches of Monmouthshire, and as
many other counties of Wales as will see fit to join us in this
important matter.' The Baptists had encouraged the same and all
over the country pastors took up the challenge. Among many,
William Jenkins of Brynmawr found his congregation praying 'as
I have never heard them pray before. A new burden seemed to press
on their hearts.'[60]

In Japan, in 1883, a week of prayer for revival was followed by
a great outpouring, and during the next seven years church membership rose from 5,000 to 30,000. Early in 1900 the churches set

themselves to pray for a work of God, and a call went out for prayer that 'the Spirit of the Lord [would] prepare the way for a meeting of Pentecostal power'. Prayer meetings were held with as many as 800 gathering at one time. A year later missionaries were speaking of a 'Pentecost in Japan'.

Jonathan Goforth, working in China at the time of revival in 1908, wrote of the great impression that the prayer life of missionaries in Korea made upon him: 'Mr Swallen of Pyungyang, [North Korea] told me how that the missionaries of his station, both Methodists and Presbyterians, upon hearing of the great Revival in the Khassia Hills of India, had decided to pray every day at the noon hour until a similar blessing was poured out upon them. "After we had prayed for about a month," said Mr Swallen, "a brother proposed that we stop the prayer meeting, saying, 'We have been praying now for a month, and nothing unusual has come of it. We are spending a lot of time. I don't think we are justified. Let us go on with our work as usual, and each pray at home as he finds it convenient.' The proposal seemed plausible. The majority of us, however, decided that, instead of discontinuing the prayer meeting, we would give more time to prayer, not less. With that in view, we changed the hour from noon to four o'clock; we were then free to pray until supper-time, if we wished. We kept to it, until at last, after months of waiting, the answer came."'[61]

Joseph Kemp described the prayer that preceded successive waves of revival at Charlotte Chapel, Edinburgh, in 1905 and 1906: 'The meetings became marked by a deeper outgoing of the soul to God in prayer than ever; and a passionately expressed desire for the salvation of men was a dominant feature. Towards the close of 1906 there were indications that the Lord was about to move in our midst once more. The attendances at the 7 a.m. prayer meetings on Lord's Days increased, and the meetings were marked by a deepening spirit of prayer. This was followed up by the same prayer spirit in the week-night meetings.'[62]

Before God began the revival that swept across Borneo in the 1970s, he had been preparing the ground by giving the missionaries a burden to pray. One missionary comments: 'At the Field Conference in 1970 and over the following years God began to work in the missionary team. There are frequent mentions of an increased urgency in prayer for revival...' But the turning-point came when a group of Bornean students spent the whole night in prayer and fellowship. In June 1972 the missionaries held a houseparty for the students and this led to an even greater desire for prayer. Two students began to pray each evening at 9.30 pm; gradually the group grew and then divided into two groups until a great wave of student prayer was reaching God for revival in Borneo.[63]

Reporting on the revival in Shillong in the Khassi Hills of India in 1905 one eyewitness commented: 'There are many who ask "How did the revival begin?" To this we can only answer that "The wind bloweth where it wants"; but we know for a certainty that many people have been praying for a revival, praying, hungering, thirsting for it. In Wales Christians were praying that the Lord in his mercy would not withhold the blessings from Khassia, and in Khassia a very earnest spirit of expectation prevailed.'[64]

Nearly forty years later in India the Spirit of God came to Madras when the Christians began to spend whole nights in prayer. One, who had never prayed like this before, described how he felt at the close of his first night of prayer: 'I thought about an hour must have passed but to my amazement I saw that it was nearly daybreak.'[65]

In 1921 even the *Yarmouth and Gorleston Times* for 10 November acknowledged: 'God has become very near and the secret of it all can be summed up in one word — prayer.'[66] That local newspaper was right! In fact the revival began in Lowestoft in the London Road Baptist Church, where for six months prior to the outpouring of the Spirit in February 1921, around sixty members had met every Monday evening to pray for nothing but revival. Jackie Richie reminds us that this revival was preceded by a time of spiritual decline: 'Yet, in the mending lofts, on the boats and along the quays there were those who had a hunger for God. Days and nights were spent in prayer before the Throne of Grace. God had moved upon the hearts of these people who had little education and whose material means were limited, but who were "far-ben" with Him...These men "whose hearts the Lord had touched", had received a vision and were willing to wait upon God until the vision became a reality.'[67]

Revival came to Lewis in 1949 as groups of Christians, here and there throughout the island, set themselves to pray. Peggy and Christine Smith prayed, alone in their cottage. Peggy was eighty-four and blind; Christine was eighty-two and crippled with arthritis.

They prayed until they knew that God was going to send revival. For months James Murray MacKay and his church leaders prayed for an outpouring of God's Spirit.[68]

Methodism in the nineteenth century knew about the importance of prayer both to call down and maintain revival. Whenever they detected a decline in the revival, they renewed their effort in prayer. The work of God in revival throughout various parts of England in the nineteenth century, and in America at the same period, may be traced to the Baptist 'Call to Prayer' in 1784, which was taken up elsewhere in Europe, and the 'Union for Prayer' in 1785 and the American 'Concert of Prayer' from 1795.[69] When God came to Redruth in Cornwall in 1814 there had been a series of special prayer meetings early in February of that year. In 1901 in Melbourne, Australia, 2,000 'home prayer circles' for an outpouring of God's Spirit resulted in the city being 'moved from end to end by the mighty movings of the Spirit of God'. These 'home prayer circles' caught on in England and elsewhere by 1902, and it is to these that the revivals in various parts of the world from 1904-1907 owe their origin. In fact there is a story of revival that came to a church in Wales in 1903, a year before the general movement of God in the Principality. Four young men, all less than eighteen years old, had gone to the mountains every night for months to pray for their church. When the secret was discovered the church was so moved that they all turned to prayer and 'In an incredibly short time the whole neighbourhood was ablaze with divine fire.'[70]

Prayer for revival should never be self-centred. If we long for the glory of God then we will be ready to invest prayer time that others too will receive the Spirit of God in revival. Following a conference in the Philippines in 1975, 200 participants returned to their home countries determined to raise prayer for China, then in the grip of Mao Tse-Tung. In Britain, for example, the 'China — Too Hard for God?' campaign led to many committing themselves to pray for that great nation. What has been happening in China can only be understood in terms of revival. In 1980 in one area of the province of Fozhou alone, 6,000 new believers were baptized. It was reported that in one city in the province of Zhejiang there were now 50,000 Christians, or one in eight of the population, meeting in some 600 house groups. Today it is estimated that there may be as many as 50,000,000 Christians in China. Not that all this has been the result of that one prayer burden in 1975, but all over the world many Christians have never ceased to pray for China since the last missionaries were expelled in 1948, when there were fewer than 1,000,000 Christians in the country.[71]

Almost 250 years earlier, Asahel Nettleton in America knew the importance of communities praying for each other. At Milton he urged the Christians to pray for revival but then added, 'Whether you do or not, it is possible there may be one, for Christians in other places have agreed to pray for you'![72] This is a reminder that in our praying for revival we should never be parochial and long for the touch of God only for ourselves; we must pray for those churches that do not pray for themselves, as well as for those that do.

Prayer for revival must surely be one kind of preparation that is never wrong; it is essentially God-centred and not man-centred. It tells God we are at an end of ourselves. The church in this country is not at that point yet. Commenting upon Zechariah 12:10, 'I will pour out on the house of David and the inhabitants of Jerusalem a spirit of grace and supplication...' the Puritan Matthew Henry remarks, 'When God intends great mercy for his people, the first thing he does is to set them a-praying.' Similarly, John Wesley was convinced that 'God does nothing but in answer to prayer.' Arthur Pierson, who for many years edited *The Missionary Review*, made the same claim: 'From the day of Pentecost, there has been not one great spiritual awakening in any land which has not begun in a union of prayer, though only among two or three; no such outward, upward movement has continued after such prayer meetings have declined.'[73]

A greatly increased interest in the prayer meeting is not only evidence of revival, it is also evidence that revival may be on the way. The ready response of the priests to Hezekiah's order to reopen the temple was not in itself the revival, but it was the early rain that promised a harvest shortly to follow. God waits to see whether those who say they are concerned for the state of the church and the nation are serious enough to get down to prayer. Is he still waiting for his church today?

No church can ever expect revival unless it is praying for it. This is not to say that revival will not come to such a church, for God is too sovereign to be limited; but he is the God of the means as well as the end, and he has invited us to ask in order that we may receive. Our prayers for revival may be frequent, but our prayer meetings for revival do not last very long. A minister in Caernarvonshire, prior to 1859, speaks for many since: 'It came to the mind of the Lord's people in this place to hold a meeting for prayer once a week; and the particular subject of the prayers was to plead that God would also visit them in the influences of His Spirit, as comforter and convicter. This meeting was quite popular for a while; but somehow or other it gradually diminished, until the attendance at the gatherings was very low.'[74] Fortunately it was the news of revival in Cardiganshire, much closer than America, that revitalized that prayer meeting and 'The dawn finally broke in the young people's Sunday night prayer meeting.' But this gradual diminishing of our determined prayer is a mark of our lack of urgency and longing for revival.

We say that we long for God to forgive our sin and heal the land, yet we seem to have forgotten that he has set his own conditions for doing just that: 'If my people, who are called by my name, will humble themselves and pray and seek my face and turn from their wicked ways, then will I hear from heaven and will forgive their sin and will heal their land. Now my eyes will be open and my ears attentive to the prayers offered in this place' (2 Chron. 7:14-15). Hezekiah knew that condition and was determined to fulfil it. Commenting on the prayer that preceded the revival in Shotts in 1630, one writer remarked that while God sometimes works without his people, he never refuses to work with them.[75]

Before revival

Response to a godly example

In 2 Chronicles 29:2 we are told that Hezekiah lived according to all that 'his father David had done'. David was not the immediate father of Hezekiah, but in Hebrew there is no word for 'grandfather', so any direct ancestors are referred to as 'fathers'. Hezekiah lived according to all that David his father had done; in other words he was interested in what God had done in the past.

But we can go further and claim that Hezekiah was interested in how David had lived, so he read what he could find on the life of David. This is how Hezekiah found those proverbs written by David's son, Solomon (Prov. 25), and he was moved by what he read. One of the great concerns that we should have today is the lack of interest that evangelical Christians have in their history. If we knew the history of revival, and the stories of some of the great Christians of the past, some among us would stop crowing and start crying; we would realize that we are not in a time of revival, and that there are greater things that God has for his people. But there is another reason why we should know our history, and especially the history of the Spirit of God at work among his people: it would encourage in us a desire for God to repeat his work.

Hezekiah inherited the rich stories of God's care for his people in the past and he could say with the psalmist:

'We have heard with our ears, O God;
    our fathers have told us
what you did in their days,
    in days long ago...'

(Ps. 44:1).

And, unlike many today, he listened to what he was told!

When Asaph felt neglected, or even rejected, by God, and when he was tempted to doubt God's love, he knew what his response should be:

'Then I thought, "To this I will appeal:
    the years of the right hand of the Most High."
I will remember the deeds of the Lord;
    yes, I will remember your miracles of long ago.
I will meditate on all your works
    and consider all your mighty deeds'

(Ps. 77:10-12).

Incredibly for many Christians today, the psalmist concluded that the best avenue for his despair was a good dose of the story of the church! One reason why revivals often fade quickly is that the generation in revival begins to neglect what God is doing. A fire needs fuel to stay burning. When the nineteenth-century Methodists saw revival on the wane, they went to prayer; but not all have been that wise. However, our need today is to alert Christians to the desperate state of the church and to the only effective answer. The problem is that we have forgotten what God has done in the past, or we are not particularly interested in being reminded. Mention 'church history' and Christians scatter. But David needed no second encouragement. When he felt hounded and hard-pressed, with a thirsty soul that was unsatisfied even after praying, he set his mind upon what God had done in the past and that gave him hope in God:

'I remember the days of long ago;
    I meditate on all your works
    and consider what your hands have done'

(Ps. 143:5)

During 1858 God was moving powerfully across America, by his
Spirit, and there can be no doubt that it was this work of revival over
the Atlantic that inflamed the minds of many in Britain for a similar
outpouring of the Spirit here. The General Assembly of the Presbyterian Church of Ireland, meeting in Dublin in 1858, agreed to send
two of its leaders, William Gibson and William McClure, to see the
revival in America at first hand; they returned with enthusiastic
reports which they shared in meetings and in a book, and people
longed for God to do the same in Ulster. Meanwhile, reports of the
same work in America were being received in Wales through the
religious press particularly.

William Jenkins, the minister of the Congregational Church at
Brynmawr, was typical of many ministers at this time: 'Ever since
the news of the outpouring of the Spirit upon the American churches
reached our country, I longed and prayed that the Lord would, in his
infinite mercy, visit poor Wales. I immediately brought the subject
before the church and earnestly exhorted them to "seek the
Lord"…I related every fact and incident I could glean…in order to
produce in the minds of my people the desire of a similar
visitation…Some of [our aged members]…prayed as I have never
heard them pray before. A new burden seemed to press on their
hearts…There were no less than eighty-five added to the church in
about six months after those prayer meetings. This was in the year
1858.'[76]

The prayer meetings for revival stopped after a while, but they
began again when the people heard of the revival in Cardiganshire
under David Morgan's preaching. And they were given fresh
incentive when news of the revival in Ireland reached them. A
young preacher called Humphrey Jones arrived back in his native
Wales from America in 1858 determined to set Wales ablaze with
revival. Scotland was affected both by news from America and also
from Ireland. Prayer meetings for revival began in Edinburgh,
Glasgow and Aberdeen and when revival began in Aberdeen in
1859 it was commonplace for people to be converted actually in the
prayer meetings for revival!

Twenty years before this in 1839, William Chalmers Burns told the congregation at Kilsyth in Scotland about revival in the church-yard at Shotts in 1630, when 500 were converted during one sermon by John Livingstone. As Burns retold the story, he felt himself so deeply moved that he pleaded with the people from this godless town to respond at once. They did, and revival came to Kilsyth. In August of the same year Burns was preaching at St Peter's in Dundee in the absence of the minister, Murray M'Cheyne, who was in Israel. For some time M'Cheyne had made it a habit to use the Thursday evening meeting not only for prayer and Bible study, but also for 'reading accounts of Missions, Revivals of Religion etc.'. When Burns related what was happening at Kilsyth the people were prepared and revival came to Dundee as well.[77]

Asahel Nettleton was preaching in America during the first half of the nineteenth century and this contagion of revival is com-mented upon by his biographer: 'These spiritual awakenings were contagious and spread from one congregation to another. Often when a pastor and his parishioners heard about a revival in a nearby town or parish they went to see for themselves and frequently caught the flame and carried it back to their own vicinity. The revival at Wethersfield, which is just south of Hartford, is an example. Jacob Brace was the pastor of a church in Newington, to the east of Wethersfield. The people in this town "heard with awe" of what was going on in their sister church, and they occasionally visited there to observe for themselves. They did not want to be "passed by"'.[78]

There can be little doubt that the Welsh revival of 1904 was one of the most influential revivals ever. In 1905 the pastor at Charlotte Chapel in Edinburgh was persuaded by his church officers to go to Bournemouth for a rest. Joseph Kemp stayed there for only a day or two because the sight of so many invalids made him feel worse! He had heard of the revival in Wales and determined to go there instead. Years later he reflected on that visit: 'I spent two weeks watching, experiencing, drinking in, having my own heart searched, compar-ing my methods with those of the Holy Ghost; and then I returned to my people in Edinburgh to tell what I had seen. In Wales I saw the people had learned to sing in a way which to me was new. I never heard such singing as theirs...'

His wife took up the story of that introduction of revival to Charlotte Chapel: 'The evening he returned from Wales was

memorable. A large meeting was in full swing when he walked
down the aisle of the chapel. The people listened eagerly as he told
of his visit and its effect upon his own soul. After telling the story
he tested the meeting, asking if there was a man willing to be saved.
About five seats from the front a man rose, saying, "I want you to
pray for me." This man was the first of hundreds who were saved
during the revival in Charlotte Chapel. The people were now on the
tiptoe of expectancy for a revival. A Conference on January 22,
1906, addressed by several workers who had visited Wales, lasted
from 3.30 p.m. until midnight. From that day it was felt that the fire
of God had fallen; and as far as Charlotte Chapel was concerned,
God had answered prayer and reviving had come.'[79]

The effect of this powerful work in Wales is seen on every
continent of the World, including Europe, Asia, Africa, Australia
and America, as 'observers' and missionaries returned to their
fields of service from furlough in Wales. The Calvinistic Methodist
Church of Wales had a number of missionaries working in India in
the Khassi and Jaintia Hills in Assam. In 1905 revival came there
in a power and intensity that equalled that in the homeland. A
missionary describes how the first news of revival in Wales began
to affect the missionaries in Assam: 'When we read of the wonderful work of the Spirit in Wales, our desire for a spiritual Revival in
India was fanned into flame. Every week when the mail arrived
bringing fresh news, the desire became more intense, and almost
unknown to ourselves we began to pray for the Spirit, and to expect
a real Revival.'[80]

Similarly, in Madagascar Thomas Rowlands, from Trefgarn in
Pembrokeshire, learned of the revival in Wales and this stirred up
a longing in many: 'If for Wales, why not for Madagascar?' On 5
May 1904 revival came and soon Rowlands' wife was writing in her
diary, 'I think it must have been like the first Pentecost...Never in
our missionary career have we had such joy and gladness.'[81] In
America the Welsh churches longed for the same spirit of revival
and received it. It spread across the border into Mexico. In France
the French Home Office was sufficiently concerned about revival
there to order an enquiry into the effects this 'religious excitement'
might have upon those suffering from 'nervous instability'.
Sweden, Denmark, Germany, Belgium and even Hungary and
Bulgaria were all touched in 1905 by revival traceable to Wales.

Africa, Australia, New Zealand, China, Korea and, as we have seen, India were all blessed by the revival contagion from tiny Wales. Edwin Orr, reflecting on this spread of revival from Wales comments simply: 'The story of the Welsh Revival is astounding.'[82]

Revival in the Manchuria district of China in 1908 was a great-granddaughter of Wales! A longing for revival among the national Christians and missionaries in Manchuria was quickened by Jonathan Goforth's description of revival in Korea the year before; that revival in Korea was itself sparked by missionaries in Pyungyong, the capital of North Korea, hearing of the work of the Spirit in the Khassi Hills of India. The revival in India in 1905 was the product of Wales!

This revival contagion is almost impossible to explain merely in terms of human psychology. Christians could attend meetings and, as for example in Korea, 'return to their homes...taking the Pentecostal fire with them'.[83] Similarly, in 1921, when the Scottish fishermen were converted in Yarmouth and returned to their fishing ports in Scotland, 'It was like moving from one revival fire into another.'[84] In the Congo in 1953 a letter sent from one missionary to another describing the revival hundreds of miles away was like a spark that began an awakening there also.

Just as Hezekiah was influenced by the life of King David, so the lives of men greatly used by God have had an equally contagious effect in the story of revival. Many have been stirred to long for God in revival by reading the life of David Brainerd, including John Wesley, who recommended that all his Methodist preachers should read carefully the life of Brainerd. James McQuilkin was moved to pray for the power of God in Ulster after reading the story of George Müller of Bristol, and Rajamani in Madras was greatly challenged by the lives of C. T. Studd and Hudson Taylor.

It is not that revival can be caught like a disease, but that the effects create a longing and thirst among those who are told of them or see them. Most of those whom God uses in revival have themselves been made aware of what God has done in the past. This is not true of all, because there are times when God comes to a part of his church that has no knowledge of such things. But that is not so with us. We have a rich history of God at work among his people in revival and we are foolish not to take advantage of learning all that we can about past revivals so that we are responsive to God's possibilities for us. We need to have our eyes upon what God can do, our minds expanded and our vision set on the power of God's mighty work. God is perhaps waiting for us to be responsive to what he has done in the past.

> 'Like cold water to a weary soul
>   is good news from a distant land'

(Prov. 25:25).

3.
During revival

When Duncan Campbell described revival as 'a community saturated with God', he did so from personal experience. He knew what it was to feel the awesome presence of God which seems to be unique to revival, and to see the evidence of that presence around him. When God saturates a community with his presence, there are certain features that generally accompany the revival. These features are the subject of this section. However, there are two things that we must never forget.

First of all, we cannot limit God to work in a particular revival in exactly the same way that he has done elsewhere; there will be common features to all revivals, but every revival is unique. In this sense a revival is a unique uniqueness! Most true revivals have majored on powerful preaching, but in some, conviction has played the major part, or prayer, or praise and worship. Most have been led by a strong and vigorous leadership, but a few have been very much a 'people's movement', with no one name above the rest. It is a fact that most revivals in history are marked by an absence of modern-day charismatic gifts, but this is not true of all; in some, phenomena like healings, faintings, visions and so on are fairly commonplace, whilst in many they are virtually unknown. All revivals are accompanied by deep emotion, but whilst some express it in loud and enthusiastic behaviour, others are quiet, controlled and even solemn. And so we could go on. It is dangerous to read one revival and assume all are like that. Even in the same period of revival expressions of it in different areas can be quite unlike each other. The leadership of Evan Roberts in the Welsh revival of 1904 gave a very different emphasis to the movement from that of R. B. Jones in the north Wales town of Rhos at the same time. The record of revival in the days of Hezekiah, together with the rest of Scripture, will keep us within a biblical framework.

Secondly, we must never fall into the trap of assuming that we have only to imitate the features that accompany true revival in order to reproduce the revival itself. This point has already been made, but it must be repeated. We can become so excited with the idea of revival, which is a good thing, that we try to copy the effects of revival, which is a bad thing. Preparation is one thing; imitation is another. It is the duty of the church to prepare for an outpouring of the Holy Spirit but never to imitate it. Sadly, it is the failure to understand this distinction that has caused confusion and has devalued the word 'revival' today.

Revival is not solemn, serious singing and long, heavy sermons; nor is it light and breezy celebrations with plenty of music and movement in the sanctuary. Awesome quietness and ecstatic noise may both accompany revival, but in themselves they neither promote nor confirm the presence of revival. It is God himself who authenticates revival, and when he comes and saturates a community, his presence is unmistakable. The report of a distant revival may leave us wondering whether or not it is a true work of God, but we have only to visit it to find a clear answer. When God is there, those who are guided by Scripture and are sensitive to his Spirit should be left in no doubt. For all our tests, true revival authenticates itself.

During revival

A revival of urgency

Revival reveals in an exaggerated way those ingredients that God expects always to be present in his church. There is an immediacy and an intensity about revival that are absent in the normal life of the church. That is why 2 Chronicles 29:36 is such a good description of revival: 'Hezekiah and all the people rejoiced at what God had brought about for his people, because it was done so quickly.' It happened suddenly and unexpectedly. When God comes down people do not go home to think; they face up to God's claim upon their lives there and then. Whatever God says, they determine that they will do it immediately. In revival, the minds of people are concentrated upon things of eternity and there is an awareness that nothing matters so much as getting right with God.

When God worked powerfully at Charlotte Chapel in Edinburgh in 1905, Joseph Kemp recorded: 'There was nothing, humanly speaking, to account for what happened. Quite suddenly, upon one and another came an overwhelming sense of the reality and awfulness of His presence and of eternal things. Life, death, and eternity seemed suddenly laid bare.'[1]

When the couriers were sent throughout Israel and

Judah (2 Chron. 30:6) they went with all speed and nothing could stop them from delivering their message. With the activity of Assyria in the land, Hezekiah must have known that the future for Israel was bleak. Hundreds of thousands had been deported into exile and more would follow (2 Kings 18:9-12). In a real sense, therefore, this was their last chance to respond to the gospel before disaster overtook them. In revival people cannot wait to get on with the work of the gospel. It was 'in the first month of the first year of his reign' (2 Chron. 29:3) that Hezekiah began his great work. He could hardly have started sooner!

This sense of urgency is confirmed in the words of Jonathan Edwards when he was writing of the outpouring of the Spirit of God in 1733 in Northampton, New England: 'God has also seemed to have gone out of his usual way in the quickness of his work and the swift progress the Spirit has made in his operations on the hearts of many. It is wonderful that persons should be so suddenly yet so greatly changed. Many have been taken from a loose and careless way of living and seized with strong convictions of their guilt and misery, and in a very little time all things have passed away, and all things have become new.'[2]

Elsewhere Edwards remarks on this 'quickness' by declaring that 'There was as much done in a day or two as, at ordinary times, with all endeavours that men can use, and with such a blessing as we commonly have, is done in a year.'[3]

In the normal life of the church we slowly nurture people into the faith. We preach to them, reason with them and pray for them; and still souls are won by a long haul. But when God's Spirit comes down he contracts time. In America, Asahel Nettleton had been preaching on the subject of repentance in the town of Nassau in 1819. He describes his own sense of urgency in the meeting as he preached, and the response of the congregation: 'Never more expecting to meet my anxious hearers in this world, I urged them, by all the solemnities of the judgement, not to pass the threshold of the meeting house that night with impenitent hearts. They seemed to hear as for their lives...'[4]

Similarly, M'Cheyne described the preaching at Dundee in 1839 and claimed that in their sermons the ministers all sought 'the immediate conversion of the people'.[5] David Brainerd preached to the Susquehannah Indians about the merits of Christ, and his willingness to save them and, Brainerd concludes, 'Therefore [I] pressed them to come without delay.'[6]

An amusing story from the life of David Morgan during the 1859 revival in Wales illustrates the urgency in the appeal of preachers during times of spiritual awakening. Morgan had been criticized by some who thought that he did not give people sufficient time to think through the implications of their response to the gospel. The minister at Blaenannerch took him to task: '"What is this that I hear about you, David, my boy?" said John Jones. "What have you heard?",asked David Morgan guardedly. "What have I heard? What means this lugging of people into church fellowship without giving them time to sit down and consider and count the cost before they build?" "What time ought a sinner to get to consider, Mr Jones?" "More than you give them, by all accounts." "You are criticizing my method; what is your idea of a reasonable period for considering this great question?" Accepting the challenge John Jones retorted, "A month is not too much at least." David Morgan saw that his enemy was delivered into his hand, and replied, "Well! Well! God's Spirit says Today; the devil says, Tomorrow; but the old evangelist of Blaenannerch says, A month hence will do."'[7]

Our sympathies may in fact be with the old evangelist of Blaenannerch, but the speed with which God works, the sheer unexpectedness of it and the way he contracts time are all found regularly in accounts of revival. When God saturates a community he accomplishes a vast amount in a short space of time. When John Livingstone preached from Ezekiel 36 in the churchyard at Shotts on the communion Monday, 21 June 1630, we are told that he saw the immediate conversion of 500 people![8] 300 years later, in Ethiopia, God did a similar sudden work. There the number of Christians increased from forty-eight in 1936, when the missionaries were forced to leave the country, to over 10,000 when they returned in 1946. And that was under the harsh Italian occupation![9]

When the Spirit of God came down at Redruth in Cornwall in 1814 the church was on occasions 'spontaneously crowded by seekers'. The same thing happened in Lewis and elsewhere; people were drawn irresistibly to where the Spirit was at work. No one advertises meetings a long way in advance during revival; no posters are put up or leaflets distributed. The Spirit is his own advertising agency. Not that preparation or advertising is wrong, but a mark of revival is that there is no need for these things. A big crusade or mission, however big, is not a revival; unless, of course, God comes and transforms it. Our very organization is evidence enough of our need for true revival. In revival very few are left indifferent to what is happening; even those who are not converted are aware of God's presence, and many are alarmed, even terrified, of being close to the revival for fear of getting converted. When God came to Rhos in North Wales in 1904, a feared fighter of the town fled to the mountains to escape the revival, and God converted him there!

Even when revival is 'in the air' and might be expected, it is often overwhelming in its suddenness. In Broughshane in Ulster in the year 1859, the people had been expecting revival; after all, it was all around them. But they admitted they were 'taken by surprise, so sudden, so powerful, and extraordinary were the manifestations of the Spirit's presence…I should say about one thousand people were suddenly, sensibly, and powerfully impressed and awakened.'[10] It is this element of surprise that makes revival so uncomfortable for those who prefer their Christianity to be nicely ordered. Diaries and appointments are of little use when the Spirit takes over the programme. Duncan Campbell comments: 'Time doesn't matter in revival.' The Spirit is unpredictable; which does not mean that he works in ways contrary to his character or holiness, or in defiance of his own revelation in Scripture, but he certainly works to an unexpected schedule.

We must never imagine that this contracting of time, and the salvation of large numbers in a small space of time, means an easy ride for Christians. On the contrary, more sermons are preached, more counselling is done and generally more effort put in during revival. Whitefield and Wesley often preached themselves to near exhaustion, and the New England pastor Jonathan Edwards speaks of thirty converts a week for five or six weeks, all in need of pastoral care. He adds that extra meetings were commonplace.[11] But there is also an unusual enlivening in revival. Christians are able to preach and pray for longer than usual, without appearing to be tired. People will stay up late at their meetings, then go off to work the next day, and again stay up late at praise and prayer. 'There was life in the air,' was how one man explained it who had himself been involved in revival. Another has described how time and tiredness vanish in revival; as meetings continue, sometimes all night, sleep becomes 'impossible or undesirable; it seemed a waste of time in such an atmosphere'. The Spirit giving life becomes true in many senses during revival.

It is this urgency and life that are so evident as you read through the story of the church in Acts. On the Day of Pentecost the crowd broke into the sermon of Peter with the demand: 'What shall we do?' (Acts 2:37) and Peter demanded an instant response. Every sermon in Acts calls for the obedience of faith — at once. Paul, for example, reminded the men of Athens that God's command to them to repent was a command *now* (Acts 17:30). Whilst it is true that people did go away to think and debate further (e.g., 'We want to hear you again on this subject', Acts 17:32), the apostles never once encouraged people to do so; they preached for an immediate response. When the Spirit of God is at work in power, 'urgency' and 'immediacy' are the two words to describe both the preaching and the response to it. It was said of Wales in 1904 that you knew revival was on the way when you heard the 'Oh' of desperation and urgency in the prayers of the Christians.

During revival

A revival of Christ-centred preaching

God only uses men in revival who have a clear commitment to the authority of Scripture; and in the same way, revivals continue by a total trust in God's Word. An evangelical theology of the inspiration of Scripture is the baseline of revival. I am not aware of any exception to this. Hezekiah was a man who relentlessly 'follow[ed] the Word of the Lord' (2 Chron. 29:15; 30:12), and everything done in the revival was 'as prescribed in the Law of Moses' (30:16; 31:3, 21). Disobedience was to do anything 'contrary to what was written' (30:18). All whom God uses in exceptional times of spiritual power, both within the Bible and since then, are men and women who trust the Word and place it at the centre of their belief and practice; they test everything by it.

Commenting upon the revival in India in 1905, one missionary unknowingly summarized the place of Scripture in all true revivals: 'At the present time, perhaps, nothing may be found to be so appropriate as the supreme importance of the Bible, the whole Bible, and fundamentally, nothing but the Bible.'[12]

Thirty-five years later in India, Bakht Singh invited his

congregations to display their Bibles by raising them above their heads — and they were told to feel ashamed if they had not brought one. Whatever we may think of that, a van-load of Bibles was sold and 'People in Madras began to read the Bible as never before'![13] And if Scripture is at the centre of revival, it is hardly surprising that great and powerful preaching is at the heart of most revivals also.

In 2 Chronicles 29-30 there are two chapters that are concerned with what took place in the temple when Hezekiah had cleared out the rubbish. We read of three major sacrifices that were re-established: the sin offering, the burnt offering and the Passover. There was only one great purpose for these offerings: they were reminders to the people of sin and the possibility of forgiveness. The Old Testament sacrifices were gospel sermons; it was the way God continually reminded his people of the enormity of their sin and the cost of reconciliation. Every sacrifice was, of course, a preparation for the coming of Christ, so they were gospel sermons with Christ at the centre. The absence of sacrifices in the life of the people denied them the knowledge of God.

True revival is a revival of gospel preaching and in the time of Hezekiah it all began when the king turned back to 'following the word of the Lord' (29:15), and had taken the people that way also. True gospel preaching majors on the person of Christ — his life, death and resurrection, but always it is the Christ of the Bible; Scripture is the authority of the preacher in revival. It should always be. Most of the names associated with revivals are of men who preached. If preaching the gospel under the power of the Holy Spirit is not a major force in something claiming to be a revival, we would do well to look again to see what the true nature of the supposed revival is. Both in Scripture and in history preaching has been one of God's chief means of reaching into the hearts and minds of men and women. Hezekiah knew the 'Word of the Lord' and he applied it to the nation.

The immediate result of Pentecost was a sermon, and from there on the apostles saw themselves as 'heralds' of the good news. The word 'herald' was a specialist word for the forerunner or ambassador of the king. In fact, in Greek and Roman society the herald was considered so important as to have special protection from the gods. Yet this is the very word Paul used to describe his ministry when he wrote to the Christians at Rome (Rom. 10:15) and Corinth (1 Cor. 1:21; 2:4). Preaching is 'heralding', and since revival reawakens those things that ought always to be present in the church, it is significant that preaching almost always holds a central place in the revivals of history.

When Peter Waldo was converted to Christ around the year 1170, and discovered the clarity and authority of Scripture, he spread the good news by sending out preachers two by two, and the Waldensian movement reached out across Europe. 200 years later John Wycliffe was sending out his 'Poor Preachers', equipped only with the newly translated English Bible. A revival commenced which prepared the ground for the Reformation a century later. Hugh Latimer was an outstanding preacher during the Reformation, and wherever he preached, hundreds flocked to hear him. When Latimer preached before the young King Edward in 1548 courtiers crowded into the royal garden to hear him, and when he preached at St Margaret's in Westminster, the people crammed into the church until the pews cracked! A century later, the Puritan ministers placed preaching above all their other public duties.

Writing of the revival in 1839 in Dundee, M'Cheyne claimed to have discovered nothing 'peculiar or different' in the work of the ministers: 'They have preached, so far as I can judge, nothing but the pure gospel of the grace of God. They have done this fully, clearly, solemnly; with discrimination, urgency, and affection. None of them read their sermons. They all, I think, seek the *immediate* conversion of the people, and they believe that, under a living gospel ministry, success is more or less the rule, and want of success the exception.'[14]

Preaching in revival times is not always graceful or polished, or even eloquent, but it is always powerful. By this word 'powerful', I do not mean only that it changes lives, though it does that, but that the sermons are real and felt by the congregation. The preaching of Asahel Nettleton in America from the 1830s onwards was described as 'vigorous and bold...it was warm, pungent and awakening'. He was never 'graceful' as a preacher, but his plain, outspoken and serious ministry gripped the hearts and minds of his listeners. His biographer comments simply: 'His hearers tended to forget about the speaker and become engrossed in his message...[the sermons] were eminently scriptural and plain, and made men feel that *they* were the men addressed, and not their neighbours.'[15] When Paul came to Corinth some considered that his eloquence, or lack of it, 'amount[ed] to nothing' (2 Cor. 10:10), but both his message and his preaching were 'with a demonstration of the Spirit's power' (1 Cor. 2:4); that was revival preaching. In revival, congregations do not discuss a man's style or eloquence, in fact they do not even debate the content; they are moved to action. Revival preaching has a power and an authority that bring the Word of God like a hammer to the heart and conscience. This is exactly what is absent from most of our preaching today.

The men who preach in revival are always unafraid and urgent, and the description of Duncan Campbell as a preacher shows how seriously they took their task: 'There was nothing complicated about Duncan's preaching. It was fearless and uncompromising. He exposed sin in its ugliness and dwelt at length on the consequences of living and dying without Christ. With a penetrating gaze on the congregation, and perspiration streaming down his face, he set before men and women the way of life and the way of death. It was a solemn thought to him that the eternity of his hearers might turn upon his faithfulness. He was standing before his fellow men in Christ's stead and could be neither perfunctory nor formal. His words were not just a repetition of accumulated ideas, but the expression of his whole being. He gave the impression of preaching with his entire personality, not merely with his voice.'[16]

When revival came to Beddgelert in Wales in 1817, 'One of the outstanding characteristics', writes Henry Hughes, 'was that the preaching of the gospel had a prominent, indeed a predominant place in it...It was preaching which had the leading part in this revival.'[17] In 1859 the wind of the Spirit was blowing powerfully through many parts of Britain, and especially in Wales. Prayer meetings were given new life and thousands poured into the times of early morning prayer. However, nothing was allowed to interfere with the preaching — not even the times of prayer. David Morgan insisted upon the centrality of the preaching and in this way many extremes and excesses were avoided. Ministers were busy preaching throughout the Principality during 1859, and although there were exceptional men, like David Morgan himself, hundreds of ministers were used to feed the flame of revival.[18]

Rhys Bevan Jones admits that this was not so much the case in the 1904 revival. Certainly there was 'an intense hunger for the Word, and the awakened ones could not tolerate anything but the Word', but frequently the ministers felt unable to preach: 'Indeed, to cease preaching, at that time, seemed to many the natural thing to do.'[19] This was undoubtedly one of the great weaknesses of the 1904 revival in Wales. Though thousands were saved, and the fire of revival in Wales spread all over the world, its failure to survive long, and the disproportionate number of those who fell away, was in large measure due to the fact that in many areas preaching was neglected. However, it would be wrong to conclude that preaching was altogther neglected. If this was a failure of Evan Roberts, it was certainly not that of R. B. Jones, who reasserted the importance of preaching and seems to have deliberately 'distanced' himself from Roberts' methods. Jones commented thirty years later that this lack of preaching in the later ministry of Evan Roberts was a vital loss: 'Indeed it is not too much to say that, when the human leader could no longer speak his characteristic, vital message, his work entered upon a new phase. The Word of God is not only pure but also purifying. Its giving forth, whether in reading, preaching, or teaching, has a vital effect upon a meeting's atmosphere and success, for it lays an effectual check upon any elements therein that may be carnal. Others of the revival's leaders...did not give up preaching and teaching the Word.'[20]

Where preaching is neglected in revival, however 'spiritual' the reason, dangerous excess and error will be lurking. Preaching was central in the New Testament, and the church in any age dare not depart from that mandate.

It is this emphasis upon living, vital and urgent preaching, together with the people's confidence in Scripture and love for it, that produces such a powerful force in revival. Revival never begins with those who deny or despise the authority of the Word, and if people who do deny Scripture are effectively influenced by the revival it will always change their theology of the Bible.

One commentator on the eighteeth-century Awakening rightly claims that 'the uninhibited and compelling urge to preach the Gospel' was a basic characteristic of all the personalities involved, whatever other gifts they might have: 'Both Harris and Wesley had keen organizing ability, both William Williams and Charles Wesley had unsurpassed genius to write hymns, Whitefield's compassionate heart and breadth of vision well-nigh encircled the globe, and Rowland's communion seasons were heavenly, but each felt deeply the absolute priority and unique authority of preaching in the power of the Holy Spirit.'[21]

Preaching in revival is not dry theory, but a living and powerful force. Few people are able to leave the sermon unmoved; they may be furious, or converted, and even those who are neither are impressed by the power of God. The story of Whitefield preaching to the miners at Kingswood, near Bristol, is familiar to those well-aquainted with revival.[22] But Whitefield frequently describes the scene and the effect of his preaching in his diary.

Here are just two glimpses from his diary taken almost at random. The first is at Kingswood near Bristol on Sunday, 25 February 1839, and the second is later in the same year at Olney in Buckinghamshire: 'At four [in the afternoon] I hastened to Kingswood. At a moderate computation, there were about ten thousand people to hear me. The trees and hedges were full. All was hush when I began; the sun shone bright, and God enabled me to preach for an hour with great power, and so loudly, that all, I was told, could hear me...The fire is kindled in the country; and, I know, all the devils in hell shall not be able to quench it.'

At Olney, 'Though it rained all the time, yet the people stood very attentive and patient. All, I really believe, *felt*, as well as *heard* the Word, and one was so pricked to the heart, and convinced of sin, that I scarce ever saw the like instance. The Word of God is quick and powerful, sharper than a two-edged sword.'[23]

As a result of this kind of living preaching, people love to hear the sermon. It is no longer the plague to be endured once a week, or the butt of cheap jokes; on the contrary, the sermon becomes central in the activity and worship of the church. Jonathan Edwards commented that the congregations of New England in 1733 were 'eager to drink in the words of the minister as they came from his mouth'; and he noticed the changed attitude towards the sermon by those who were converted: 'Persons after their conversion often speak of religious things as seeming new to them; that preaching is a new thing; that it seems to them they never heard preaching before...'[24] To an extent that is true whenever someone is converted, but in revival the whole thing is intensified. When William McCulloch reported on the revival at Cambuslang in Scotland that took place in 1742, and at which Whitefield was one of the preachers, he listed the number of sermons before the communion service: 'Four on the Fast day, four on Saturday, on Sabbath I cannot well tell how many, and five on Monday.'

Robert Murray M'Cheyne commented upon the attention of the people to the Word of God in 1839: 'I have observed at such times an awful and breathless stillness pervading the assembly; each hearer bent forward in the posture of rapt attention.'[25] Of those days in Madras in the 1940s, one who was a leader through it all comments: 'I tell you, God's Word came alive to us then.' The evidence of this is clearly seen in the description of an evening in October 1940, during the monsoon season: 'The skies were dark and threatening and we thought it would be necessary to go inside: but a very large crowd had gathered, far more than the church could accommodate, and after prayer brother Bakht Singh decided we should carry on in the open. Suddenly it began to rain very heavily. He urged the people not to stir, but just to protect their Bibles by putting them under their clothes. He himself continued to preach with his Bible wide open. People just sat on the ground in the pouring rain with rivulets of water running beneath them. Though soaked to the skin they went on listening to God's saving Word. Only after a long time did it stop. There were mothers with babies in their arms, yet no one stirred until the meeting was over, and no one was anxious for it to conclude early. For a wind of God was blowing through Madras and the showers that watered our hearts were showers of blessing.'[26]

Shortly before this, at Carloway on the Isle of Lewis in Scotland, a revival between 1934 and the outbreak of war was noted for 'the eager attention with which young and old listened to the preaching of the Word'.[27]

Commenting upon revival in Borneo in the 1970s a writer declares of the people: 'Their readiness to submit themselves to the Word was awesome.' And the evidence of this commitment is noted by the fact that three years after the revival a missionary visited the Kelabit Highlands for a Bible-teaching tour and one of the first Kelabits to become a Christian in the revival followed him from village to village to get more teaching.[28]

But revival is not only a revival of preaching that is loved by the people and effective in their lives, it is also a revival of preaching in which Christ is at the heart. In the time of Hezekiah the blood of the sacrifice was central (2 Chron. 29:20-24). Seven bulls, seven rams, seven lambs and seven goats were brought to the temple and they were slain in the prescribed manner. We are told in verse 22: 'They slaughtered the bulls, and the priests took the blood and sprinkled it on the altar.' The people had stopped doing that; they did not feel it was necessary, and could think of better things to do with the meat than simply offer it as a burnt offering. And yet this sacrifice was God's way. And when the Spirit of God came, the sacrifice of the blood offering became central to all their worship. The priests and Levites were once again listened to.

This was God's way of salvation in order to show the people the sinfulness of their sin and the severity of judgement upon sin. They had been taking sin lightly. And therefore when God's Spirit came it was inevitable that the sacrifice of blood should become central once again. They returned to the blood of the covenant, and the covenant sealed by blood. Christ is our atonement, our covering; again and again the apostles came back to this great theme of the blood of Christ.

> There is propitiation through his blood (Rom. 3:25).
> We are justified by his blood (Rom. 5:9).
> We are redeemed through his blood (Eph. 1:7).
> He made peace through the blood of his cross (Col. 1:20).
> We were redeemed with the precious blood of Christ
>   (1 Peter 1:19).
> The blood of Jesus Christ, God's Son, purifies us from
>   sin (1 John 1:5).
> He has washed us from our sins in his own blood (Rev.
>   1:5).

This emphasis on the blood of Christ as the way of salvation has never been popular. Recently a university chaplain referred to it as 'this repulsive theory', and one modern Bible paraphrase tried to avoid references to the blood of Christ wherever possible, by substituting the word 'death'.

The sermons of the apostles were full of Christ. They loved to recount the historical facts of the gospel because they had no doubt that their Christ was the Jesus of history. So they declared that he had been 'killed, murdered, put to death, crucified, condemned, raised to life', and so on. But all this was because of who he was. Christ was 'glorified by God, the holy and righteous one, the author of life, Prince and Saviour, the Righteous One, Son of Man, Judge of the living and dead'. In other words, the historical facts of the life of Jesus, and the implications of these for who he was, were at the very heart of the New Testament gospel. And even though the Jews were offended at it, the apostles did not avoid the issue of the cross and the blood of Christ (Acts 2:36; 1 Cor. 2:2).

In revival Christ, and the blood of the cross particularly, is central to the preaching. Perhaps this is why many records of revival refer to the special blessings experienced at communion services when the blood of Christ is preached both from the Word and through the bread and wine. At Cambuslang in 1742 the presence of God was so real at the communion service held on 11 July that it was agreed they must celebrate it again, and very soon. Untypically for the Scottish Presbyterians, they arranged another service for 15 August and this was attended by some 20,000 people! Though only a few thousand were allowed to participate, hundreds were converted.[29] There are references to times of great spiritual blessing at communion services in revivals as far apart, historically and geographically, as the churchyard at Shotts in 1630 and Madras in 1940, and many revivals between. In eighteenth-century Wales, Howel Harris gave great prominence to this service, which he called 'the Royal Feast'. One writer has concluded that the root of the Methodist revival lay in the Lord's Supper.[30] The revival began at Herrnhut in 1727 whilst the community was at communion.[31]

In the eighteenth century Whitefield and Wesley found that the preaching of the cross was hated, just as it is hated now. But thousands found in the blood of Christ justification, redemption, propitiation, peace, reconciliation and cleansing, whether or not they understood all those terms. Joseph Kemp returned from a visit to Wales in 1905 and reported to his congregation at Charlotte Chapel in Edinburgh that the dominating note of the Welsh revival was 'redemption through the Blood'.[32] Whenever we hear or read that the Spirit is at work we can assess the genuineness of the work by how central the blood of Christ is to the preaching and the worship. And if the cross is central in the preaching and the worship then it will be central in the lives of the converts.

There are times when, in revival preaching as in any faithful preaching, the law of God must be thundered. But always the message must come back to the cross. Duncan Campbell was often criticized for declaring the wrath of God night after night, but he saw this only as a backcloth to the gospel. Hezekiah did the same thing. He began by reminding the people of past unfaithfulness and the 'dread and horror' when the 'anger of the Lord has fallen on

Judah and Jerusalem' (2 Chron. 29:8-9). But once having fixed this
backdrop in place, he went on immediately to the offer of
forgiveness and reconciliation in the sacrifice. It is said of Duncan
Campbell that those who listened to him could almost see his face
glow with light when he turned to the great theme of the love of
Christ and God's welcome to returning sinners; his after-meetings
were designed especially for those seeking salvation, and these
occasions were full of Christ.

David Brainerd comments that he saw the greatest effect of his
preaching among the Susquehannah Indians of North America in
the 1740s, 'when I insisted upon the compassions of a dying
Saviour, the plentiful provisions of the Gospels, and the free offers
of Divine grace to needy distressed sinners'.[33]

When Jonathan Edwards wrote of the revival in Northampton,
New England, in 1733 he described the centrality of Christ and the
cross in the lives of the people: 'In all companies, on other days, or
whatever occasions persons met together, Christ was to be heard of,
and seen in the midst of them. Our young people, when they met,
were wont to spend the time in talking of the excellency and dying
love of Jesus Christ, the glory of the way of salvation, the wonderful, free, and sovereign grace of God, his glorious work in the
conversion of a soul and the truth and certainty of the great things
of God's word...'[34]

Whitefield travelled to Scotland in 1742, and he arrived at
Cambuslang to find that God was already at work in revival and
hundreds had been converted. One who was present at that time
reported on the response of the crowds to the preaching of the
gospel: 'During the time of divine worship, solemn, profound,
reverence overspread every countenance. Many cry out in the
bitterness of their soul. Some...from the stoutest man to the tender-
est child, shake and tremble and a few fall down as dead. Nor does
this happen only when men of warm address alarm them with the
terrors of the law, but when the most deliberate preacher speaks of
redeeming love...Talk of a precious Saviour, and all seem to
breathe after him.'[35] In this revival at Cambuslang in 1742, there is
no doubt that it was the loveliness of Christ and the benefits of his
cross that formed the central part of the preaching.

In one of Count Zinzendorf's letters he described the kind of
preaching that was typical of the Moravian revival in 1727: 'Our
method in proclaiming salvation is this: To point out to every heart

the loving Lamb, who died for us, and although He was the Son of God offered Himself for our sins…as his Mediator betwen God and man, his throne of grace, his example, his brother, his preacher of the law, his comforter, his confessor, his Saviour, in short, his all in all; by the preaching of His blood, and of His love unto death, even the death of the cross; never, either in the discourse or in the argument, to digress even for a quarter of an hour from the loving Lamb; to name no virtue except in Him, and from Him and on His account; to preach no commandment except faith in Him; no other justification but that He atoned for us; no other sanctification but the privilege to sin no more; no other happiness but to be near Him, to think of Him and do His pleasure; no other self-denial but to be deprived of Him and His blessing; no other calamity but to displease him; no other life but in Him.'[36]

In the same way Paul wrote to the Corinthians: 'I resolved to know nothing while I was with you except Jesus Christ and him crucified' (1 Cor. 2:2). Powerful preaching is a hallmark of true revival. It is God's greatest and most effective weapon. In times of spiritual decline the church will resort to all kinds of antics to gain a crowd and stir enthusiasm, some of which will undoubtedly prove successful and a few of which will win souls, but revival shows where God's real interest lies. In a day when powerful preaching is rare, and even good preaching is scarce, it is inevitable that it will be dismissed. But our response should be to cry to God for such an awakening that will put preaching back in the centre of our worship and evangelism, and Christ back in the centre of our sermons. God is not pleased when the sermons go over the heads or out of the mind; he has always intended the sermon to change thoughts and inflame hearts. In revival it always does.

Always in a time of revival there is a hunger and a thirst for what God has to say. We are in the age of 'Be your own Bible student'. People listen to the sermon and consider that their own opinion is as valuable as that which they hear from the preacher. If they agree, they agree and if they do not, they have every reason not to. But in revival, it is almost always true that there is a respect for God's Word not only written but preached, expounded and explained. In 2 Chronicles 30:12 this readiness to submit to the authority of the Word through the leaders is clear: 'Also in Judah the hand of God was on the people to give them unity of mind to carry out what the king and his officials had ordered, following the word of the Lord.'

Jonathan Edwards complained, in 1733, that the young people, especially, were very careless and were not interested in listening to what God had to say through their parents or through the ministers of the gospel. But when the Spirit of God came in revival, 'The young people declared themselves convinced by what they heard from the pulpit, and were willing of themselves to comply with the counsel that had been given; and it was immediately, and I suppose, almost universally, complied with.'[37]

Submission to leadership is a biblical condition of worship and it runs right through both Old and New Testaments. The description of the Christians in the Acts of the Apostles was that they were dedicated to the apostles' teaching (Acts 2:42). And when revival comes, one of its hallmarks is not independency, but a holy dependence upon Scripture and a respect for those whose task it is to explain and apply it.

During revival

Conviction of sin and a revival of holiness

Holiness can never be separated from revival. If some kind of spiritual experience in an individual, or among a community, has the label 'revival' pinned to it, we should always look at the lives of the Christians and the new converts. Are they a holy people who fear only God and sin, and who allow God's Word to rule their lives? If not, then we are not looking at revival. Neither loud excitement nor sombre quietness, and not even love and gifts, are any necessary evidence of revival. But a deep conviction of sin and biblical holiness are. God prefers light to heat, and holiness to happiness. Some-one has described revival as the top blowing off. It is, but not before the bottom has fallen out!

In 2 Chronicles 29 not only did the Levites 'consecrate themselves' (v. 15) but they and the priests 'went into the sanctuary of the Lord to purify it' (vv. 15-16). They went into the sanctuary. The Revised Standard Version reads, 'the inner part of the house of the Lord', and there are two things to notice about the inner part of the house of the Lord.

First, it was that part of the temple which was *furthest from the eyes of men*. They could have overlooked this and few would have seen it. The priests could have shovelled away all the dirt from the outer court and swept spotlessly around the great altar outside; they could have emptied out the stale, stagnant water in the great bath in front of the altar and filled it with fresh water. Everybody would have been very impressed. But instead they went into the sanctuary and started there, furthest from the eyes of men. God judges the secrets of man. And holiness begins with an alarm at the sin lurking in the dark corners of life.

Paul never encouraged his readers merely to make promises to God, but always to take action. He writes in a blunt way to the Christians at Rome: 'Do not offer the parts of your body to sin, as instruments of wickedness, but rather offer yourselves to God, as those who have been brought from death to life; and offer the parts of your body to him as instruments of righteousness' (Rom. 6:13).

Christ said, 'Blessed are those who mourn,' which refers to those who feel their sin and cry over it. Sin is always a problem to the Christian who is longing for revival, and revival always deals uncomfortably with those things the world around us does not see. Revival throws light into the dark places. In encouraging his congregations in Wales in 1904 to prepare for revival, Evan Roberts would remind them that the Spirit would not come until the people were prepared: 'We must rid the churches of all bad feeling — all malice, envy, prejudice, and misunderstandings. Bow not in prayer until all offences have been forgiven: but if you feel you cannot forgive, bend to the dust, and ask for a forgiving spirit. You shall get it then.'[38]

But the second thing about the sanctuary is that it is *nearest to the eyes of God*. It was the holy place, representing God's presence among his people. Only the clean Christian can live close to God. In the same verse in 2 Chronicles 29 we are told that the Levites dealt with 'everything unclean', and they threw all the rubbish into the valley of Kidron. The Kidron Valley begins north of Jerusalem, passes the temple and the Mount of Olives and ends in the Dead Sea. Most of the year the Kidron Valley is a dry sun-baked river-bed, but in the rainy season it becomes a torrent. It was the city rubbish tip, because rubbish left here would eventually be swept downstream. Kidron represented a total removal, a complete clean-up. These Levites did not just leave the rubbish outside the temple. For the same reason, Moses ground Aaron's calf to powder, King Josiah crushed the pagan altars and scattered them in the Kidron Valley, and the Ephesians burnt their books of magic. When Jesus spoke of cutting off an offending limb he meant that there is no sacrifice too great to make us fit for God to use. In revival Christians will weep over their sins — sins that at present they entertain.

In fact it is this shame over sins that were once acceptable that we read of in 2 Chronicles 30:15: 'The priests and the Levites were ashamed and consecrated themselves.' All their past seemed to come before them as a great cloud of sin and they were sick of what they had been entertaining for so long. When Hezekiah reminded the leaders of the people of the disgrace of the past (29:6-9), he did so for this very reason: he wanted even the spiritual leaders to become painfully aware of how far the nation had fallen — including themselves! It must be admitted that when revival comes, those who have longed most for it may suffer most conviction in it. Revival always touches the conscience of those who long to serve him most. It was as the priests and Levites were busily engaged in the revival that they became most acutely ashamed of their past. According to 2 Kings 18:4 the emblems of idolatry and the worship of the fertility goddess, Asherah, had to go; the idols of the Baal god were also removed (2 Chron. 28:2). Worse still, many of them were reminded of the child sacrifice they once indulged in (28:3) — their own children cruelly put to death! All this came vividly before them and they were ashamed.

It is a sad fact that in normal times Christians hold on to those things that revival will snatch away from them. In Korea and Borneo Christian leaders held on to their fetishes and charms, but the revival made them so ashamed that these things were publicly confessed. The present-day secret sins of Christians will be brought into the open in revival, or at least into the mind of the Christian, and there will be no peace until all is confessed and put right.

This desire to be holy becomes a burning passion in revival, and Christians persist in fighting against sin in their lives: 'They began the consecration on the first day of the first month, and by the eighth day of the month they reached the portico of the Lord. For eight more days they consecrated the temple of the Lord itself, finishing in the sixteenth day of the first month' (2 Chron. 29:17).

Here was a sixteen-day spring-clean until everything unclean was removed from the temple. The priests started at the centre and a week later they came to the vestibule and then they started all over again! They never gave up on their warfare against all the rubbish that had accumulated in the temple. And then the priests reported to Hezekiah: 'We have purified the entire temple of the Lord, the altar of burnt offering with all its utensils, and the table for setting out the consecrated bread, with all its articles. We have prepared and consecrated all the articles that King Ahaz removed in his unfaithfulness while he was king. They are now in front of the Lord's altar' (vv.18-19).

Revival is always a revival of holiness. And it begins with a terrible conviction of sin. It is often the form that this conviction of sin takes that troubles those who read of revival. Sometimes the experience is crushing. People weep uncontrollably, and worse! But there is no such thing as a revival without tears of conviction and sorrow.

In January 1907 God was moving in a powerful way in North Korea, and a Western missionary recalled one particular scene: 'As the prayer continued, a spirit of heaviness and sorrow for sin came down upon the audience. Over on one side, someone began to weep, and in a moment the whole audience was weeping. Man after man would rise, confess his sins, break down and weep, and then throw himself to the floor and beat the floor with his fists in perfect agony of conviction. My own cook tried to make a confession, broke down in the midst of it, and cried to me across the room: "Pastor, tell me, is there any hope for me, can I be forgiven?" and then he threw himself to the floor and wept and wept, and almost screamed in agony.

'Sometimes after a confession, the whole audience would break out in audible prayer, and the effect of that audience of hundreds of men praying together in audible prayer was something indescribable. Again, after another confession, they would break out in uncontrollable weeping, and we would all weep, we could not help it. And so the meeting went on until two o'clock a.m., with confession and weeping and praying...'

He went on to describe a meeting a few nights later when many Christians were brought to a deep conviction of sin: 'My last glimpse of the audience is photographed indelibly on my brain. Some threw themselves full length on the floor, hundreds stood with arms outstretched toward heaven. Every man forgot every

other. Each was face to face with God. I can hear yet that fearful
sound of hundreds of men pleading with God for life, for mercy. The
cry went out over the city till the heathen were in consternation.'[39]

Scenes like these are typical of almost every recorded revival.
There is no revival without deep, uncomfortable and humbling
conviction of sin. It is this terrible conviction of sin that led the
Congolese Christians, during the revival in 1953, to sing a chorus
of their own making:

Receive salvation today,
This is the hour of judgement.

The missionaries wanted to change the words to 'This is the hour of
mercy,' but were pointed to Malachi 3:2-3: God had come as 'a
refiner's fire'.

In 1949, on the Isle of Lewis off the west coast of Scotland,
Duncan Campbell witnessed similar scenes of conviction over
personal sin: 'The awful presence of God brought a wave of
conviction of sin that caused even mature Christians to feel their
sinfulness, bringing groans of distress and prayers of repentance
from the unconverted. Strong men were bowed under the weight of
sin and cries for mercy were mingled with shouts of joy from others
who had passed into life.'[40]

Revival in China in 1906 was 'marked by a wholly unusual
conviction of sin'[41] In 1921, in the revival that began in the East
Anglian fishing ports of Lowestoft and Great Yarmouth, strong
fishermen were literally thrown to the floor under conviction, until
one eyewitness reported: 'The ground around me was like a battlefield with souls crying to God for mercy.'[42] When God came to
Borneo in the 1970s a headmaster, a professing Christian, stood
before his school and confessed his sin of holding on to some of his
most powerful charms.[43]

But this is not a twentieth-century experience alone. When God
came to Cornwall in 1814, the people spoke of the 'penitential pain'
when men and women were in great distress over their sin. At
Tuckingmill a meeting lasted from Sunday until Friday, with
people coming and going all the time. During this 'meeting' this
'penitential pain' was extreme in some cases: 'Hundreds were
crying for mercy at once. Some remained in great distress of soul for
one hour, some for two, some six, some nine, twelve and some for

fifteen hours before the Lord spoke peace to their souls — then they would rise, extend their arms, and proclaim the wonderful works of God...'[44]

In the first half of the nineteenth century God used the ministry of Asahel Nettleton in revival for over thirty years, and during his preaching scenes of deep conviction were commonplace. One observer described a meeting at Calway near Saratoga Springs in the summer of 1819: 'The room was so crowded that we were obliged to request all who had recently found relief to retire below, and spend their time in prayer for those above. This evening will never be forgotten. The scene is beyond description. Did you ever witness two hundred sinners, with one accord in one place, weeping for their sins? Until you have seen this, you have no adequate conceptions of the solemn scene. I felt as though I was standing on the verge of the eternal world; while the floor under my feet was shaken by the trembling of anxious souls in view of a judgement to come. The solemnity was still heightened, when every knee was bent at the throne of grace, and the intervening silence of the voice of prayer was interrupted only by the sighs and sobs of anxious souls. I have no time to relate interesting particulars. I only add that some of the most stout, hard-hearted, heaven-daring rebels have been in the most awful distress.'[45]

The same terrible conviction of sin was experienced in the previous century under the preaching of David Brainerd among the Susquehannah Indians in North America: 'I stood amazed at the influence which seized the audience almost universally and could compare it to nothing more aptly than the irresistible force of a mighty torrent or swelling deluge, that with its insupportable weight and pressure bears down and sweeps before it whatever is in its way. Almost all persons of all ages were bowed down with concern together, and scarce one was able to withstand the shock of this surprising operation.

'Old men and women who had been drunken wretches for many years, and some little children, not more than six or seven years of age, appeared in distress for their souls, as well as persons of middle age. And it was apparent these children (some of them at least) were not merely frightened with seeing the general concern, but were made sensible of their danger, the badness of their hearts, and their misery without Christ, as some of them expressed it. The most stubborn hearts were now obliged to bow.'[46]

In October 1791 there was a powerful work of God in Bala, North Wales. It began during the preaching of Thomas Charles one Sunday evening, and by ten o'clock that night, 'There was nothing to be heard from one end of town to the other but the cries and groans of the people in distress of soul.'[47]

At Cambuslang in 1742, Dr John Hamilton of Glasgow observed: 'I found a good many persons under the deepest exercise of soul, crying out most bitterly of their lost and miserable state, by reason of sin; of their unbelief, in despising Christ and the offers of the gospel; of the hardness of their heart; and of their gross carelessness and indifference about religion...not so much...from fear of punishment as from a sense of the dishonour done to God.'[48]

The priests in the time of Hezekiah were ashamed because their behaviour had dishonoured God. This is often forgotten today; our shame at sin should be the dishonour it has brought to almighty God. Revival never lets men and women forget that fact.

At Cambuslang — and the experience was by no means exceptional in the story of revivals — men and women suffered such agony and distress over their sin that some would faint or cry out under the burden. One of the ministers, James Robe, freely admits that at first he did not approve of this and tried to stop it, even asking that these people should be carried away from the scene! However, he later admitted that this was wrong because always such suffering led eventually to a great peace and joy in forgiveness.[49]

King David knew something of the physical pain of a tortured conscience:

'O Lord, do not rebuke me in your anger
    or discipline me in your wrath.
For your arrows have pierced me,
    and your hand has come down upon me.
Because of your wrath there is no health in my body;
    my bones have no soundness because of my sin.
My guilt has overwhelmed me
    like a burden too heavy to bear...
My heart pounds, my strength fails me;
    even the light has gone from my eyes...
I am like a deaf man, who cannot hear,
    like a mute, who cannot open his mouth;

I have become like a man who does not hear,
   whose mouth can offer no reply...
I confess my iniquity;
   I am troubled by my sin'

(Psalm 38:1-4, 10, 13-14, 18).

Does this account for Paul falling to the ground outside Damascus, and the vivid language of Acts 2:37, '...cut to the heart'? So universal is this work of conviction in revival that Jonathan Edwards puts it at the top of his list in describing how the sinner is converted: 'Persons are first awakened with a sense of their miserable condition by nature [and] the danger they are in of perishing eternally.' But in coming to this position, Edwards admits that 'Persons are sometimes brought to the borders of despair, and it looks as black as midnight to them a little before the day dawns in their souls. Some few instances there have been, of persons who have had such a sense of God's wrath for sin, that they have been overborne; and made to cry out under an astonishing sense of their guilt, wondering that God suffers such guilty wretches to live upon the earth...'[50]

Not infrequently this deep conviction leads to open and public confession. In Korea it was commonplace for times of confession, where wrong relationships were put right, to follow conviction of sin: 'Sometimes a man would get up and make only a partial confession of his wrongdoing, holding back the part he was really ashamed of; but the next night would find him back, pale and tortured, ready to rise at the first opportunity and confess his double sin in hiding his great sin the night before. Once the Spirit convicted a man, he seemed to get no rest day or night till he had unburdened his heart to the church and done what he could to repair the injury.'[51]

For two reasons I have deliberately laboured this aspect of revival and given a number of examples. In the first place we must be fully aware that this deep and painful conviction of sin is an inevitable part of true revival. If all this appears to be a frightening prospect, it is well to understand that God will bring it, and that a deep, uncomfortable, and at times overwhelming, conviction of sin is an indispensable part of revival. We often have a tinted view of revival as a time of glory and joy and swelling numbers queueing to enter the churches. That is only part of the story. Before the glory and the joy, there is conviction; and that begins with the people of

God. There are tears and godly sorrow. There are wrongs to put right, secret things, furthest from the eyes of men, to be thrown out, and bad relationships, hidden for years, to be repaired openly. If we are not prepared for this, we had better not pray for revival. Revival is not intended for the enjoyment of the church, but for its cleansing.

None of this should surprise us if we understand the ways of God in the Bible. The terrible judgement upon Uzzah for his careless contempt of disobedience (2 Sam. 6:6-7) is paralleled with the remarkably similar story of Ananias and Sapphira in the early church (Acts 5:1-11). The purpose was the same: 'Great fear seized the whole church and all who heard about these events' (Acts 5:11). In revival there are none in the church and few in the community who take sin lightly; God turns his anger into mercy but still he makes people 'feel' their sin. We have an unholy church today because Christians do not feel sin or fear it. The God who punished the sin of Uzzah, and before him, that of Achan and of Nadab and Abihu, is still as holy now as he was then; his view of sin has not changed.

Secondly, it must be understood that this experience of conviction, and the physical crying and fainting that not infrequently accompany it, can be fraudulently copied by men. There is always the danger that foolish men try to ape the work of the Holy Spirit. To set out to create these physical responses, whatever name we give to them, is a dangerous and sinful meddling with the work of God. It is not difficult to work people up to such a degree of intensity that they show the symptoms of conviction without the lasting fruit of peace in Christ and a holy life. Conviction of sin, and everything that goes with it, is God's work, and it is the wise Christian leader who leaves it in his capable hands.

Those who long most for revival should begin by examining their hearts and lives before the searchlight of a holy God and his Word. If we cover our sin and do not confess it now, when revival comes we may find ourselves confessing it to the church. When God came to the Congo in 1953, it was two months before the unbelieving world was touched; but those were a painful two months for the church, with missionaries, pastors, elders and evangelists confessing their sin. The reason why this deep conviction of sin is so much part of true revival is simply that the presence of a holy God is so real. A holy God makes the Christian aware of the gravity of even the smallest sin. When Isaiah went into the temple and stood in the presence of God, his response was devastatingly self-condemning: 'Woe to me!...I am ruined! For I am a man of unclean lips, and I live among a people of unclean lips, and my eyes have seen the King, the Lord Almighty' (Isa. 6:3).

The reason there is so little repentance among our congregations today is not just that our sermons are not directed against sin, but that God is not felt among us. Those who know themselves to be in the presence of a holy God are always aware of personal sin. Daniel is one example: 'We have sinned and done wrong. We have been wicked and have rebelled; we have turned away from your commands and laws. We have not listened to your servants the prophets, who spoke in your name to our kings, our princes and our fathers, and to all the people of the land' (Dan. 9:5-6).

Nehemiah was even more specific about his own personal sin when he cried to God for the derelict city of Jerusalem: 'I confess the sins we Israelites, including myself and my father's house, have committed against you. We have acted very wickedly towards you. We have not obeyed the commands, decrees and laws you gave your servant Moses' (Neh. 1:6-7).

An illustration of this is clearly seen in the experience at Baria in Borneo in 1973. One national Christian, Taman Ngau, records the time when the entire village seemed to be going to the church: 'There in the church we found the Lord. The whole place was full of the Spirit of the Lord. Young people were praying and worshipping. Some of them were confessing their sins and we began confessing too. We didn't realize we had sinned before, but we saw how filthy we were in the presence of a holy God.'[52]

But all this is only the beginning. Duncan Campbell declared again and again that true revival is a revival of holiness and that holiness is more desirable than happiness. One man, converted under the preaching of Campbell, claimed that his conversion cost him $10,000; he had to return to America and work for a year 'to make restitution for things I had done as a sinner'.

200 years earlier Jonathan Edwards commented that one effect of revival is to bring sinners 'immediately to quit their sinful practices'.

This deep work of conviction always leads to a freedom and joy in the new-found experience of forgiveness. Following the 'smiting of the heart' come the 'outbursts of the joy of salvation'. We shall return to the subject of joy in revival later, but revivals do not start there. It is not our happiness that God is concerned with, but our holiness; it is impossible to read the story of revivals without understanding this. If there are three things that are common to all true revivals they are prayer, preaching and a conviction of sin. If we are to expect revival in these days, we must expect it to hurt. In recent years we have been busy trying to convince the world by our Christian clowns and comedians, and by our big, happy events, that Christianity is fun. The reason why the world does not take Christianity seriously is because Christians don't! Revival does not persuade the world that the Christian faith is *fun*, but that it is *essential*. There is a colossal difference. The first work of the Spirit is not to tell us that we can be happy, but that we must be holy — because God is.

We saw earlier the kind of men God uses in revival. They were men who trembled at sin and whose conscience was sensitive to the approach of sin; men who did not try to justify their lazy, careless habits, but who lived disciplined and determined lives. If there is one thing common to the men God uses in revival it is that they fear nothing but God and sin. The reason for this is that revival is *always* a revival of holiness, and therefore the vessels God uses must be holy. A man may be extreme or even unwise in his leadership, but if he crosses the boundary into sin then God will set him on one side. Humphrey Jones was greatly used in Wales in 1859 until his pride robbed God of the glory, and then his effective ministry was ended.

As the leaders, so the people; there is no honour to God in an unholy people. When we look at the fruits of revival we shall see how great a reformation any revival brings to society. But the reason for deep conviction is so that the people will feel their sin and hate it. The deeper the pile-driving, the higher the building can rise. When revival comes, priorities are focused on what pleases God. Public houses and dance halls close, betting shops are abandoned, even sports are set on one side; work output increases, and honesty is the norm. In Wales, during the revival early this century, it was claimed that the pit ponies stopped work because they no longer understood the orders from the men — no one was swearing at them!

In the light of this, how many of us are ready for revival? Have we shown God we want a revival? There is a preparation that must begin *now*, and a concern to be holy will show God that we care. We will be saying to God, 'Lord, I long for revival, and this is how much I long: I want to be as holy as a saved sinner can be.' And if there is still no revival, we shall at least have done our duty and God asks us to do no more than that. The outcome is his, the preparation is ours.

> 'The Lord will indeed give what is good,
>   and our land will yield its harvest.
> Righteousness goes before him
>   and prepares the way for his steps'
>
> (Ps. 85:12-13).

During revival

A revival of prayer

'In the first month of the first year of his reign, [Hezekiah] opened the doors of the temple of the Lord and repaired them' (2 Chron. 29:3). That is not merely a statement about a new piece of ecclesiastical carpentry; on the contrary, it is possibly the most significant statement in this entire story of revival. Hezekiah began at the temple because by reopening the house of the Lord he was making it a priority that the people should come into the presence of God in prayer. Unless they came to God in *his* way, through the proper sacrifices offered in the temple, there could be no access to the Father. When the Hebrews entered the temple to worship that was their approach to God in prayer. Without this initial action by the king, the statement of 2 Chronicles 30:27 would be impossible: 'The priests and the Levites stood to bless the people, and God heard them, for their prayer reached heaven, his holy dwelling-place.'

There are therefore two periods of prayer implied here. The first was just *before the work of revival began*; it was the prayer that longed for revival and, from a human point of view, brought revival down. The second was prayer offered *during the revival itself*. All revival begins and continues in the prayer meeting. Before revival the prayer meeting is not always attended by many; sometimes only by a few, but someone is always praying. When revival comes the prayer meeting is among the first to benefit. Someone has called prayer 'the great fruit of revival'.[53] The meeting that is frequently the Cinderella of the church becomes the focal point of the life of the Christian community, and Christians who have avoided a prayer meeting for years are now longing for the next occasion to call to God. Prayer is no longer a burden, though it may be a battle.

When God began to move through the ministry of Whitefield he recorded: 'Sometimes whole nights were spent in prayer. Often we have been filled as with new wine. And often have we [been] overwhelmed with the Divine presence and crying out, "Will God indeed dwell with men upon earth? How dreadful is this place! This is none other than the house of God and the gate of Heaven!"'[54]

Murray M'Cheyne commented on the number of prayer meetings he found in his parish in Dundee when he returned from Israel in 1839: 'I found thirty-nine such meetings held recently in connection with the congregation, and five of these were conducted and attended entirely by little children. At present [March 1841, two years after the beginning of the revival]...I believe the number of these meetings is not much diminished.'[55]

M'Cheyne described these prayer meetings, at which, 'Serious men covered their faces to pray that the arrows of the King of Zion might be sent home with power to the hearts of sinners,' and many were 'bathed in tears'. The effect of such meetings was to 'spread a sweet influence over the place'.

It is far easier to allow the records to speak for themselves than for someone at a distance to try to describe these prayer meetings in times of revival. There is something always so living, urgent and real about them that second-hand descriptions must fail; in fact even the eyewitness reports can hardly do justice to the fresh life and enthusiasm that Christians have for prayer in times of revival.

One of the great marks of the 1904 revival in Wales was the meetings for prayer and perhaps one of the most moving descriptions came from a reporter on the *Western Mail* of the prayer meetings deep underground in the coal pits: 'The workmen on the night shift had gone down half an hour earlier than the usual time so as not to interfere with the operations of the pit. Seventy yards

126

Revival!

from the bottom of the shaft, in the stables, we came to the prayer meeting. One of the workmen was reading the 6th chapter of Matthew to about eighty comrades. He stood erect amongst the group, reading in a dim, fantastic light that danced with the swinging lamps and vanished softly into surrounding darkness. A number of lamps were attached to a heavy post closely wedged to support the roof, and around the impressive figure the colliers grouped themselves…Earnest men, all of them; faces that bore the scars of the underground toiler; downcast eyes that seemed to be "the homes of silent prayer"; strong frames that quivered with a new emotion.'[56]

A similar scene, though this time among a fishing community on the east coast in 1921, describes a Sunday prayer meeting at Cairnbulg in Scotland: 'Every Sunday morning from 6.30 to 9.30 a.m. there was a prayer meeting. It was held in a net loft above a wash-house close by the sea and known as "Mary Clarke's Joe's loftie". Heat came from a small fire and light from a paraffin lamp, but the fellowship was sweet. Ages ranged from 16 years to 60 years and the spirit of prayer was tremendous. One man who was there told me how these folks "grasped hold of the horns of the altar binding the powers of evil in the name of Jesus".'[57]

One result of the revival in Ulster in 1859 was the rapid growth of prayer meetings. In the Connor district alone, 100 weekly prayer meetings commenced. During this revival in Ulster prayer meetings could be found everywhere, even in graveyards and gravel pits! In Ballymena the large Presbyterian Church in Wellington Street could be 'crowded in all its parts by a prayer meeting' and this on Saturday, the weekly market day, when at normal times 'a dozen persons could scarcely have been convened for such a purpose'.

An eyewitness has left a vivid account of one of these prayer meetings. It could be multiplied many thousands of times all over Ulster during that eventful year: 'For some time before the appointed hour, many of the younger converts assemble to sing together some favourite hymns. A little later the people pour in rapidly and soon every seat is occupied, men of business sitting beside their workers, all in their usual attire. A large proportion is made up of the scholars and of the lower classes, who were specially visited during the awakening. Some seem very anxious and all are solemn. On the faces of the recent converts there is such a beaming gladness that even a stranger can tell their story at a look...The prayer which follows bears greatly on the three classes of worshippers, the converted, the anxious and the unawakened, and contains earnest pleadings for the Spirit's presence for the spread of the revival work...'[58]

Sometimes a burden of prayer has so overwhelmed a congregation that everyone prayed at once. There are reports of this in revivals in Korea, Borneo, India, even Wales, and elsewhere. In Korea in 1907 the missionaries felt a tension as if everyone longed to pray. Dr Lee said simply, 'If it helps you all to pray together, then pray in that way.' The reporter continued: 'Then a tide began to sweep through the church. There was no confusion; it was a single harmony of prayer, as if the voices of all the praying congregation merged together to form a single cry to God. There was not the slightest disorder. The Holy Ghost welded them all together into one. As on the day of the first Whitsun, all souls were tuned to the same note, and unity of the Spirit held sway.'[59]

Joseph Kemp described similar prayer meetings a year earlier in Scotland at Charlotte Chapel. During the revival there most of the converts were born in the prayer meetings, which though 'held by invisible hands', were 'usually of a tumultuous sort': 'One does not readily take in the meaning of simultaneous praying, in a meeting of from 100 to 200 people, full to overflowing of a strong desire to pour out their hearts before the Lord. How could there possibly be time for each to pray separately? After all, what need is there to wait? His ear finds no difficulty in dealing with the simultaneous prayer of a revival meeting.'[60]

However, this simultaneous praying is not a necessary mark of revival. In reviewing similar forms of prayer around the world the reporter from Korea comments wisely: 'There is a great difference between communal prayer inspired by the Holy Ghost, and communal prayer that merely represents a fading tradition harking back to some great event in the past. In general, traditions lack the wonderful harmony of the Holy Ghost.' But simultaneous praying is an indication of the great burden for prayer that revival brings with it.

Before revival comes, prayer is often a battle that is more easily entered than fought. But in revival, whilst the battle is still evident, God himself takes control. Occasionally the coming of God's Spirit is felt among God's people just as it was in Acts 4:31: 'After they prayed, the place where they were meeting was shaken. And they were all filled with the Holy Spirit and spoke the word of God boldly.' An example of this happened at Arnol on the Isle of Lewis in the 1940s. Towards the close of a prayer meeting in the home of an elder, the local blacksmith was asked to pray. His prayer turned to the promises of God and to his own thirst for God and concluded: 'O God, your honour is at stake, and I now challenge you to fulfil your covenant engagement and do what you have promised to do.' At that moment the house shook and 'Dishes rattled in the sideboard, as wave after wave of Divine power swept through the house.' When this group of praying people closed the prayer meeting and went outside, they found 'the community alive with an awareness of God'.[61] We cannot explain this, neither do we need to; it is simply an example of the powerful presence of God in revival prayer meetings.

In meetings like this, timid tongues are released to join in prayer. In 1938 a missionary visited the Lun Bawang people in Borneo. God had revived the tribespeople in the absence of missionaries and it was the times of prayer that particularly impressed him: 'At home prayer is so often laboured. Young Christians have to be urged to pray in front of others. Not so in the isolated jungles of Borneo. With no direct teacher other than the Holy Spirit, these people pour out spontaneous full-hearted prayer.'[62]

In a previous chapter we have seen the revival of prayer among the Moravian Community at Herrnhut in Saxony, when the Spirit of God came powerfully among them in August 1727. Adults covenanted to cover each of the twenty-four hours in prayer and by the end of the month the children were holding their own prayer meetings, spending many hours in 'praying, singing and weeping'. In 1905 in the Assam district of India there were occasions when work actually stopped as people came to the church at all hours of the day and night to pray; though instances of prayer interfering with work are not common. During the 1859 revival in England a Christian newspaper reported on the growth of prayer meetings in London. In August a prayer meeting was started at the Crosby Hall and within a month 100 people were meeting. By October there were six daily prayer meetings in the metropolis and by the end of the year the paper reported 120.

In revival, prayer becomes a delight and joy. And, as in so many aspects of revival, the form of the meetings may vary considerably. The vast prayer meetings attended by 18,000 people in Wales in 1859 were led by men specifically chosen to stand in a cart and pray whilst the great crowd added their 'Amen' or prayed silently. On the other hand prayer meetings are reported across the world where the whole congregation prayed simultaneously like the waves crashing in unison against the shore. This may be reflected in Acts 4:24: 'They raised their voices together in prayer to God.' There is no kind of prayer labelled 'revival'; as with singing in revival, when the Spirit of God comes he takes up the church's corporate prayer and breathes new life and zeal into it.

There is hardly a more powerful description of the part that prayer plays, both before and during revival, than that given by Joseph Kemp. Revival had come to Charlotte Chapel in Edinburgh in 1905 and two years later the church was still in the full experience of it. The members had prayed urgently for revival when their pastor returned from Wales in 1905, and when it came even that insistent prayer was transformed: 'What can I report about our Prayer Meetings? Did ever anyone see such meetings? They used to begin at seven o'clock on Sunday mornings, but that was felt to be far too late in the day for the great business that had to be transacted before the Throne of the Heavenly Grace! The meetings now begin at six o'clock and go on for almost seven days a week, with occasional intervals to attend to business, household duties, and bodily sustenance! Some of you who are strangers may smile — many of us did — but we don't now. It is that continuous, persevering, God-honouring weekly campaign of prayer that has moved the mighty hand of God to pour upon this favoured people the blessings of His grace in such rich abundance; and if ever you should be asked the secret of this church's great spiritual prosperity, you can tell them of the prayer meetings, and especially of the gatherings of God's people — forty to sixty strong — in the Upper Vestry every Sunday morning at six or seven o'clock — summer and winter, wet day and fine — to pray. Yes, that is the secret — the secret of our church's success and prosperity.'[63]

During revival

A revival of worship

Someone has described revival as 'the top blowing off', and that is very true. But the top does not blow off before the bottom has fallen out. Revival always begins by dealing with the people of God: alarm at sin, a longing for holiness and a revival of prayer are always marks of a true work of the Holy Spirit. From here, revival touches the worship of the church in a powerful way.

Possibly more than anywhere else in our evangelical church life, there has been over the last two decades what we can only describe as a revolution in worship. For richer or for poorer, we can only describe where we are today as radically different from where we were in the late 1950s and '60s. But if we have before us in the story of Hezekiah an illustration of revival then at least we have a very useful yardstick to measure things by, and it is always good to have a biblical yardstick; otherwise anything goes. Revival is bound to affect our worship, not necessarily by doing new things, strange things, or different things, but by injecting new life into what we do. Although it will affect our worship, it will not necessarily change any of the ingredients in our worship; it will simply bring a new quality into what is done. When the Spirit of revival came to the Isle of Lewis earlier this century the churches, then as now, still sang their metrical psalms slowly and without accompaniment, but there was a new life and reality in the old ways.

So what accompanied this revival, 700 years before Christ? First of all, Hezekiah 'opened the doors of the temple' (29:3). Sooner or later revival always prompts a rush for the house of God! People who have not attended church in years now long to be there. No one talks of the unbeliever feeling a stranger in the place of worship; you can hardly keep him away from it, unless he is afraid of being converted. In 1839 when M'Cheyne returned from Israel to his church in Dundee he reported: 'There was not a seat in the church unoccupied, the passages were completely filled, and the stairs up to the pulpit were crowded, on the one side with the aged, on the other with eagerly-listening children.' And for over four months, 'It was found desirable to have public worship almost every night.'[64]

A little over a century later, Martyn Lloyd-Jones was minister in Aberavon in Wales when God came in revival to the church in 1931. The description is typical of what takes place in revival. It was the 'eagerness with which the congregations gathered' that impressed one observer: 'On a Sunday evening the building would start to fill as much as an hour before the 6.30 hour of service, with sometimes not a seat remaining empty by 6 p.m. The Monday and Wednesday meetings had both to be removed to the church itself on account of the numbers attending. Shopkeepers would arrive straight from their business without an evening meal. Night-shift workers, due to report for work at 8.30 p.m., would come in their working clothes, preferring to miss part of the meeting rather than the whole.'[65]

The same thing happened in the Isle of Lewis in 1949. At the close of meetings others arrived; people could not be kept away from the house of God. Revival always seems to start here. There was an irresistible power on Lewis, so that when the congregation moved out of the church and began to go home they were met by the people of the town moving in spontaneously, wanting to know where God could be found.[66] In Borneo, when God moved in 1973, we are told that the whole village seemed to be going up to the house of God. Everybody was longing to open the doors and worship God

again.[67] So we are not surprised, therefore, that the very first thing
that happened when the Spirit of God began to move in the time of
Hezekiah was that the doors of the temple were opened and people
began to worship God again.

Solemn respect for God

But what kind of worship was going on in the temple? Perhaps the
most marked aspect of it was a holy seriousness and respect for
God: 'The whole assembly bowed in worship...When the offerings
were finished, the king and everyone present with him knelt down
and worshipped' (2 Chron. 29:28-29). There were some noisy
scenes in their worship, which we shall look at in a moment, but
their attitude to God is revealed in the phrase, 'The whole assembly
bowed in worship.' The presence of the choir and the orchestra is
no necessary barrier to revival; nor is it necessary evidence of it
either.

There are various ways of worshipping God and we should be
careful before we criticize others. Culture and temperament all play
their part, even in revival. So when the Spirit came to Wales, there
were frequent outbursts of praising at the preaching services.
Sometimes the preachers were interrupted and not able to continue
because the praising was so great. On the other hand, a little before
this, in Dundee, an awful and breathless stillness pervaded the
assembly, 'each hearer bent forward in the posture of wrapt attention'. The experience of simultaneous praying, which has been
common in revivals in Asia, occurs less frequently in accounts from
Europe.

There is something characteristic about these differences.
Revivals are not all according to the same identical pattern. They do
not all come out of a mould in heaven called 'revival'. Sometimes
meetings in revival are quiet and controlled. An early biographer of
Asahel Nettleton describes many of the meetings in America under
the preaching of Nettleton as, 'No bustle...all was orderly, quiet,
and Scriptural,'[68] whereas many of the gatherings under the
preaching of Evan Roberts in Wales in 1904 were 'go-as-you-
please for two hours or more...People pray and sing, give
testimony; exhort as the Spirit moves them,'[69] though it was
remarked that there was no confusion or disorder even under

Roberts. As Joseph Kemp remarked from Edinburgh in 1905, 'The confusion never gets confused.'[70]

God deals with us in different ways, just as he converts people in different ways. One man may be converted suddenly, in a moment, and in a great passion and agony of soul. Another man reasons and thinks and works his intellect until one day God gives him faith and he too is converted. Either way they come to the same cross, but by different routes. Of course, there are some things that have no mandate from the Word of God, but even within Scripture there is a fair degree of liberty to worship as God leads us and as we find best. No one today, or in any day, has the only right style of worship.

'The whole assembly bowed in worship…The king and everyone with him knelt down and worshipped' (2 Chron. 29:28-29). The one constant factor that appears again and again in revival worship is this sense of the awful holiness of God. The people are serious. M'Cheyne in 1839 wrote of the revival in Dundee: 'It pleased God…to bring an awfully solemn sense of divine things over the minds of men…There is far more solemnity in the house of God.'[71] Under Nettleton, it was said: 'There seems to have been an increasing solemnity while the work continued.'[72] In fact this affected the whole community. From Ulster during 1859 it was reported: 'During the service there were indications of an unusual solemnity, the most intense earnestness being depicted on every countenance…'[73] A contemporary newspaper claimed that the most striking feature of the revival in Wales in the same year was 'a pervading and overwhelming solemnity…'[74] When Whitefield took part in the preaching and communion service at Cambuslang in 1742 one report claims, 'The thing most remarkable, was the spiritual glory of this solemnity…,' and Alexander Webster of Edinburgh described the 'solemn, profound reverence [that] overspread every countenance' during the services at Cambuslang.[75] Revival came to Carloway on the Isle of Lewis between 1934 and the beginning of the war, and an elder in the Free Church recalls: 'The churches were full, and the solemnity at these services was awe-inspiring…'[76] And so we could continue. No one caught up in the spirit of revival can ever take it lightly and flippantly; joy there may be, but not jollity. A holy seriousness is a hallmark of true revival. 'Solemnity' appears to be a key word in describing revival meetings.

Rhys Bevan Jones described a scene at Amlwch, Anglesey during one of the most powerful meetings he ever experienced in Wales in 1904: 'The whole place at that moment was so awful with the glory of God — one uses the word "awful" deliberately; the holy presence of God was so manifested that the speaker himself was overwhelmed; the pulpit where he stood was so filled with the light of God that he had to withdraw! There; let us leave it at that. Words cannot but mock such an experience.'[77]

The presence of God

This is the key to understanding what revival is. If there is one aspect of worship today that is lacking, it is the felt presence of God. Whatever our label or style, whatever our claims or convictions, Christian churches today are not generally noted for the over-whelming sense of the presence of God. That is why we can behave so carelessly in worship. The deep work of the Spirit in revival is always noted for the experience that convinces us that God is present. Of course we believe the promises of God that he is always with us, and especially when Christians meet together; even without a sense of his presence, we are right to believe that he is a promise-keeping God. However, revival is altogether different. God is *known* to be there, and even the unbeliever is compelled to admit, 'God is really among you' (1 Cor. 14:25). In revival the presence of God becomes a tangible, felt experience.

The presence of God was familiar to many of the greatest leaders in the Old Testament and the phrase 'the face of God', which is well translated 'the presence of God', occurs often. In Exodus 33:14-16 God promised that his presence would go with the Israelites, and Moses was so insistent upon this that he refused to consider a forward march unless God kept his promise. For Moses, it was one great hallmark of their worship and activity that distinguished the Israelites from the surrounding nations. This 'felt' presence of God was convincing evidence that these people were in favour with the Sovereign Lord: 'Then Moses said to him, "If your Presence does not go with us, do not send us up from here. How will anyone know that you are pleased with me and with your people unless you go with us? What else will distinguish me and your people from all the other people on the face of the earth?"' (Exod. 33:15-16).

The presence of God is part of the gospel and it is the very thing that man forfeits by his sin. Adam hid from God's presence, and Cain 'went out from the Lord's presence' (Gen. 4:16). Salvation is God restoring his presence; and the Christian church is marked by that very thing. Sadly, in normal times the presence of God is hardly felt among his people, but in revival it becomes so evident that at times it is overwhelming.

A prayer meeting attended by thousands in Wales in 1859 left one man aware only of God. He walked away in silent awe. 'A friend stopped him, and said, "What a glorious sight that was, when the thousands were engaged in silent prayer at Mr Morgan's request! Did you ever see anything like it, Mr John?" He answered solemnly, "I didn't see one of them: I saw *no one but God*. I am going home," he said suddenly. "How terrible is this place! It is too terrible for me. My flesh is too weak to bear this weight of glory..."'[78]

On Wednesday, 13 August 1727 God came among the small community of exiles at Herrnhut on the estate of Count Zinzendorf in Saxony: 'A sense of the nearness of Christ was given to us all at the same moment...what the Lord did for Herrnhut, from that time till the winter of the same year, is inexpressible. The whole place appeared like a visible tabernacle of God with men.'[79]

One report of the revival in Cambuslang in 1742 speaks of the 'gracious and sensible presence of God'.[80] Over a century later in Wales we meet the same word: 'The house was often so full of the divine presence that ungodly men trembled terror-stricken...'[81] During the 1904 revival people could feel the presence of God even at a distance from a town; it was something felt and tangible. And a year later, far away in Australia God was at work; at meetings in Bowden Methodist Church the congregations were reluctant to leave and 'Manifestations of the Divine Presence and power were marked and felt by all present.'[82] In 1906 Joseph Kemp described the coming of the Spirit to Charlotte Chapel in Edinburgh: 'Quite suddenly, upon one and another came an overwhelming sense of the reality and awfulness of His presence and of eternal things.'[83] In January 1907, when God came down among his people in North Korea a missionary records: 'Each felt as he entered the church that the room was full of God's presence...That night in Pyungyang...[there was] a sense of God's nearness impossible of description.'[84]

Among the fishing ports of the east coast of Britain in 1921, tough, burly fishermen were giving testimony to how God had dealt with them: 'As these recently converted people got up and told how and when they were saved, the atmosphere was charged with the presence of God.' In fact it is recorded that in Yarmouth that year, 'The entire town was in the grip of the presence of God.' So evident was this that even the *Yarmouth & Gorleston Times* of 10 November reported: 'God has become very near.'[85]

In 1949 Duncan Campbell was at Arnol on the island of Lewis, off the west coast of Scotland; when God came down the community became 'alive with an awareness of God'. In another place, during the revival of 1949 in the Western Isles, a man came to the home of a minister in great concern for his spiritual welfare. The minister asked, 'What touched you? I haven't seen you at any of the services', to which the man replied, 'No, I haven't been to church but this revival is in the air. I can't get away from the Spirit.'[86] The small island of Bernea lies off the coast of the Isle of Harris in Scotland with a population of just 400 people. In April 1952 God came down and the minister of the Church of Scotland, Angus MacFarlane, was suddenly conscious that God had come upon the congregation. Duncan Campbell commented, 'Perhaps the most outstanding feature in this part of Harris was the awe-inspiring sense of the presence of God...'[87] Frequently it was the awful presence of God that brought a deep conviction of sin upon a congregation. When the presence of God is an inescapable fact, then we are in revival. It was this tangible experience of the presence of God that led Duncan Campbell to describe revival as 'a community saturated with God'.

This 'presence of God' defies human explanation, but it accounts for the exceptional experiences of revival. It is also this ingredient today that is so sadly absent from our meetings. Duncan Campbell claimed, 'I have no hesitation in saying that this awareness of God is the crying need of the church today.'[88] It cannot be made up for by the counterfeit of religious sobriety or enthusiastic wildness. It is altogether different from anything the church normally experiences, and it certainly cannot be created by human devices. But it is this sense of God's presence that compels a reverent awe of God. "'Should you not fear me?" declares the Lord, "Should you not tremble in my presence?"' (Jer. 5:22).

Joy and singing

Singing has always been part of the worship of God. From the moment of creation the morning stars and the angels themselves have worshipped God in song (Job 38:7). The Israelites sang when God set them free from slavery in Eygpt (Exod. 15) and David 'sang to the Lord' when God rescued him from his enemies (2 Sam. 22); he then established a choir for the temple worship. Psalm after psalm encourages us to sing out our worship of God and this was David's own natural response to God's personal deliverence: 'He put a new song in my mouth, a hymn of praise to our God' (Ps. 40:3). When God brought his people back from their exile in Babylon, Psalm 126:2 describes their response: 'Our mouths were filled with laughter, our tongues with songs of joy.' Revival brings to thousands a greater liberty than a return from a land of exile: it brings a new life and new peace with God. It is hardly surprising, therefore, that those who have been suddenly rescued from hell should have their tongues filled with 'songs of joy', and even the regular singers have a new song to sing. It was in this long tradition of choral worship that Hezekiah encouraged his priests and Levites to 'praise the Lord with the words of David and of Asaph' (2 Chron. 29:30).

The deep repentance of sorrow over sin in revival, which crushes the spirit and makes even the body weak, soon gives way to rejoicing 'with an inexpressible and glorious joy' (1 Peter 1:8). In a simple letter to his friends in England, an elder in the church of Bario in Borneo revealed this change from tears of sorrow to songs of joy. He was writing on 7 November 1973, shortly after revival had come to the church there: 'The services are so different from what I have ever experienced before. When the Holy Spirit comes down upon the congregation, people begin to cry out in loud wailing (sometimes twenty and thirty people at the same time) calling out to God for forgiveness of sins and some calling the names of people with whom they have been quarrelling in a desperate desire to get reconciled. Many pending court cases have been cancelled because the parties involved have been reconciled in a very dramatic manner with tears and embraces of godly love. After the sin problems have been dealt with by the Lord and forgiveness granted, then the service goes on with loud singing of praises while tears of joy are still flowing down.'[89]

Singing is the natural response to the great joy that inevitably accompanies revival. The young church of Pentecost was found praising God 'with glad and sincere hearts' (Acts 2:46-47), and even prison could not silence their hymn-singing (Acts 16:25). For the early church enjoying the new experience of the Holy Spirit among them in revival power, 'psalms, hymns and spiritual songs' formed a significant part of their Christian worship, and it was both joyful and heartfelt (Eph. 5:19; Col. 3:16). It is these two things, singing and joy, that are found together in 2 Chronicles 29-30.

'They sang praises with gladness' (29:30).
'All the people rejoiced at what God had brought about' (29:36).
They 'celebrated for seven days with rejoicing' (30:21).
'For another seven days they celebrated joyfully' (30:23).
'There was great joy in Jerusalem' (30:26).

These people were not being whipped to worship; nor was their joy manipulated by the leaders of worship. There was a spontaneous joy and gladness, and a longing to worship God together.

Jonathan Edwards writes of revival in Northampton, New England, 'This work of God...soon made a glorious alteration in the town: so that in the spring and summer following 1735, the town seemed to be full of the presence of God: it was never so full of love, nor of joy, and yet so full of distress, as it was then. There were remarkable tokens of God's presence in almost every house. It was a time of joy in families on account of salvation being brought unto them; parents rejoicing over their children as new born, and husbands over their wives, and wives over their husbands...God's day was a delight...'[90]

That is typical of what happens when the Spirit of God comes. When God came to Cambuslang in 1742, the phrase 'joy unspeakable and full of glory' is found often in the records.[91] It was the only way that the writers could adequately express what God was doing in the lives of so many. The revival that came to Beddgelert in Wales in 1817 was noted for its expression of gratitude to God: 'The outbursts of the joy of salvation [were] more powerful than were seen in some previous revivals.'[92] In 1859 in Wales there were frequent outbursts of praising at the preaching services. In 1839 in Dundee, 'The private meetings for prayer have spread a sweet influence over the whole place.'[93]

In faraway Assam, the effect of the 1904 awakening in Wales was carried back with a missionary, John Roberts, who had returned from furlough in Wales. The scene that at first shocked the Presbyterian missionaries was that of the rejoicing Khassi tribesmen, converted from head-hunting. When their conviction of sin gave way to unfettered rejoicing, 'In a united presbytery meeting of fifteen hundred folk, the singing overwhelmed the preaching, many of the awakened people dancing with joy, their arms outstretched, their faces radiant. Missionaries were astounded to see principal men and leading elders jump for joy. At first some missionaries disapproved, changing their minds as the revival transformed the Christians and won hundreds of non-Christians to the fellowship.'[94]

Merely to imitate this kind of behaviour, which is not hard to do, will never produce a revival; but when such a spontaneous explosion of joy is genuine, there will be the accompanying sense of the presence of God. However, it is just as much part of revival when the response is quietly controlled. David Brainerd was working among the North American Indians when revival came; these were a people who were used to high excitement in their religious ceremonies, and whom we might therefore expect to be extravagant in revival. In fact Brainerd noted an absence of undue excitement in the meetings, and commented that often 'When their hearts have been glad they could not help crying.'[95] M'Cheyne particularly noted the same in Scotland, though deep emotion was certainly there. And it was said of a revival in Connecticut in 1799 that the people convicted were 'by no means noisy or boisterous'.

Sometimes the leaders themselves have a significant influence on the degree of excitement. So there were more emotionally extravagant responses under the preaching of Wesley, who approved of them, than under the preaching of Whitefield, who disapproved. Similarly the Welsh revival of 1904 under the leadership of Evan Roberts was noted for its noisy emotion, whereas a revival in Rhos at the same time under R. B. Jones was quietly controlled, and revival in Norway a year later, under Albert Lunde, lacked many of the marks of the Welsh revival but was none the less real.

The presence of deep emotion, whether of joy or conviction, is not necessarily demonstrated by extravagant excitement, or bois- terous antics. We can never limit God in revival; the more we learn of his ways in revival, the less we can be sure of what he will do. But we can be certain of this: you do not judge the presence, or absence, of the Holy Spirit by simply listing the outward responses of the people.

However, singing almost always forms a significant part of a true spiritual revival; it is the natural overflow of the emotion of joy in forgiveness. Jonathan Edwards commented from his experience in New England in the early eighteenth century: 'Our public praises were then greatly enlivened; God was then served in our psalmody, in some measure, in the beauty of holiness...There has been scarce any part of divine worship, wherein good men amongst us have had...their hearts so lifted up in the ways of God, as in singing his praises...They [sang] with unusual elevation of heart and voice, which made the duty pleasant indeed.'[96]

This singing was the Psalms of David, 'sometimes set to none too good a metre', as someone has unkindly remarked. But the Spirit in revival did not seem to trouble about bad metre. And in 1839 M'Cheyne noted that the psalm singing in Dundee was 'so tender and affecting, as if the people felt that they were praising a present God'.[97] In Ulster, in 1859, 'The singing of the psalms was a perfect outburst of melodious sound.'[98] However, when a new wave of revival came to America under the ministry of Nettleton less than a century later it brought with it a new vogue of singing, and the result was a new hymnbook, *Village Hymns*. When God came to the Herrnhut community in Saxony in 1727 Count Zinzen- dorf wrote some excellent hymns for his people.

The eighteenth-century revival in England was accompanied by a fashion of 'modern' hymns. Philip Doddridge and Isaac Watts had both prepared the way, preceded in the seventeenth century by men like William Burton, Richard Baxter, Matthew Henry, John Mason and John Bunyan. The badly metred and poorly sung psalms were giving way to something a little more 'swift and jocund', though not to everyone's liking. Isaac Watts had published *Hymns and Spiritual Songs* and *Divine Songs for Children* by 1715, and these were followed by *Divine and Moral Songs*. But the revival

under Whitefield and Wesley gave a strong boost to hymn-writing.
John Newton, the ex-slave-trader, now converted and preaching at
Olney in Buckinghamshire, and one of his parishioners, William
Cowper, our national poet, published *Olney Hymns* in 1779. John
Wesley wrote and translated a number of hymns, but it was his
brother Charles whose output was phenomenal: he is estimated to
have written as many as 6,000 hymns! Singing formed such a major
part of the worship of the early Methodist societies that John
Wesley compiled some 'Rules for Methodist Singers':

1. Learn the tunes.
2. Sing them as printed.
3. Sing all. If it is a cross to you, take it up and you will
   find it a blessing.
4. Sing lustily and with a good courage.
5. Sing modestly. Do not bawl.
6. Sing in time. Do not run before or stay behind.
7. Above all, sing spiritually. Have an eye to God in every
   word you sing. Aim at pleasing him more than yourself or any other creature. In order to do this, attend
   strictly to the sense of what you sing and see that your
   heart is not carried away with the sound, but offered to
   God continually.

Howel Harris described the revival meetings in Wales during
March 1743, particularly when Daniel Rowland was preaching; he
commented upon the felt power of God and especially noted, 'Their
singing and praying is indeed full of God.' R. B. Jones commented
on the singing in Wales in 1904 that it was 'truly magnificent and
stirring' — and that from the land of song! One witness, quoted by
Rhys Jones, described the singing in this way: 'No need for an
organ. The assembly is its own organ as a thousand sorrowing or
rejoicing hearts found expression in the sacred psalmody of their
native hills.'[99] The stirring words and tune of 'Here is love, vast as
the ocean...' were sung so often that it became the love song of the
1904 revival; it was sung all over the world. The now familiar 'Just
as I am, without one plea...' was composed by Charlotte Elliott in
1836 and twenty-three years later was probably the most popular of
the hymns sung in the revival.

Joseph Kemp, the pastor of Charlotte Chapel in Edinburgh,

visited Wales in 1905. When he reported what he had seen to his own congregation it was evidently the singing that impressed him greatly: 'In Wales I saw the people had learned to sing in a way which to me was new. I never heard such singing as theirs. They sang such old familiar hymns as "When I survey the wondrous Cross," and "There is a fountain filled with Blood," and "I need Thee, oh, I need Thee." They needed no organist or choir or leader. Their singing was natural. The Holy Ghost was in their singing as much as in any other exercise. They had the New Song. People tell us our religion is joyless. Well, if the saints of the Living God have no joy, who has? Jesus Christ has given us to see that joy is one of the qualities He imparts to the saints of God. The world knows nothing of it...When a revival from God visits a congregation it brings with it joy.'[100]

In 1905 God was at work in the Khassi Hills of India. 5 March was the day the Holy Spirit revived the church in the village of Nongspung. During the opening hymn of the Sunday Service, 'The people sang and sang forgetting everything until one old man cried out asking someone to explain the hymn, which was done by one of the Christians, then the people began to sing it again, until the whole place was full of weeping tears of joy that they had such a wonderful Saviour.'[101]

On Lewis in 1949, 'Groups of converts, unwilling to go home, would gather on the roadside or sea-shore singing praises to God and sharing together what God had done for them. One night in Ness the crowd was so great that they spilled out of the house into a field and sang 'until it seemed the angels were joining with them'.[102] Singing caught hold of the fishermen around the east coast of England in 1921: ' On the Denes [dunes] where most of the curing yards were, and across the river at Gorleston in the yards there, the songs of Zion were sung. Far out at sea as the boats lay at their nets, the singing of men who were redeemed wafted over the waves.'[103] Up in Fraserburgh Jock Troup saw scores of Scottish fishermen converted in services that were 'characterized by joyful singing'.

In 1973 in Borneo it is recorded: 'Somehow the singing was different. There was something beautiful, sweet and real about it all.'[104] And in Indonesia at about the same time one eyewitness comments, 'Nothing I have heard before compares with the singing I was enabled to hear in the actual revival centre on Timor. The wealth of songs in the revival churches is indeed amazing.'[105] Festo

Kivengere confesses that, before his conversion in the Uganda revival that began in the 1930s he was annoyed at the Christians singing everywhere, and found it offensive that the women should be singing Christian hymns as they filled their water-pots. Madras in the 1940s was filled with such joy as the Christians worshipped God and sang almost everywhere that one Hindu remarked, 'It looks as though Sennai Pattana has become a Christian city.'[106]

It is clear, therefore, that singing from the heart, which is vital, living, God-directed singing, is a natural overflow of the joy experienced in true revival. But it is a dangerous deceit to imagine that if we get our singing right we will get revival. There is no one kind of singing that God blesses in revival; he takes what the church normally uses and fills it with his Spirit. When revival came to Scotland and Ulster, only metrical psalms were sung, and without any instrument to accompany the singing. In England, Charles Haddon Spurgeon led his congregation at the Metropolitan Tabernacle in hymns as well as psalms, but, for him the organ was 'the devil's whistle' and it found no place at the Tabernacle. Elsewhere psalms and hymns or hymns without psalms or hymns and songs and psalms were all sung, with or without accompaniment. There is no 'right' kind of singing in revival. *What* we sing has nothing to do with the presence or the absence of the Holy Spirit, but when he comes he will certainly change *how* we sing. David loved singing, whether alone on the hills or among the great congregation, but when God came and rescued him he described his singing as 'a new song' (Ps. 40:3), and the returning exiles described their singing as 'songs of joy' (Ps. 126:2). In revival, singing is neither coldly formal nor thoughtlessly repetitious. On the contrary it is real, living and vital. It is the best we have in 'normal times', made better by the Holy Spirit.

Longing for worship

Another feature of the revival of a community's worship is the love people have for worship and the spontaneous lengthening of services that results. 2 Chronicles 30:23 describes this: 'The whole assembly then agreed to celebrate the festival seven more days; so for another seven days they celebrated joyfully.' These people had celebrated the festival of the Passover for a whole week and they had enjoyed every minute of it. They did not have a meeting beforehand to decide that it would be spiritual to go on for another seven days! But when they came to the end of the seven days there was a spontaneous decision: this is too good to leave, let's do it again! This may be unprecedented in the Old Testament, but in revival people long to be in the presence of God and to stay there. It is not planned that way but God seems to contract time; in more than one revival the claim was made that 'Clocks have gone out of fashion.'[107]

It was exactly this that happened at Cambuslang in 1742. Unusually for the church in Scotland, who normally celebrated communion only on a few occasions in the year, the session decided that in view of the great blessing of God during the revival they would arrange another service within a month.

A minister reported of a revival in 1832 in Rhode Island, New England: 'Ordinarily ministers of New England preached twice on the Sabbath day and once in the evening of a week. Of late however the number of services have been much increased.' What he meant was three times at least on Sunday and many times during the week. If we ever think revival is a short cut from hard work, be warned! In 1839 at St Peter's, Dundee the services occasionally went on until midnight because the people refused to leave. Just prior to this, at Kilsyth, William Chalmers Burns preached in a great revival and on 22 September more than 12,000 people poured into the town and the Sunday services continued throughout the day and concluded at daybreak on Monday.

In 1904 in Wales, Joseph Jenkins of the Calvinistic Methodist Church in New Quay recorded in his diary: 'The revival goes on. I cannot leave the building…until twelve and even one o'clock in the morning — I have closed the service several times and yet it would break out again quite beyond the control of human power.'[108] On 8 November 1904, at the Baptist Church in Rhos, the minister began what was planned to be a ten-day mission. The closing service of the mission commenced at ten o'clock in the morning and went through to ten o'clock in the evening. At this point the town of Rhos was 'ablaze' with a revival that lasted well into the following year.[109]

The 1859 revival in Ulster witnessed many scenes of meetings continuing long after the normal time for a service to close: 'The usual time for dismissal came, but they were heedless about the hour of the night. The day brightened in the heavens, the morning star was succeeded by the rising sun, but they still remained exhorting, praying, and praising the Lord. They did not leave the spot till five o'clock in the morning.'[110] The fisherman's revival in 1921 on England's east coast also saw meetings continuing until the early hours of the morning: 'Whenever work was finished, meetings were held. Often due to bad weather the boats would tie up and many would gather together at all hours in different places. Meetings would often go on until three o'clock in the morning.'[111]

During the early part of the Second World War meetings in Madras would sometimes last until ten or eleven at night, with three-hour sermons: 'But still they kept attending. It was unbelievable. No man could have brought it about; only God could create such a hunger for His Word.'[112]

In 1949 in Lewis, there was such a hunger to hear the Word of God that when the services finished in the small hours of the morning the people assembled again a short distance away in the police station where many found the Saviour. At Barvas and Lochs the churches were crowded, with services continuing until three o'clock in the morning. Work was largely put aside, as young and old were made to face eternal realities.[113]

However, revival does not normally mean that work is neglected. More often the people find that the Spirit is invigorating, and long meetings into the night plus a full day's work go side by side. In the Welsh coal pits in 1904, for example, men who had been at prayer meetings until the early hours rarely failed to report for work on time in the morning.

One of the longest meetings in revival on record took place at Tuckingmill in Cornwall. The year was 1814 and revival had spread from Redruth like a prairie fire. A service began in the Methodist chapel on Sunday, 27 February and the Holy Spirit was present in such power that the meeting could not be closed until the following Friday morning. People came and went, but the meeting continued. During the course of that week it was claimed that 2,000 people had professed Christ.

The following report from Ulster in 1859 is possibly the best summary of this love for worship in times of revival, which ignores the normal length of services and the need for rest: 'In this town [Ballymena] at present, at public worship on Sabbath, the churches are thronged — pews, alleys, and vestibules. The open-air services, whether in town or country, on any evening of the week, are attended by thousands; and these services though so numerous are often not far distant from each other. Our congregational weekly prayer meeting was attended by some fifty persons ordinarily. During the three months past, whether held four times or seven times a week, it is attended by more than twenty times that number. The difficulty used to be to get the people into the church, but the difficulty now is to get them out of it. One night and morning we had three services. The first of these was three hours and a half. I pronounced the benediction intending to dismiss the people, but no, they kept possession, only a very few left. After some half hour we engaged in prayer and praise again. I pronounced the benediction, intending to dismiss the people, but no, they still kept possession, only a few left.'[114] That minister left the meeting at two o'clock in the morning and commented, 'Many remained'!

It would be untrue to suggest that in revival no meeting ends at the stated time, or that all services continue for many hours. However, these examples are not untypical, and in revival time often appears to stand still. Or, as Duncan Campbell commented, 'In revival time doesn't matter.' It is not our long services that will bring about revival; this shortening of the hours is the fruit of revival, not the cause of it. But it demonstrates one of the marks of a true awakening by the Holy Spirit, when things once considered dull and tedious become alive and meaningful in such a way that they cannot be left alone. Prayer, preaching and worship become the most enjoyable activities in life for both young people and old. People cannot wait to get to the prayer meeting; it becomes the high point of the day. Today we have a carelessness in our churches, where many will not attend more than one service in a day and a number of fellowships have followed the continental pattern and abandoned the Sunday evening service altogether. In revival the churches are overcrowded with people who only attend once — not because the congregation will not turn out for the evening, but because they will not go home in the morning!

During revival

A revival of evangelism

One of the inevitable results of revival is found in 2 Chronicles 30:1-12: 'Hezekiah sent word to all Israel and Judah and also wrote letters to Ephraim and Manasseh, inviting them to come to the temple of the Lord in Jerusalem and celebrate the Passover to the Lord, the God of Israel...They decided to send a proclamation throughout Israel, from Beersheba to Dan, calling the people to come to Jerusalem and celebrate the Passover to the Lord, the God of Israel...At the king's command, couriers went throughout Israel and Judah with letters from the king and from his officials...The couriers went from town to town in Ephraim and Manasseh, as far as Zebulun...'

Always when the church of Christ is revived by the Holy Spirit evangelism and mission are the natural and inevitable outflow. Evangelism therefore becomes a test of a genuine work of the Spirit of God. The success of the gospel during the centuries in which the Waldensians spread across Europe, which one historian describes as 'one of the most remarkable missionary movements that have ever occurred',[115] and during the Reformation, from Wycliffe onwards, was due to evangelism riding on the crest of revival. There is no other way of explaining the spread of the Reformation except through evangelism with the Word of God, and there is no better way of accounting for such evangelistic zeal other than by the word 'revival'. Before Hezekiah celebrated the great Passover feast he sent out letters to the whole of Israel and Judah to join with him. It was a grand effort of evangelism, and we will never find an outpouring of the Holy Spirit without a revival of evangelism. Hosea chapter 14 is a familiar passage to those concerned for revival:

> 'Return, O Israel, to the Lord your God.
>   Your sins have been your downfall!
> Take words with you
>   and return to the Lord.
> Say to him:
>   "Forgive all our sins
> and receive us graciously,
>   that we may offer the fruit of our lips"'

(Hosea 14:1).

As a result of that, God continued in verses 4-6:

> 'I will heal their waywardness
>   and love them freely,
>   for my anger has turned away from them.
> I will be like the dew to Israel;
>   he will blossom like a lily.
> Like a cedar of Lebanon
>   he will send down his roots;
>   his young shoots will grow.
> His splendour will be like an olive tree,
>   his fragrance like a cedar of Lebanon.
> Men will dwell again in his shade.
>   He will flourish like the corn.
> He will blossom like a vine,
>   and his fame will be like the wine from Lebanon.'

The prophet uses the picture of a lily, but somehow it seems altogether too inadequate; there is a beauty in a lily which is neither strong nor widespread, so Hosea changes to the picture of the cedar of Lebanon, which is strong, spreading and powerful. An outpouring of the Holy Spirit will be both attractive and powerful, reaching out and affecting multitudes. There is an effectiveness in the dew of God. The same is true in Isaiah with this picture of the nations hearing about the great work of God:

> 'Oh, that you would rend the heavens and come down,
>   that the mountains would tremble before you!
> As when fire sets twigs ablaze
>   and causes water to boil,
> come down to make your name known to your enemies
>   and cause the nations to quake before you!
> For when you did awesome things that we did not expect,
>   you came down, and the mountains trembled before you.
> Since ancient times no one has heard,
>   no ear has perceived,
> no eye has seen any God besides you,
>   who acts on behalf of those who wait for him.
> You come to the help of those who gladly do right,
>   who remember your ways'

(Isa. 64:1-5).

Reading about revival in Scripture and in history is intended to awaken the same thirst: 'Lord, you have not done these things for a long time now; very few have seen your power. But do it again. That is what we want. We remember the kind of God you are. We want you to come and we want to be ready for you to come.' God says to people like that, 'I will come and I will make the enemies know who my people are and who I am, and I will make the nations tremble.' That is revival, when the nations can see what is happening. The disgrace of the people of God today is that the nations do not take us seriously, and the locality in which we live does not even know we exist.

Here, in 2 Chronicles 30, was a great overflow of evangelism by Hezekiah. And it was an overflow. Much of our evangelism today is an effort; Christians have to be driven to it, and preachers are like pumps trying to get a large body of water out of a deep pit. But there is no effort in an overflow. Hezekiah and the people were so thrilled with their new relationship with God, and so grateful for all that it meant, that it was only natural they should want to share it with others. Evangelism comes naturally to a grateful heart.

The situation in Israel was that for 200 years the north and south had been bitterly divided. It had begun in the time of Rehoboam the son of Solomon. A terrible division came in, and the north and south went their own ways: Rehoboam in the south, with the tribes of Judah and Benjamin centring on Jerusalem; and Jeroboam in the north, with the rest of the tribes of Israel centring upon Samaria. By the time of Hezekiah, there had been eighteen kings in Israel, but in the year 722 B.C., just six years before Hezekiah came to power, Assyria conquered Samaria in the north and, after plundering the land, deported nearly 30,000 inhabitants. In their place he settled thousands of foreigners who had been deported from their own lands conquered by Assyria. So the tribes of the north were a conquered and defeated people and, adopting the religions of their conquerors and the settlers, they had also become a pagan people.

There is a very significant decree in 2 Chronicles 30:5. The proclamation was to be sent throughout Israel from 'Beersheba to Dan'. That expression means from the bottom to the top, because these two towns were at the extreme south and north of the land. The entire nation was to receive the invitation to return to the Lord. There had been nothing like this for 200 years. It was a brand new thing that was being done. And, significantly, it was a brave thing to do in a land teeming with foreign settlers and Assyrian petty lords. It was also a last chance for Israel before the Assyrian army pillaged its way back through the land a few years later. Knowing the uncertainty of the times, it would have been all too easy for Hezekiah to forget the north and look only to secure his own borders. Hezekiah was aware of the dangers, but there was an urgency about the sending of the couriers: 'How will they hear without a preacher?' The couriers were thorough and went 'from town to town' (2 Chron. 30:10). And the reference to Zebulun in the same verse was a mark of particular mercy since this tribe had felt the full force of the Assyrian invasion, and Hezekiah may well have urged his couriers to reach Zebulun with the gospel at all costs. 'Ephraim and Manasseh' (2 Chron. 30:1) were settled on the east side of the Jordan, furthest from Israel or Judah, and deeper into regions beyond.

Evangelism is always a hallmark of revival. In fact, in revival it is not ordinary evangelism but a desperate concern, amounting to a passion, for those who have never yet received the invitation to return. Evangelism is an inevitable outflow in revival because revival makes eternal issues a reality. Without Christ men go to hell. Nothing happens today when we talk about hell; we do not feel very much. In revival, both evangelist and hearers feel the horror of hell and the reality of eternal issues. And they feel the glories of heaven also. Things that are ordinarily so remote and distant to us become so real and so vital in revival.

Just as Christ and the apostles preached both heaven and hell with equal conviction, so men who lead in revival are always men with a sharp awareness of eternity and the reality of heaven and hell. I am not aware of any great preacher in times of revival who doubted the terrors of hell or the desperate danger of those without Christ. Some of these men experienced visions of the lost in hell, and all of them were urgent to turn men and women away from the road to eternal punishment.

Duncan Campbell's biographer described the evangelist's terrifying vision of the reality of hell: 'He seemed to be in a trance gazing into caverns of death, witnessing the agonies of hell. With horror he saw thousands from the Highlands and Islands of Scotland drifting to their doom, and heard a voice calling: "Go to them, go to them."'[116]

In 1743 David Brainerd began his great missionary work among the Indians of North America at the forks of the Delaware River. He was himself the product of revival and he had a longing to reach the Indians. Brainerd recognized that to the eyes of reason, 'Everything that respects the conversion of the heathen is a dark midnight.' Everything was against it. Brainerd was well spoken of by the presbytery, and had received one or two offers of attractive pastoral charges, but he had a passion for the Indians. He set himself particular times to go into the woods where he would walk and pray. There were times when he was caught up into heaven almost out of himself, pleading for the Indians. No one else cared much about them. Brainerd lived in the North American frontier, during the cowboy and Indian age. When he went among the Indians it was dangerous, because the poor Indians were being pushed out of their land. Their livelihood was being swept away from them. Yet

Brainerd was praying. There was an occasion when he had been praying in the woods and, he tells us in his diary: 'All things here below vanished and there appeared to be nothing of any importance to me but holiness of heart and *the conversion of the heathen to God*.'

That is what happens in revival: holiness of heart and a passion for the conversion of the lost. Brainerd continues, 'When I was asleep, I dreamt of these things and when I waked, as I frequently did, the first thing I thought of was this great work of pleading for God against Satan.'[117] This frail Puritan missionary set out on a journey of 420 miles in uncharted territory on the dangerous journey to the Susquehannah Indians, and there a great revival broke out — because one man had a passion for the lost.

Evan Roberts describes the spiritual experience he had before God used him so powerfully in the 1904 revival in Wales, perhaps the most influential revival of all times. The Spirit of God broke him into obedience until he was willing to do anything; then he was overwhelmed by the love of God. What followed sums up what so many have felt in times of revival: 'Then the fearful bending of the judgement day came to my mind, and I was filled with compassion for those who must bend at the judgement, and I wept. Following that, the salvation of the human soul was solemnly impressed upon me. I felt ablaze with a desire to go through the length and breadth of Wales to tell of the Saviour; and had it been possible, I was willing to pay God for doing so.'[118]

Similarly, Howel Harris in Wales during the eighteenth-century Awakening had declared to his brother: 'Yet shall I be more satisfied when I am an instrument to bring one soul to the knowledge of God than if I got £1,000.'[119] In a less sophisticated way, a half-deaf, wizened old Penan tribeswoman in Borneo expressed the same thing when, having found Christ and the assurance of salvation, she hurried off 'to tell the ones in the jungle about this'.

There is a pattern in 2 Chronicles 30. Verse 6 tells us of the content of evangelism. It is very simple. Today we run our training courses in evangelism, telling people just what to say and how to present the gospel. These are all very necessary simply because we have no passion for evangelism. When we call for a door-to-door team in the church few come. When we say we are going down the market-place to do some witnessing only a handful follow. That is one test of the state of our churches; another is the prayer meeting. But when revival comes everybody follows. Everybody will be down in the market.

Here in the days of Hezekiah the message was very simple: 'Return to the Lord…that he may return to you' (30:6). Hezekiah was not concerned to add to the number of his citizens. He did not sit down and reason that if he brought all the north down to the south it would be a great political *coup* and he would more than double his kingdom. His concern was a call to repentance and faith and reconciliation to God. He had a love for the gospel and the people. And the evangelists that he sent out shared with him in this urgency and passion. It is quite clear from the prayer that the king urgently offered to God when Assyria turned its attention in his direction, that Hezekiah held a firm theology of the sovereignty of God: 'O Lord, God of Israel, enthroned between the cherubim, you alone are God over all the kingdoms of the earth. You have made heaven and earth…' (2 Kings 19:4). But this did not lull him into the belief that he could just wait for the north to return to the Lord. He sent out evangelists! And if we go out and evangelize, that same Sovereign God of election will show us just how many of the elect live in our area!

These people had a 'unity of mind to carry out what the king and his officials had ordered, following the word of the Lord' (2 Chron. 30:12). Their unity was on the basis of the gospel and the desperate need of the people. And the invitation was to come to the Passover sacrifice and worship at the altar in Jerusalem (30:8). The invitation of the gospel has not changed. It is that men and women might be brought to the knowledge of Jesus Christ. That is the content of evangelism: an invitation — in fact, a command — to come and be reconciled to God through the blood of the sacrifice. It is a very simple message.

You will notice also the confidence of these evangelists: 'If you return to the Lord, you will be shown compassion…for the Lord your God is gracious and compassionate…He will not turn his face from you if you return to him' (30:9). Men and women involved in revival are utterly convinced that there is no other gospel and that God is faithful to his promises. These people knew there was no other way. Commenting on the work of God in Dundee in 1839, Robert Murray M'Cheyne referred to the expectations of the ministers: 'They all, I think, seek the immediate conversion of the people, and they believe that, under a living gospel ministry, success is more or less the rule, and want of success the exception.'[120]

We have already referred to the courage of these evangelists. In verse 10 we are told that they 'went as far as Zebulun'. Zebulun, after the invasion of Tiglath-Pileser of Assyria, was virtually swallowed up in the Assyrian Empire. So in reality it was hardly part of Israel any more; it was one of the frontier posts of the Assyrians. This was a missionary thrust for the regions beyond. These men were evangelists, not just messenger boys; they had caught the faith and vision of the rest of the nation. The couriers went, we are told in verse 10, 'from town to town'. There must have been many of them because there was a large area to cover and the Passover was getting close. It was a dangerous work in enemy-occupied territory; the jibes of the unbelieving Israelites were the very least they could expect.

The outflow of revival has always been a courageous evangelism. We are in danger today of scorning the early pioneer missionaries. We scoff at the typical picture of the missionary of a past generation, with his pith helmet, his big Bible under his arm, and his train of native porters behind him. But we ought to be careful that we do not touch God's anointed. Africa is littered with the graves of these pioneer missionaries. They went out knowing that a high proportion of them would never return. And the great thing about these missionaries is that they went because they were compelled by God to go.

The Moravian missionary work, which was a direct result of the revival among the community at Herrnhut in 1727, is legendary. Over the next sixty years their evangelists travelled to almost every country in Europe and covered vast areas of North and South America, Asia and Africa. Half a century before William Carey went to India the Moravians had spread the gospel in places barely known. They had become slaves to evangelize the negroes, and reached as far as Greenland, which so impressed our national poet William Cowper that he described their work in the following words: '[They] plant successfully sweet Sharon's rose on icy plains and in eternal snows.' Someone has claimed that the Moravians achieved more in twenty years than the entire evangelical church had done in two centuries. It is estimated, for example, that they

gained 13,000 converts in the West Indies before any other missionaries arrived. William Carey and John Newton are among many
who acknowledge the challenge of these Moravian missionaries to
their own lives, and the great evangelist John Wesley was converted
through the witness of Moravians.

Reflecting on the revival in Kilsyth in 1839, William Burns
included the following as third on his list of benefits: 'There is a
close connection betwixt Missionary work and revivals. Our newly
organized Missionary Society, in January this year [1839], has been
marked by several people as an era. No church can be in a lively state
when nothing is done for the heathen.'[121]

In the year of revival, 1859, David Livingstone made an appeal
to the university students which led directly to the Universities
Mission to Central Africa. In North America Dwight Moody
arranged a meeting in 1886 which resulted in the Student Volunteer
Movement, with its slogan, 'The evangelization of the world in this
generation.' This movement sadly took a wrong doctrinal direction
later, but its early goals were good. At the turn of the nineteenth
century there were 14,000 Protestant missionaries around the
world; the revivals of 1904-5 gave a further influx, so that by 1925
this figure had doubled. Geographically the world was opening up.
In 1800 one third of the globe was unknown to Europeans, whereas
a century later almost every country was known and open to
missionaries. God was preparing the world by quicker and easier
travel just as he had prepared the Roman Empire for the first-
century Christian missionaries. But the expansion of missionary
activity cannot be explained solely in terms of colonialism and the
steam engine; the greatest thrust behind world-wide evangelism in
the nineteenth and early twentieth centuries is undoubtedly revival.

As a result of the 1859 revival the Evangelisation Society,
which is still with us today, was born. At the same time there was
a great expansion in the London City Mission, and the Salvation
Army, which then had the gospel at the very heart of its activity,
came into being. That same period of revival saw the birth of some
of our greatest overseas missionary activity. Churches today have
a concern for what Francis Schaeffer, shortly before his death,
called 'sensationalism and style'. But we have not very much
passion for evangelism. The souls of the lost do not trouble us.
Revival brings a personal passion for the lost. Among the benefits

of the awakening in Ulster in this same year, 1859, one historian records 'a forward movement in philanthropic and missionary enterprise' which included the 'China and Zenana Missions'. During the 1904 revival in Wales the challenge was laid down that the genuineness of the work would be seen in its missionary results. R. B. Jones had no doubt, from his own experience that, judged on this ground, the fruit of the revival stood the test. He traced missionaries from 1904 carrying revival to India, Madagascar, Africa, Poland, South America, Japan and many more places. Rhys Jones concludes: 'The records of all the Missionary Societies could bear eloquent testimony to the practical, lasting result of the Spirit's work in those days.'[122]

Great names from the eighteenth and nineteenth centuries were products of revival: Carey, who went to India; Martyn, who went to Persia; Judson, who went to Burma, and Taylor, who went to China. But far back in the dark period of the twelfth century God had moved in the life of Peter Waldo of Lyons and the revival that followed sent out hundreds of Waldensian preachers all across Europe. The same was true two centuries later when John Wycliffe gave England its first English Bible; his 'Poor Preachers' went out into the nation, penetrating Scotland and Wales with the gospel until half the population seemed, to its opponents at least, to be 'Wycliffites'. A little over a century after Wycliffe, the radical reformers of Zurich (incorrectly known by history and their opponents as Anabaptists), set out to evangelize Europe. Missionaries went out in small groups until, in spite of persecution from both Reformers and Catholics, their evangelistic zeal had captured the lives of scores of thousands.

Evangelism in revival is a spontaneous 'people movement'. In 1958 a missionary in Borneo asked permission from the government's District Officer to enter a particular area with the gospel. The disgruntled official replied, 'In fact you have already occupied the area.' The missionaries had not been there at all, but the Tagal tribespeople who had been converted simply gossiped Christ. This was exactly the response of the first-century Christians who evangelized wherever they went (Acts 8:4). When God came to the Kelabit Highlands in Borneo in 1973 even schoolchildren went out in evangelistic teams during their school holidays.[123]

Commenting on the effects of the revival in the Khassi Hills in

India in 1905, one writer concluded, '...and above all an intense passion for souls and untiring efforts made to bring outsiders to the Saviour'.[124]

When the north of China experienced revival in 1906, two things particularly marked it as a movement from God: 'a wholly unusual conviction of sin and great anxiety for the conversion of friends and neighbours'.[125]

During the revival in Madras men came straight from their offices to the church to collect a pile of Gospels and then they would go out, two by two, on their 'Tapping-the-Door Campaign'. Their aim was to introduce the Scriptures to every house in the city and each evening they walked miles to bring the gospel to these homes. A year later, in 1944, 'Gospel Raids' were started when, for several days at a time, a large group of Christians would visit distant towns and villages with the good news. One visit took them 300 miles from Madras, and occupied them for three weeks. In 1947 the teams entered the slum areas of their city with the gospel. They did not offer financial help or food, but had with them only the message of salvation; and many were led to Christ.[126]

Similarly, Festo Kivengere reports that in Uganda God 'kept sending us out. We went, whether we were invited or not, on foot, an assorted "ad hoc" team spilling over into neighbouring valleys, usually leaving "Jesus people" behind when we came back home. Ordinary folk, bound together in a true love-fellowship, can be a powerhouse for evangelism.'[127] The same thing was happening all over East Africa, from Rwanda to Burundi and Tanganyika.

When revival began in 1907 in Pyungyang, now the capital of North Korea, students from the theological seminary were involved and, together with others caught up in the Spirit's fire, they set themselves the task of spreading the gospel through the whole of Korea within a year. They determined to penetrate areas where no missionary had ever been and, as an aid to their witness, 1,000,000 copies of Mark's Gospel were printed — and 700,000 were sold in the first year. Many went abroad as missionaries, and wherever Korean settlements were found, these gospel couriers settled also. Some went to Siberia, some to remote islands and others to China. The 'Movement of the Millions', reaching out to China's vast population, was born in the Korean revival. Some of the best young men from the seminary were sent out in this wave of evangelism.[128]

The same thing happened under the preaching of Dwight Moody in America in the 1880s; thousands of university students volunteered for missionary service. A missionary involved in the revival in the Shantung province of China in 1932 observed, 'Everywhere I went, the Christians had a zeal to search out the lost and win them to Christ...Little children, old men and women, people of all ages where lives had been changed, thus witnessed.'

When the Holy Spirit came down at Pentecost Peter demonstrated the same courage. Here was the man who had locked himself indoors because he was terrified of the Jews and the Romans, now standing in the open air. He did not stand at the window and shout and then shut the window, quickly pulling the shutters down, in case they saw where the voice came from. Peter was standing in the streets, preaching openly. He did not know 3,000 people were going to be converted. As far as Peter knew he might have been dragged off and thrown into prison, and then crucified like his Master. That was not his business. His business was to do what God was telling him and he had to preach. It was a burning fire. The Spirit of God came down and Peter had to evangelize.

The reason we have to be faithful in the present day is because the Christian who knows God's command and loves God and the gospel does what he is told even when he does not feel like it. The Christian does not simply react to feelings. So we go on preaching because that is God's way. We go on evangelizing because we know it to be right. But the plus factor in revival is that we not only know it but we have a heart for it. There is a passion that cannot be explained except in terms of the Holy Spirit. What sent David Brainerd to the Indians compelling him to travel miles in dangerous frontier territory? Because whenever he prayed he saw those Indians falling into a Christless eternity. Eternal issues became vital realities. Brainerd did not go out there to give the Indians a little bit of culture. He went out to convert them to Christ.

In times of revival Christians go out spontaneously. You cannot stop them. Nobody can stop them. Revival is a spontaneous combustion of evangelism. And this is one of the things we must long for when we long for revival.

During revival

A revival of giving

William Sprague, in his *Lectures on Revival*, comments that 'It is amidst the effusions of the Spirit of God that men are trained to engage actively and efficiently in the great enterprise of Christian benevolence. Here they have their hearts and their hands opened on behalf of those who are sitting in the regions and the shadows of death.'[129] Giving for the support of the ministry and the work of the gospel is yet another indication of whether or not God is at work.

During the years of spiritual decline in Jerusalem, the support for the priests and the temple maintenance had virtually disappeared. As a result, the priests and Levites were forced to give up their full devotion to the service of God and spend much of their time earning their living in working the land. In the Old Testament there were two barometers by which the spiritual life of the nations of Judah and Israel could be judged. One was their observance of the sabbath and the other was their giving of the tithe. The tithe, one tenth of the people's income or produce, had been demanded by God to provide for those working full-time in the temple service (Num. 18:21-24; Lev. 27:30-33). This tithe was the minimum that the people were obliged to give; in addition there were 'first-fruits', the first portion of their harvest, and 'freewill offerings', which they gave out of glad and generous hearts.

When the people held back the tithe, God had no hesitation in accusing them of robbing *him*, not the Levites, of what belonged to him: '"Will a man rob God? Yet you rob me. But you ask, 'How do we rob you?' In tithes and offerings. You are under a curse—the whole nation of you—because you are robbing me. Bring the whole tithe into the storehouse, that there may be food in my house. Test me in this," says the Lord Almighty, "and see if I will not throw open the floodgates of heaven and pour out so much blessing that you will not have room enough for it"' (Mal. 3:8-10).

For God's people in the Old Testament there was a direct relationship between giving the tithe and receiving the blessing of God. Giving our tithe to God is a necessary preparation if we long for revival, but it is also an inevitable result of revival. When God comes in power he always touches the pockets of his people. In revival there are very few who rob God; on the other hand, spiritual slackness makes people selfish. Everywhere today we hear of missions and gospel causes that are hindered from advance, not only because of a shortage of workers, but through lack of funds. That will never happen in revival.

When the Spirit began to move in Jerusalem during the reign of Hezekiah, the king 'ordered the people living in Jerusalem to give the portion due to the priests and Levites so that they could devote themselves to the Law of the Lord' (2 Chron. 31:4). Although this was a royal command which could not be disobeyed, the people responded immediately and generously (31:5) so that a large pile of tithes soon gathered in the temple, and when Hezekiah asked about the progress he received the encouraging reply from Azariah, the chief priest: 'Since the people began to bring their contributions to the temple of the Lord, we have had enough to eat and plenty to spare, because the Lord has blessed his people, and this great amount is left over' (31:10). The whole-hearted response of the nation is evident from the expressions: 'The Israelites generously gave...They brought a great amount, a tithe of everything...They piled them in heaps...This great amount is left over.' They added to the tithe their first-fruits (31:55) and freewill offerings (31:14).

The Isle of Lewis has received a number of spiritual awakenings in its history and one such occasion was between the years

1824-1835 when Andrew McLeod was ministering on the island. Among the results of this revival, McLeod commented particularly on the generosity of the people, and how they would have given more if only their poverty had allowed them to do so: 'Considering the circumstances of the people, I bear testimony, that their liberality and zeal in this case have cause to provoke very many to similar duties. It was most delightful to see the hoary head, and the young scholar of eight or nine years, joining in this contribution. The will preponderates over our purse, so that we cannot do exactly what we would.'[130]

In the autumn of 1839 the church at St Peters in Dundee held a thanksgiving service, and M'Cheyne records: 'A thank-offering was made among us to God for his signal mercies. The times were hard, and my people are far from wealthy, yet the sum contributed was £71. This was devoted to Missionary purposes.'[131] That figure probably represented the equivalent of the annual stipend of the minister.

Twenty years later, when God saturated Ulster with his presence, the same spirit of giving came from his people. Writing half a century after the event, Thomas Sinclair listed some of the long-term advantages of the revival, which included, 'the creation of a new spirit of Christian liberality; a forward movement in philanthropic and missionary enterprise, of which the Sabbath School Auxiliary to Mission, the Orphan Society, and the China and Zenana Missions are lasting fruits; and, finally, a sense of generous loyalty to the church which enabled her to surmount successfully the financial perplexities'.[132]

Between 1906-1910 the church in Korea doubled its membership, adding 80,000 new believers to the churches; three years later it almost doubled again. With this great work of God came a feature that one observer claimed never to have met elsewhere in the world: 'Another characteristic of Korean Christians is their readiness to make sacrifices…Many of these devout people are rice farmers. In spite of the biblical rule that the labourer shall be the first to enjoy the fruits of his toil, Korean Christians do not take advantage of the latitude allowed them; they sell their rice and buy millet, which is half the price. They give their profits, that is to say, fifty per cent of their earnings, in aid of missionary work, to send missionaries to neighbouring countries and so spread the Gospel. They give not a tenth, but a half of all they earn.'[133]

The same commitment was found among the Ethiopian Wallamo Christians when missionaries discovered the results of a revival that broke out during their wartime absence from the country. At a conference in 1949 the churches gave to the support of forty evangelists and then promised that in future, half of all the local church offerings would go to support evangelists. The following year these Wallamo Christians, who earned little enough to live on, made promises of what they would trust God to help them give over the next year. A missionary continues the story: 'The idea immediately caught fire. Christians stood by the score to make similar faith promises: a sheep, a donkey, a horse, a blanket, ten dollars, the produce of ten coffee trees. These promises were not made lightly but as serious obligations between the individual and the Lord...During the following year each one worked hard to pay the promise in full, often in small instalments. By the next conference, a careful check showed that every penny promised had been paid.'[134]

Even the women, who had little to call their own, would make promises and gifts at their Bible classes. The same missionary tells of one old woman who rushed into the class just as they were taking the offering; she was out of breath but gasping: 'Oh, thank you Lord! Oh, thank you for bringing me here in time!' Later she explained that she had longed to make an offering to the work of the gospel, but had almost nothing to give. With just a few pennies she bought some cotton and sat up late each night spinning it into thread. Finally she walked for five hours to get to market, sold her thread, and returned just in time to place the proceeds in the offering. Where is that kind of longing and zeal among Christians in the West today?

When the Spirit came to the naturally generous Penan tribespeople of Borneo in 1959 a missionary commented, 'Penans were always careful to share out everything, but the gospel had given them joy in much greater generosity.'[135]

Joy in much greater generosity is a hallmark of revival today, as it was in the time of Hezekiah. One of the great and practical benefits of revival is that gospel work is not held up because of a lack of finance. It often takes revival to loosen our hold on this world and create such an awareness of eternity that Christians see investment in the gospel as the most profitable use of their money.

During revival

A revival among children and youth

An unexpected ingredient in revival is the effect it has upon young people and even very young children. Generally we think of revival in terms of adults longing and praying for God to move, and then of adults being changed under the powerful influences of the Spirit. When Hezekiah sent his evangelists throughout the northern territories, the promise of blessing included the children. There is a significant phrase in 2 Chronicles 30:9: 'If you return to the Lord, then your brothers and your children will be shown compassion by their captors and will come back to this land, for the Lord your God is gracious and compassionate...'

It was not long afterwards that the prophet Isaiah promised a time of revival among the people which certainly included the next generation:

> I will pour water on the
> thirsty land,
> and streams on the dry
> ground;
> I will pour out my Spirit on
> your offspring,
> and my blessing on your
> descendants.
> They will spring up like
> grass in a meadow,
> like poplar trees by
> flowing streams.

One will say, "I belong to the Lord";
   another will call himself by the name of Jacob;
still another will write on his hand, "The Lord's",
   and will take the name Israel'

                                                            (Isa. 44:3-5).

The form of these words has no necessary reference to children or young people; they may simply refer to the next generation when it is grown to adulthood, but there is too much in the Bible that reveals God's concern for children to assume there is no reference here to the children who, in youth, would be blessed by the revival.

Tragically, in normal church life we have a low spiritual expectation for our children. We do not expect much from them because we do not expect much from ourselves; we drag the next generation down to our own level of spiritual backsliding. In many evangelical churches the presence of children, or even teenagers, in our weekly prayer meetings is unthinkable because we do not pray as families; we never hear our children pray. If they asked to come to a prayer meeting, most parents would suggest that it was not really for them! We do not expect our children to read the Bible or have a hunger for it, because we don't ourselves. Because of our own coldness of heart, we would be astounded if our children wanted to go out and witness for Christ. The tragedy is that our children reflect us; we pass our spiritual life on to the next generation. They are what we are. We can't listen to sermons, so we assume our children can't; we don't go to the prayer meeting, so we assume they couldn't. One generation creates the environment that either stifles or invigorates the spiritual growth of the next.

However, God is concerned, even though we are not. And he promises that when he comes in power by his Spirit he will bless the next generation. God's concern for children is found throughout the Bible.

In Deuteronomy 6:4-9 parents are given specific instructions concerning their responsibility towards children. The Word of God must be impressed on them and talked about with them; it must be 'tied, bound and written' into their lives.

When the walls of Jerusalem were rebuilt at the return from exile, there was a grand dedication ceremony during which Ezra read the law of God to 'men and women and all who were able to understand', from daybreak until noon. And later 'all who [were] able to understand' entered into a binding covenant to obey the Lord (Neh. 8:3; 10:28).

When the prophet Joel urged the leaders to call a solemn assembly and bring the people to repentance, the children, even those still at their mother's breast, were included:

> 'Blow the trumpet in Zion,
>   declare a holy fast,
>   call a solemn assembly.
> Gather the people,
>   consecrate the assembly;
> bring together the elders,
>   gather the children,
> those nursing at the breast'
>
> (Joel 2:15-16).

During his earthly ministry, our Lord invited children to be brought to him. 'And he took the children in his arms, put his hands on them and blessed them' (Mark 10:16).

On the Day of Pentecost the gospel was offered 'for you and your children' (Acts 2:39), and we have no need to take that as a vague reference to future generations.

Without doubt Christ reserved some of his most solemn warnings to those who cause children to be offended at the gospel: 'If anyone causes one of these little ones who believe in me to sin, it would be better for him to have a large millstone hung around his neck and to be drowned in the depths of the sea' (Matt. 18:6). This is not only what Christ thinks about parents who deny their children the right to hear the gospel; it is also what he thinks about Christian parents who stifle the spiritual growth of their children by their own backsliding.

What is particularly significant is that in times of revival it is not infrequently the children and young people who are especially challenged and changed, and in many instances they are the ones who are most sincerely longing and praying for revival, and amongst whom it begins. References to the part played in revivals by children and teenagers are abundant. This is an aspect of revival which, in spite of being well reported, receives too little attention from those who analyse the common factors of revivals.

Two years before the revivals at Kilsyth and Cambuslang in 1742, the minister at Kilsyth, James Robe, discovered that sixteen children in a nearby town were meeting together in a barn to pray, and in his own parish, 'Several young girls...from ten to sixteen years of age, had been observed meeting together for prayer in an outhouse they had access to.' All this 'made deep impressions both upon young and old'. It is hardly surprising that when revival came many children, some only eight years old, were brought to salvation.[136]

When God came down among the Susquehannah Indians of North America in the 1840s Bavid Brainerd recorded in his diary: 'Old men and women who had been drunken wretches for many years, and some little children, not more than six or seven years of age, appeared in distress for their souls...And it was apparent that these children (some of them at least) were not merely frightened with seeing the general concern, but were made sensible of their danger, the badness of their hearts, and their misery without Christ, as some of them expressed it.'[137]

In a letter dated 26 March 1841, M'Cheyne reviewed the revival which had taken place two years previously in Dundee and noted, 'The ministers...believing that children are lost, and may through grace be saved, have, therefore, spoken to children as freely as to grown persons; and God has so greatly honoured their labours, that many children, from ten years old and upwards, have given full evidence of their being born again. I am not aware of any meetings that have been held peculiarly for children, with the exception of the Sabbath-schools, the children's prayer meetings, and a sermon to children on the Monday evening after the Communion. It was commonly at the public meetings, in the house of God, that children were impressed; often in their own little meetings, when no minister was present.'[138]

The revival in Aberystwyth in 1805 began in the Sunday School and Thomas Charles described the 'powerful awakenings among the young people and children...Hundreds of children, from eight years old and upwards, might be seen in the congregation, hearing the word with all the attention of the most devout Christian and bathed in tears.'[139]

At Berry Street Presbyterian Church in Belfast in 1859, 300 children attended a midday children's meeting and a third of them found peace in Christ.[140]

Amy Carmichael described how a new awakening came among the Tamils in Dohnavur in 1906: 'It was at the close of the morning service (22nd October) that the break came. The one who was speaking, was obliged to stop, overwhelmed by sudden realization of the inner force of things. It was impossible even to pray. One of the older lads in the boys' school began to try to pray, but he broke down, then another, then all together, the older lads chiefly at first. Soon many among the younger ones began to cry bitterly and pray for forgiveness. It spread to the women.'

Amy Carmichael found it hard to recall all the details of that eventful day: 'It was so startling and so aweful — I can use no other word — that details escaped me. Soon [many] were on the floor, crying to God, each boy and girl, man and woman, oblivious of all others. The sound was like the sound of waves or strong wind in the trees...For the next fortnight, life was apportioned for us much as it was for the apostles when they gave themselves continually to prayer and to the ministry of the word. Everything else had to stand aside. At first the movement was almost entirely among convert boys, schoolboys, our own children and workers, and some younger members of the congregation.'[141] Seven months later she reported: 'Nearly all our children were out and out converted.'

In 1973 in Borneo, even 'little children' were brought to tears of repentance when God came down at the Vacation Bible School at Bario.[142]

But it is not only that children and young people are converted in revival; their involvement in praying for revival and their prayer during revival are noted regularly in the records of God's powerful work.

In 1727 at Herrnhut in Saxony revival broke out on 13 August. In part the revival owed its origin to Count Ludwig of Zinzendorf praying desperately for his class of young girls, who showed no evidence of spiritual life. By 26 August forty-eight men and women had covenanted to pray for twenty-four hours, dividing the time between them. The next day the number increased to seventy-seven. Then the children set up a scheme of their own! 'The children of both sexes felt a most powerful impulse to prayer, and it was impossible to listen to their infant supplications without being deeply moved and affected. A blessed meeting of the children took place in the evening of the 26th of August, and on the 29th, from the hours of ten o'clock at night until one the following morning a truly affecting scene was witnessed, for the girls from Herrnhut and Berthelsdorf spent these hours in praying, singing and weeping. The boys were at the same time engaged in earnest prayer in another place. The spirit of prayer and supplication at that time poured out upon the children was so powerful and efficacious that it is impossible to give an adequate description of it in words.'[143]

A few years after this, in Northampton, New England, Jonathan Edwards witnessed the same thing. He found that the largest number of children converted in revival were between the ages of ten and fourteen and, writing nearly ten years after the event the ever-cautious Edwards recorded: 'In the summer and autumn, the children in various parts of the town had religious meetings by themselves, for prayer, sometimes joined with fasting; wherein many of them seemed to be greatly and properly affected, and I hope some of them savingly wrought upon...Now we had the most wonderful work among children that ever was in Northampton.'[144]

George Whitefield had noted in his diary, towards the end of 1741, that many small children sat on the pulpit steps while he preached in the open air; they were listening to the preaching and handing up to him notes from the crowd. What impressed Whitefield was the fact that these children often received the eggs and filth that were thrown at him, and yet they appeared to be unconcerned for their own welfare. In an age when children were little noted, this is a significant entry in the diary of one of England's greatest preachers.[145]

In 1742 God moved in the parish of Baldernock in Scotland, and children in the local school were particularly moved. The schoolmaster, James Forsyth, wrote of a young people's prayer meeting in his school, through which many were converted, 'None of them were above thirteen years of age — a few of them were so young as eight or nine.'[146]

Just before the revival in Beddgelert in Wales in 1817, a spirit of prayer was noted not only among the church members, but among the children as well.[147]

In Wales in 1859 the children were particularly noted as having been moved by revival. In many places children were used by God to bring the fire of revival into the adult community and some of the most powerful effects of the Spirit were felt in the children's prayer meetings. One minister in Aberaeron reported on 16 May: 'The youth of our congregations are nearly all the subjects of deep religious impressions. Many of them seem as if filled with the Spirit of prayer. Very young people, yea, children from ten to fourteen years of age, gather together to hold prayer meetings, and pray very fervently...' One minister compared the children to steam tugs sent out by the Spirit to draw the larger vessels into port![148] At Fishguard in the same year the first evidence of revival came through the prayer of young children.

The same thing happened in 1904 in Wales. Children met frequently for prayer, even using their playtime at school for that purpose. They held meetings in their own homes, and in barns, even in empty pigsties. The records are full of children taking part in the meetings. The *North Wales Guardian* for 27 January 1905 reported on meetings in Dolgelley which included reference to a 'Sunday afternoon children's prayer meeting' when 'Several very young children took part, and at the conclusion a short service was held in the public square.'

About the same time in India a missionary commented upon the children in the prayer meetings during the revival in the Khassi Hills: 'Two boys prayed afterwards and one prayer in particular was very beautiful. I never knew what a child's prayer could be before.'[149]

In the same year God moved among the congregation at Charlotte Chapel in Edinburgh and the pastor, Joseph Kemp, recording the many conversions in the Sunday School commented that 'So keen were the children that they started prayer meetings of their own, and a sympathetic leader was appointed to guide them.'[150]

During the 1859 revival in Ulster, great gatherings were held in the Botanic Gardens in Belfast; numbers were so large that the crowds broke into smaller groups which included prayer meetings composed entirely of young people. One observer reported: 'In many parts of the gardens groups of boys and girls, some of them ragged, who had evidently belonged to the outcast classes, and were recently converted, prayed in language most affecting and impressive.' When the revival came to Belfast, Berry Street Presbyterian Church was the first to experience its power and in that church a midday children's meeting was attended by 300 children, of whom a third found peace in Christ. At Coleraine the large school of the Irish Society was swept by the Spirit, and almost the entire school, both boys and girls, came under conviction of sin.[151]

It is not only children that are affected. Older teenagers are frequently at the centre of revival benefits. Jonathan Edwards admitted that 'At the latter end of the year 1733, there appeared a very unusual flexibleness, and yielding to advice, in our young people.' He went on to describe what they had been like previously, which proved them to be much like every generation of young people! Then Edwards continued: 'The young people declared themselves convinced by what they had heard from the pulpit, and were willing of themselves to comply with the counsel that had been given: and it was immediately, and, I suppose, almost universally, complied with...'[152]

Following the preaching of George Whitefield at Lyme in Connecticut about the same time as Edwards' report, a minister in the town, Jonathan Parsons, wrote of his young people who had been careless before. He said they were so changed that 'Whenever they fell into companies the great salvation was the subject of their conversation.'[153]

When Asahel Nettleton arrived in Boston in the spring of 1819, large numbers of teenagers were converted: 'The volatile youth could no longer resist the influences of the Holy Spirit, but in deep solemnity were daily enquiring what they should do to be saved. Vain amusements were entirely suspended. Scenes of pleasure were forsaken and the trifles of time were lost in the awful concerns of eternity.'[154]

Joseph Jenkins, the Calvinistic Methodist minister at New Quay in Cardiganshire, Wales, described how God's Spirit came in 1859 first to the young people's after-meeting, when about sixty were present. He wrote of 'an overpowering sense of God's presence' that morning and it affected the whole church.

It was the same at Mynydd Llandygai in Caernarvonshire: 'The dawn finally broke in the young people's prayer meeting where, under the influence of the Spirit, some prayed for deliverance, others wept bitterly, and others praised God for having at last visited His people. This went on for some hours and proved to be the firstfruits of a mighty awakening which soon spread to neighbouring churches.'[155]

In 1903 and 1904 in Denmark, 'a landslide' of young people

began to fill the prayer meetings. In 1904 at Fransch Hoek in South Africa a Young People's Society heard of the work of the Spirit elsewhere and a prayer meeting of forty-two was soon attended by 600.[156]

In October 1973 revival broke out among the students of the Junior Secondary School at Bario in Borneo. Two boys began to pray together and gradually the whole school was drawn in until the headmaster himself, opposed to the work of the Spirit at first, was brought to repentance.[157]

It would not be an exaggeration to claim that the amazing work of God in China, during the 1960s and '70s especially, has drawn millions of young people to Christ. In Swatow, north of Canton, where the church suffered so severely in the 'Cultural Revolution' of 1966, membership has grown to 500, of whom eighty per cent are young people. A ninety-year-old pastor, who had been permanently disabled by the Red Guard, told visitors to China recently that he was caring for over 5,000 baptized Christians, of whom a large number were young people. In 1981, in one small conference in Kaifeng, eighteen young people were commissioned as local preachers.[158]

Children and young people, when drawn into revival, have the same evangelistic passion that adults have. The great missionary movement that drew thousands of young people to Africa in the nineteenth century was the result of revival among youth.

When God came to the Khassi Hills in India in 1905 a missionary reported home: 'The young people now begin to feel that it is their duty to speak to others. In one place where a very large market is held, about forty children went to the chapel to pray at noon, others soon joined them, and the Spirit of God was among them. Some went out of the meeting to speak to the people in the market and a great crowd from the Bazaar ran to the chapel and filled it, and the service which the children held with them was a very powerful one. When these returned to their work others took their place and thus it went on for hours. One writes, "At 10 o'clock at night we only seemed to be just beginning and I do not know when our meeting came to an end, but it was sometime in the morning." These children's meetings are becoming more general.'[159]

In Korea in 1907 even little children would run up to people on the street and plead with them to accept Christ as their Saviour. In

Wales children prayed urgently and boldly for their parents. A young Christian at Rhosesmor was heard to pray: 'My father is ungodly; I am afraid to go home because of his swearing. Oh come and save him, Lord! Thou hast knocked at his door many times; compel him to open, and if he refuses, take the door off its hinges, Lord!' And when children were converted, 'They instantly crave permission to have family prayer, and thus divine worship is established in nearly every family in the country.'[160]

Perhaps of all the blessings revealed among children in revival is their awareness of the reality of God. On 22 October 1905 at Dohnavur in India one little girl expressed her understanding of the revival as the time 'Jesus came to Dohnavur'.

R. B. Jones related the following conversation between two children at Rhos in North Wales at the time of the 1904 revival:

'Do you know what has happened at Rhos?'

'No, I don't, except that Sunday comes every day now.'

'Don't you know?'

'No, I don't.'

'Why, Jesus Christ has come to live in Rhos now!'[161]

It would require a book on its own to describe all that God has done among children and young people in times of revival. God does not overlook the needs of the youngest when his Spirit comes, but frequently uses them as his instrument in promoting the revival; this should give us good cause to pray for revival if only for the sake of the next generation. Our Sunday Schools and youth meetings will be transformed when the next generation experience 'a community saturated with God'. But do we care? In Madras in 1949 the Sunday School teachers were so concerned for their children that they got up at 4.00 a.m. to pray for them. It is not surprising that revival soon followed among the children.[162]

4.
After revival

'Manasseh...did evil in the eyes of the Lord' (2 Chron. 33:1). It is sadly true that revivals very rarely outlast one generation. The son of the great King Hezekiah is known in Scripture as one of the most evil kings in Judah, at least until his own conversion. One of the most common questions from those who read or hear of revivals is: 'But why and how did it fade?' The answer to this question is often impossible to discover, but one thing is sure: few revivals continue for long. Whilst it is true that some, like the work of God during the preaching of Wesley and Whitefield in the eighteenth century, may continue for half a century or more, others pass within a few weeks. Sometimes we can discover reasons for the fading of revival; it may be that God deliberately withdraws his hand because too much attention is being focused on the men involved or on the phenomena accompanying the revival. But whether or not we can find reasons, what is more important is to look for the lasting fruits of revival.

Manasseh was not born until the revival under the leadership of his father had passed its peak, but he must have known of the great work of God, and he must also have seen the benefits in the nation. But hearing stories of revival, or even living in the results of revival, is not the same as experiencing the power of revival. The tragedy of the story of Manasseh is that it took him only a few years to turn the clock back to his grandfather, Ahaz, and nearly half a century to realize his terrible mistake. Whilst the effects and experience of revival never wholly leave those who are touched by it, a whole generation can grow up completely neglecting that which their parents experienced. Speaking with those who have been involved in revival, even fifty years after the event, you cannot help but realize that something of the glory has never fully faded from their lives. As one confessed, 'When you have lived through revival you can never be the same again.' But there is a generation growing up today that is not even aware of what revival is; sometimes even in churches that were touched with revival in the lifetime of their parents or grandparents. Every generation needs its own revival, and though, as we shall see, revivals always have a marked effect upon their own society and leave a legacy of good, that legacy is a passing thing unless God comes a second time. After Manasseh, came his grandson, Josiah, and it was during the time of Josiah that a fresh wave of revival and reformation came to the land.

After revival

Statistics
of revival

Most people think of revival as a time of phenomenal growth in the numbers attending church. In fact, some would even define revival in just this way: a time when crowds flock to church in order to hear the gospel, a sudden and startling numerical increase in church membership and attendance as a result of many conversions. It should be clear by now that this is not the most significant thing about revival. Revival is not the conversion of thousands of unsaved, but the awakening of the church, making it holy and alive once again. The crowds and conversions are the result of this, but we must never lose sight of this essential order. Even if the conversion of sinners comes hand-in-hand with the revival of the church, God's purpose in revival is first and foremost the awakening of his own people. If we pray for revival only because we want to see many converts and full churches, we have missed the whole point. We can only pray for revival when we face up to the condition we are in as Christians. God must begin with the church and sometimes, as in the Congo in 1953, it may be months before he turns his attention to the unconverted.

In the days of Hezekiah the revival started in Judah and

Jerusalem, representing the people belonging to God. They were the ones who now longed to go to church and longed to be holy. From these revived people the evangelists went out to the northern territories and although many 'scorned and ridiculed them' (2 Chron. 30:10), 'A very large crowd of people assembled in Jerusalem' (30:13), and the chronicler can speak of 'the many people who came from Ephraim, Manasseh, Issachar and Zebulun...' (30:18). No one counted heads, but they knew there were many people from the north. Revival always has this spill-over to the unsaved. Exactly the same happened in the early church, except that someone was prepared to write down statistics: first there were 3,000 (Acts 2:41), and later the number grew to about 5,000 (4:4). As the work of the Spirit continued, 'More and more men and women were added to their number' (Acts 5:14). The rest of the story of the early church concerns its growth throughout the empire.

There is no doubt that revival always marks a leap forward in the numerical growth of the church; there cannot be a great outpouring of the Holy Spirit so that a whole community is saturated with God, without eternity being impressed onto the minds of men and women who before were careless and indifferent. One of the most remarkable occasions in revival occurred on 21 June 1630 when John Livingstone preached in the churchyard at Shotts in Lanarkshire, Scotland; it is estimated that 500 people were converted as a result of this single sermon.

Jonathan Edwards was pastor of a large church in Northampton, New England, in the eighteenth century, but during the time of revival he noted especially that people 'thronged' to worship in a way they never had before, and although he was naturally cautious in giving numbers of those converted, he allowed himself this conservative estimate: 'I hope that more than three hundred souls were savingly brought home to Christ, in this town, in the space of half a year, and about the same number of males as females.'[1] This was in 1734 in just one town in the New World, and during one five-week period Edwards saw thirty people saved each week. But this Great Awakening was going on all over New England in the early eighteenth century, and it is estimated that out of a total population of 340,000, between 25,000 and 30,000 were converted.[2] If we take the lowest figure this means that over seven per cent of the population was converted during the revival!

In London at roughly the same time, George Whitefield was preaching to probably the largest crowds ever to hear the gospel in England up to that time. There was no accurate way of counting the vast crowds that listened to Whitefield in the open air from the late 1730s onwards, and it is even more difficult for us to judge 250 years later, but even if we halve the estimate given at the time — which Whitefield's biographer, Arnold Dallimore, says we should — the great preacher at times addressed up to 40,000 listeners! Dallimore suggests this may be the largest number of people ever reached by the unamplified human voice in the whole history of mankind; and this by a young man of twenty-four![3]

In 1742 God worked in a powerful way in Cambuslang in Scotland, partly under the ministry of Whitefield. Nearly six months after the revival, a local minister estimated that more than 500 had been converted and were still following Christ.[4]

When John Wesley died in 1791 the membership of his Wesleyan Methodists in Britain was around 72,000; sixty years later it had increased fivefold.[5]

When God came to Wales in 1859 it is estimated that 110,000 were added to the churches, and only slightly fewer were added between 1904-1905.[6] In each case the Calvinistic Methodists received the largest influx of 36,000 and 24,000 respectively. On 27 January 1905 the *North Wales Guardian* reported 70,000 added to the churches in Wales; but a week later, on 3 February, it increased the figure to over 74,000! The paper went on to comment that in Anglesey Professor Mavis Jones of the University College estimated the number of converts at ten per cent of the total population. He put this down to systematic house-to-house visitation inviting non-chapelgoers to attend the revival meetings.[7]

The revival that swept Ulster in 1859 claimed another 100,000 for Christ, and some, reporting at the time, considered that estimate to be too conservative.[8]

The first missionaries arrived in Ethiopia in 1928 and at that time there were no known believers in the country. In July 1935 they received orders from the American and British embassies to evacuate. The missionaries could count only seventeen Wallamo believers, and they ignored the orders and stayed on. In April 1937, when they were forced to leave after nine years' work, there were still only forty-eight believers. In 1943, less than six years later and after the cruel occupation of Ethiopia by the Italians, the missionaries were able to return and were greeted by more than 100 church leaders, representing around 10,000 Christians! In one church alone 400 believers gathered. One Christian commented: 'When you missionaries left it was difficult to find a Christian in Wallamo country. Now it is difficult to find a man who is not a Christian.' By 1945 there were 15,000 believers.[9]

Surveying the scene of revival across the world, Edwin Orr points out that in Korea between 1906 and 1910 the net gain of all the churches was nearly 80,000, which was more than the total number of Christians in Japan after half a century of Protestant effort.[10]

Similarly what has happened to the church in China in the last few decades can only be understood in terms of revival. When the missionaries were expelled in 1949 after 140 years of missionary activity there were fewer than 1,000,000 national believers. Today some estimates suggest that there may be nearly as many Christians in China as the entire population of the United Kingdom! By 1980 Bishop Peter Hsieh of Fuzhou reported that in his city of 1,000,000 people there were 20,000 Christians. On one of his pastoral journeys he discovered 7,000 new Christians in seven remote mountain villages. In this same year Christians throughout the whole province were known to number at least 600,000, and in one area alone, in one year, 6,000 new converts were baptized! In some rural areas it is estimated that over ninety per cent of the population is Christian and that as many as 27,000 people have been converted each day in China between 1980 and 1983. One elderly pastor in China commented: 'Before the Communists came, I remember that shepherds were searching for sheep. But now, all over China, it is the sheep who are searching for shepherds!'[11]

We often think of revivals only as these great periods when vast numbers over a wide area are brought to Christ, but the story of God's church reveals many more local, and sometimes very short, outpourings of the Spirit. In 1794 an awakening came to the north of England, and in Sheffield, under the preaching of John Moon and Alexander Mather, the presence of God was unusually felt. One chapel meeting began quite normally until God came down and it then continued until two in the morning. During this meeting as many as seventy found peace with God and the power of God was present for another three days until around 100 had been converted.

In the same year revivals broke out in West Yorkshire, and in the Leeds Methodist circuit 2,000 new members were added in that one year.[12]

1799 was a year of God's favour for Cornwall. At Penzance there were 100 new members; at Zennor the Methodist Society increased from seventeen to 100 and at Walls eighty were added in two months. In St Ives the Methodists grew from 160, a figure that had been static for many years, to 550. And so we could go on.[13]

In 1814 God began a work in Redruth which spread throughout Cornwall and in a period of only a few weeks it was estimated that 5,000 were added to the Methodist churches. In the course of one week, 2,000 people were converted at Tuckingmill during a meeting that lasted from Sunday, 27 February, through to the following Friday, with people coming and going all the time![14]

During the early 1830s the name of James Caughey was well known in the Midlands. Converted in revival in the United States, he returned to Britain. After a short time in Dublin he preached in Liverpool where over 12,000 were converted. The same success accompanied him in Nottingham, where William Booth was converted, and at Huddersfield, Goole, Sheffield, York, Chesterfield and Birmingham. It was here in Birmingham in the Methodist church (which seats 2,000) that 600 were brought to Christ and the revival left the 'bar-rooms and beershops vocal with lonely grumblers'.[15] When the revival that started in Lowestoft on the east coast of England in 1921 spread to the Scottish fishing ports, whole communities were transformed. At Cairnbulg, with a population of only 1,500, over 600 professions were recorded in two weeks.[16]

In the early 1970s hundreds were converted in Borneo and at one convention over 200 were baptized.[17] The same thing was happening in India at the turn of the century.[18] But whilst revival touches whole towns, counties or provinces, it is in the local church that the real effect is felt.

When Joseph Kemp came as pastor to Charlotte Chapel in Edinburgh in 1902, only thirty-five of the 100 members attended his induction. Three years later God began to work in the chapel in such a way that the building was soon outgrown by the congregation and by 1907 the membership stood at 609. Joseph Kemp records: 'Under these influences the crowds thronged the chapel, which only three years before maintained a "sombre vacuum". After the first year of this work we had personally dealt with no fewer than one thousand souls, who had been brought to God during the prayer meetings...I have yet to witness a movement that has produced more permanent results, in the lives of men, women and children.'[19]

But statistics are dangerous things. At a distance of time we can never be sure how accurate they are; some are over-generous in counting heads, and others are too conservative. Some statistics we know are accurate because of the careful records kept; others are good, or bad, guesses; some may be wishful thinking!

Keri Evans, in Wales in 1905, gave a timely reminder that in times of revival many are convicted of sin who never come to salvation: 'Conviction is not conversion, neither does an awakening mean conviction. The real thing is the Holy Spirit passing through the imagination and feelings to the conscience — so creating conviction — then through conscience to the will — so leading to conversion.'[20]

But however we read the records, it is impossible to avoid the conclusion that revival always brings with it a new and vigorous growth in the numbers regularly attending the places of worship and claiming allegiance to Jesus Christ. But do they all stand the test of time?

Doubtless there were those who went back on their commitment when Manasseh came to the throne. Certainly there were some in the early church whose profession was false: Simon the sorcerer was one, but there were others. Demas did not stay the course, and Alexander and Hymenaeus were hardly a credit to the gospel. Overall, however, the converts of the New Testament church stood the rigorous tests of time and persecution. In true revival the numbers professing Christ are so much greater than in the 'normal' life of the church, but it is a matter of debate whether the percentage of false professions is more or less. Honest men involved in revival have always been concerned with this question of whether the converts stand or fall away.

Reporting on the work of the Spirit in Dundee in 1839, Robert Murray M'Cheyne noted that 'Not fewer than from six hundred to seven hundred came to converse with the ministers about their souls...With regard to the consistency of those who are believed to have been converted, I may first of all remark, that it must be acknowledged, and should be clearly understood, that many who came under concern about their souls, and seemed, for a time, to be deeply convinced of sin, have gone back again to the world.' M'Cheyne explains this by the fact that very few who came to the meetings were completely untouched by the Word of God; thus many came for counselling who were not converted.

However, he continues: 'Confining our view to those who, as far as ministers could judge by the rules of God's Word, seemed to be savingly converted, I may with safety say, that I do not know of more than two who have openly given the lie to their profession. Other cases of this kind may have occurred, but they are unknown to me.'[21] Here is a cautious minister who distinguishes between those who make a profession and those whom the ministers judged to be converted, and four years later M'Cheyne concluded that most of the latter were still continuing well.

Thomas Jones was deeply involved in the Welsh revival of 1859 and he faced this same question, concluding: 'I have gathered from enquiry that not one person in every fifty of those who have assumed a profession of religion within the last four or six months, has relapsed into the world.' One estimate, given as late as 1897, claimed that only one in twenty failed to continue their profession.[22]

One reason for this high level of continuing is that the churches were careful never to allow people to conclude that a mere profession was enough to guarantee true conversion. In 1860 Thomas Phillips wrote down the way the churches had taken care of those who made a profession: 'On every occasion care is taken to instruct the people in the true and unchangeable principles of religion. They are cautioned against resting in a mere outward profession. They are told that excitement is not conversion, that an awakening of the conscience to a sense of guilt and danger does not always result in a change of heart. It is strongly and constantly urged that whatever hope or confidence they may have in their own minds as to their having "passed from death unto life", it is a mistake, a delusion, unless it is accompanied by hatred to sin, and a renunciation of it in every shape or form; love to holiness, and the practical discharge of every moral duty. They are told that the Bible is to be the standard of religious feeling, as it is of religious faith. In short, they are admonished to seek a thorough change of heart, and to furnish evidence thereof in holiness of life.'[23]

Much the same was true of the work of God in Ulster at the same time. One minister, writing of the results in his own locality could report: 'I do not yet know of a single backslider.'[24] Of course, among the many scores of thousands who professed Christ during that eventful year, there were some who did go back on their commitment, but the proportion was small and no one could doubt the value of the revival because of them.

Though the numbers involved were much smaller, David Brainerd was able to report that of the forty-seven Indians who were converted at the Forks of Delaware in the early 1740s, 'None of them as yet have been left to disgrace their profession of Christianity.'[25]

The ministers involved at Kilsyth and Cambuslang in 1742 were concerned and honest in their assessment of the numbers that slipped back after a profession of faith during the revival. They freely admitted that, like the seed that fell on unsuitable soil in the parable told by Christ, there were many whose profession lasted only a while. The ministers were alert to this possibility at the time, and were not willing to accept a profession merely by outward appearances, least of all by the bodily trembling that some experienced. However, in a letter written by William McCulloch to James Robe, nine years after that memorable event, the incumbent at Cambuslang records: 'I have now before me, at the writing of this, April 27th 1751, a list of about four hundred persons awakened here at Cambuslang in 1742 who from that time to the time of their death, or to this, for these nine years past, have been all enabled to behave in a good measure as becometh the gospel...'[26]

Strangely, the revival that had the most widespread influence also appears to have had the greatest percentage of losses. The 1904 revival that began in Wales spread throughout the world as missionaries returned to their fields of service and the stories spread across every continent. Yet it is estimated that during the five years following the revival something around twenty per cent slipped away from the churches. This figure needs some explanation, because not all these fell away from following Christ; some changed their church allegiance. However, twenty per cent is a high figure and is probably due as much to Evan Roberts' later indifference to preaching and the teaching of young converts as to anything else. In spite of this, it is reported that ten years later, in 1914, 80,000 of the converts were still in the membership of the churches 'in spite of leakage to mission halls and emigration overseas'.[27] That is hardly a statistic of failure!

Statistics do not tell the whole story. Another way of assessing the consistency of the converts is to look at the lasting changes to the community. For example, the following figures for total convictions for drunkenness in Glamorgan were released by the Chief Constable of Cardiff four years after the outbreak of revival in Wales in 1904 which continued into 1905:

1902	9,298
1903	10,528
1904	11,282
1905	8,164
1906	5,490
1907	5,615

This leads us directly to look at the longer results of revival in the life of a community that is saturated with God.

After revival

Benefits of revival

A time of spiritual revival is always a time of benefit to the community. 2 Kings 18:7-8 are very significant verses: 'The Lord was with him; he was successful in whatever he undertook. He rebelled against the king of Assyria and did not serve him. From watchtower to fortified city, he defeated the Philistines, as far as Gaza and its territory.'

The nation was sufficiently strong in the time of Hezekiah to throw off its slavery; the revival gave the people of Judah moral and military fibre and it was this that led Hezekiah to make a bid to secure spiritual unity in the nation after 200 years of warfare between the north and the south. This was Israel's last chance to come back to the covenant of David. The revival was also a time of Hezekiah's brilliant engineering. A tunnel was built to bring water into the city in times of siege: a subterranean passage 1,700 feet long which was started from both ends, with only a small kink in the middle! It was an incredible feat of engineering which can still be seen today. It was a time when great stores of food were laid up and a strong armoury was built. In the time of Hezekiah Jerusalem was the strongest it had ever been since the time of

Solomon. And when the Assyrians approached Jerusalem in the year 701 B.C. the city was secure. Sennacherib describes in his own records how he shut up Hezekiah in Jerusalem like a bird in a cage. He could shut up Hezekiah like a bird in a cage but he could not get into the cage! The key to it all is found in 2 Chronicles 31:21: 'In everything that he undertook in the service of God's temple and in obedience to the law and the commands, he sought his God and worked wholeheartedly. And so he prospered.'

A revival always has an effect upon the nation. Edwin Orr, one of the greatest authorities on the history of revivals, claims that the evangelical awakening in the eighteenth century saved Britain from the revolutionary experience that ravaged the continent of Europe at that time. Wesley, the English evangelist, defeated Voltaire, the French philosopher and Deist.

The historian Dr Stoughton, in his book *The History of Religion in England*, speaks of the Evangelical Awakening in the eighteenth century in this way: 'It laid hold upon multitudes of Englishmen with a firmer grasp and in a greater number of instances than ever before. It was exhibited under its most benevolent aspects...as the helper of the poor, the friend of the prisoner, the liberator of the slave, the visitor of the sick, the comforter of the dying.'

It is equally true that the period of revival across America after 1800 saved that nation from the godless French philosophy that had influenced almost every college by the close of the eighteenth century. Most students boasted of their unbelief and nicknamed each other Voltaire, Rousseau, D'Alembert and so on. At Princeton, Dr Green knew of only two professing Christians among the students. The College of William and Mary in Virginia was a 'hotbed of French politics and religion'. Almost certainly the period of revival saved America from the tragedy of the worst elements of the French revolution.

In the eighteenth and nineteenth centuries there were staggering benefits of revival in the social life of England, and some of the worst effects of the Industrial Revolution were avoided. Whatever men may think or say about revival, they cannot doubt its benefit to society as a whole. Revival gave the nation a social conscience and produced the men and women who campaigned for the abolition of slavery and brought the women and children up from the mines and the boys down from the chimneys; revival contributed also to a greater concern for prisoners and the insane, a reduction in hours of work and a care for the living conditions of the poor. To claim that every benefit to society in these two centuries was directly the result of revival would be foolishly inaccurate, but revival was certainly one of the principal causes of social reform.

Before 1857 America was similarly in a desperate condition. One writer describes the time before and after the revival like this: 'Banks and business houses failed, factories and railways closed down, vast numbers were soon unemployed, and it needed the quietness of shut-out industry and transport in order for a nation to hear the still small voice of God! In 1857 God spoke to America...Millions of converts were added to the churches of all denominations. And what proved the genuineness of the revival was the ethical result, for the social effects of the revival continued for almost half a century.' [28]

Murray M'Cheyne reported of Dundee in 1839 that the revival 'spread a sweet influence over the place,'[29] and that was a parish of 60,000 inhabitants!

Drunkenness

In a day when even the government is concerned about the rise in drunkenness, when 10,000,000 working days are lost every year as a result of it and when local authorities are openly reporting alcohol as 'our favourite drug' costing the nation twenty-six billion pounds a year, it is incredible how Christians are actually boastful of their 'freedom' to use the drug. The voluntary services of one local authority in the United Kingdom reported in its autumn newsletter for 1988 that alcohol was involved in thirty-three per cent of all child abuse cases in the borough, seventy-eight per cent of all assaults, forty-one per cent of thefts, fifty per cent of wife battering, and sixty-six per cent of suicides. We may add to this the national statistic that alcohol is responsible for forty per cent of all road deaths. The only thing that is new about all this is that we have the statistics to prove it. Historically, revival has always transformed the drinking habits of a large number of people in society.

Jonathan Edwards wrote a letter to a minister in Boston dated 12 December 1743. He was describing some of the effects of the revival in Northampton, New England, between 1740 and 1742 and particularly noted what he called 'a great alteration, amongst both

old and young, with regard to tavern-haunting'. Edwards continued: 'I suppose the town has been in no measure so free of vice in
these respects...for sixty years, as it has been these nine years
past.'[30]

The work of God at Cambuslang in 1742 'embraced all classes,
all ages, and all moral conditions. Cursing, swearing and drunkenness were given up by those who came under its power.'[31]

The powerful work of the Spirit that swept across Kentucky in
1800 left the state entirely changed and, as one observer explained:
'I found Kentucky as remarkable for sobriety as they had formerly
been for dissoluteness and immorality...A profane expression was
hardly ever heard. A religious awe seemed to pervade the
country.'[32]

In some mines in Wales in 1904 the work came to a standstill
because the pit ponies could no longer understand the orders that
were given to them; the hauliers, classed as the worst group of men
in the pits, proverbial for their profanity and cruelty, were no longer
cursing their commands and the ponies were confused![33]

The ministry of James Caughey in Birmingham in the 1830s
was said to have left many public houses 'vocal with lonely
grumblers'.[34]

All the best attempts of the temperance movements were unable
to stem the flow of drunkenness in Bala, North Wales, but when
revival came in 1858-59 the 'drink market' was so greatly affected
that the revival in this town was known as the 'temperance revival'.
Although it was not made a condition of membership, total absti-
nence was strongly recommended to the new converts, 'as a
safeguard to themselves and as an example to others'.[35]

We have already seen the statistics of the Chief Constable of
Cardiff for 1907 which were a direct result of the 1904 revival.[36] In
fact local statistics were even more impressive. David Lloyd-
George spoke of a tavern in his constituency which, at the time of
the revival, took just fourpence-ha'penny (less than two and a half
pence!) on the drinking night of the week. R. B. Jones reports on the
1904 revival that it greatly affected the drink trade; breweries were
worried by it all, and publicans went bankrupt. In some towns men
who were never converted in the revival were nevertheless
ashamed to go into the public houses.[37]

In March 1905 the Chief Constable of Glamorgan commented
that 'The decrease in drunkenness has undoubtedly been most

marked where the Revivalists have had the largest following.'
Judge Gwilym Williams, reporting to the meeting of the Glamorgan
County Council, specifically drew attention to the results of the
work of Evan Roberts; the judge claimed he was not interested in
the methods of Mr Roberts but 'the results were everything'.[38]

About the same time the Bishop of Dorking wrote of a recent
visit to Wales; he spoke to a police sergeant and asked for his
opinion of the revival and the reply he received was: 'This is a pretty
rough part; and [they] don't think much of kicking a policeman like
a football; but there's been none of that these two months. There are
twenty-two licensed houses in my district and they are not drawing
enough beer to pay the gas; the men are all in the chapels.'[39]

It is not hard to imagine the effect of all this upon the families
of men who normally spent their earnings on drink before they
arrived home at the end of the week.

When God came among the Lun Bawang people of Borneo in
1938, he did so without the presence of the missionaries. When the
missionaries came to the villages they knew how to test the
genuineness of the work: 'Where is your borak [rice beer] now?',
they asked. The reply was instant: 'Oh, we've given that up long
ago!' Among these people this change had another, unexpected
effect. The whole village was clean and tidy; to the extent that one
missionary wrote that the place was swept so clean that there was
no place to put the discarded banana skins! The longhouse used to
be the foulest in Sarawak, but was now the cleanest and best kept.
Nearly forty years later, in 1973, when the Spirit of God was at work
in Borneo, even discipline in the school changed and honesty
affected every part of the life of the communities. One Kelabit
Indian described the change by simply observing, 'The oranges are
still on the trees.' The children would no longer steal the fruit![40]

Restitution

Drunkenness and swearing are only two results of the work of God
in revival. In the Congo in 1953 so many stolen goods were returned
to the authorities that a colonial official asked the people to take
them to the missionaries, who would arrange for a lorry to carry
them all to the Belgian office in one go!

The same thing happened in Uganda in 1939 when at times so

many people were waiting outside the District Commissioner's office to return or pay for things that the official complained it was hard for him to get on with his work. Festo Kivengere writes of the effect of this kind of restitution in Uganda. One chief, Festo's uncle, was confronted by a man driving eight fine cows. The man, known to be a pagan and a rich man in cattle, addressed the chief: 'Your honour, I have come for a purpose. These cows are yours; I have brought them back to you.' 'What do you mean, they are mine?' responded the chief. 'Well sir, when I was looking after your cattle, I stole four of them when I told you we had been raided. These four are now eight. I have brought them to you.' 'Who discovered this theft?' demanded the chief. 'Jesus did, sir. He has given me peace and told me to bring them.' When revival touched children it had the same effect. One child owned up to his father that he had received too much change from a shopkeeper eighteen months prior to the revival; the father promptly sent the change to the store.[41]

In Korea in 1907 one Chinese business man was amazed when a Christian returned a large sum of money that he had received from the merchant in error.[42] No one can argue against this kind of morality in society; and revival always has this effect. It is the experience of Zacchaeus on a grand scale! And stories of property being restored and debts paid in revival come from all over the world.

Early in 1905 the *North Wales Guardian* reported on a sermon by Dr Oliver, the Secretary of the North Wales Federation of Free Church Councils: 'Referring to the revival, Dr Oliver said a South Wales shopkeeper had told him that many of his customers whose debts he had written off his books as "bad" were now paying them, and he knew of one tradesman who had just received a sum of £37 which would never have been paid him but for this revival. Referring to those cold, callous, self-complacent people who derided the revival, he said it was part of the current cant of materialism to throw doubt on all forms of religious enthusiasm. He believed the present revival was from God, and he thanked God for it from his heart.'[43]

Christian love

It must be evident already that the benefit of revival for the church is vast: renewed love towards God, reality in worship, holiness of life and zeal for evangelism; it is inevitable therefore that the community around will notice that God is among his people. One of the marks of the first-century Christians was that they 'enjoyed the favour of all the people…[and] were highly regarded by the people' (Acts 2:47; 5:13). The people could not help but notice the love and care that the Christians had for one another. Paul reminded the young converts at Corinth that they were the aroma of Christ both 'among those who are being saved, and those who are perishing' (2 Cor. 2:15). That should be true always of the life of the Christian community, but it is especially so in revival. The greater the work of God, the greater the effect across the nation. From the Khassi Hills in India came the description of 'Christians becoming more holy, more forgiving, more loving…'[44]

Festo Kivengere wrote at length of the deep Christian love that was evident even to the unbelieving world. Christians met daily in Uganda to care for and help each other. It was a new experience for many. Kivengere comments: 'I have seen many methods devised in attempting to produce a love-fellowship. But the only known power for keeping together a group of believers — intact in love, fruitful and not ingrown — is the presence of the Author in the midst who is listened to and obeyed. It is not a product of man's desire for socializing. It is a fruit of Christ's self-giving love, which always draws us together and creates a community wherever people have opened their hearts to Him. When the Lord is in the midst, the Holy Spirit makes us alert and sensitive to each other's needs. This is what the prophet calls "the heart of the flesh" in place of a cold, stony heart. The Spirit is the One who sets us "free to serve one another in love". This serving is done in practical ways which are visible to onlookers. There were many in Uganda, and eventually in all East Africa, who echoed the words of the pagan Romans which Tertullian tells us about, "Behold these Christians, how they love one another!" A widow whose house is in disrepair may find the believers together building a new one for her. A hungry family may find a bag of grain at the door in the morning. A young person may find that his school fees have been paid…'[45]

Unity

One of the greatest benefits of revival lies in its effects upon human relationships. In society, those converted to Christ are reconciled not only to God but to neighbours, workmates and others. Family feuds are healed, gossiping and slanderous tongues are silenced and class and social barriers are pulled down. The gospel that makes us 'all one in Christ Jesus' and the Saviour, in whom there is 'neither Jew nor Greek, slave nor free, male nor female' (Gal. 3:28), unite those who are unnecessarily divided.

It was reported from Wales in 1904 that women who 'sued one another in the courts, [now] prayed side by side in the same meeting'. An old miner, speaking of the feuds between union and non-union members prior to the 1859 revival in Wales, claimed: 'I have seen neighbours refuse to speak to each other, although they had been great friends. I have seen some refuse to descend the mine in the same cage with men who did not belong to the Federation, or to speak to them below ground, except with an oath. The Revival has stopped all that, and colliers look upon each other, spite of all the differences, as friends and companions. Some of the Non-unionists were among the best of men, and, at the meeting I have just left, one of them was leading the prayers, and Unionists joining in!'[46]

Nowhere is this seen more obviously than in the life of the churches. One of the sad marks of the church in its normal life is that it is often found uniting with those from whom it should separate, and separating from those with whom it should unite. Too often denominational ties and traditions are far more important than loyalty to the truth. Revival, as we have already said, is an evangelical experience; it is the glory and gift of the evangelical churches, whatever their denomination. Revival highlights the big issues that unite, rather than the secondary issues that divide. Of course, this is not always the case, but it stands as a general truth.

When Hezekiah sent the evangelists to the north, he sent them to men who had much in common with the south — but also much that was contrary to the law of God. The invitation was not primarily to come south and unite, but to 'return to the Lord...submit to the Lord...serve the Lord' (2 Chron. 30:6-8). And this inevitably included submission to God's law. In other words, it was a gospel of uniting in absolute obedience to God and his Word. In the life of the infant church Paul had a clear yardstick for assessing preaching: whatever a man's motives may be, the apostle was concerned to know whether Christ was preached or not (Phil. 1:15-18).

On the basis that revival is a thoroughly evangelical experience,

it is noticeable how often all other distinctions are lost sight of.
There are sad exceptions, such as the opposition to Bakht Singh[47]
and Jock Troup[48] because they were not ordained preachers, the
criticism of Duncan Campbell because he did not fit everyone's
theology precisely,[49] and the Associate Presbyteries' strong opposition to Whitefield because, as an ordained Church of England
clergyman, he was 'a limb of anti-Christ'.[50] In the case of Bakht
Singh in Madras it was, ironically, the churches' preoccupation
with 'church union' that caused the denominational churches to
overlook and even oppose the work God was doing in the city.[51] But
this was exceptional.

On the other hand, William Haslam who, as a proud, unconverted Anglican, once boasted he would be glad to bury every
dissenter as a breed of 'no goods', found some of his greatest
fellowship and support from these dissenters once he had been
converted and experienced revival in his church. A report in
Scotland in 1839 claimed: 'As the revival swept Kilsyth, the
various denominations worked together in perfect harmony.'[52]

Similar reports came from the Welsh press in 1860 and 1905.
The *Wrexham Advertiser* for 4 August 1860 commented upon a talk
given by the Rev. J. Baillie of the Church of England. He was
speaking of the revival in Ulster and reported that 'To ask what
denomination a convert belonged to, would excite a smile of pity,
and that it is considered there are but two sects in the world, the one
for Christ and the other against him.'

A similar report was carried in the *North Wales Guardian* on 17
March 1905. It was of a meeting in Rhosllanerchrugog where the
evangelical vicar was sympathetic to the revival, and the reporter
continued: 'One of the most remarkable scenes witnessed since the
inception of the revival was enacted here on Monday afternoon.
The Vicar has taken keen interest in the meetings from the
commencement, and has worked in co-operation with the
Nonconformists throughout. The Welsh Church was filled with a
vast congregation, composed mainly of Nonconformists, and with
a few exceptions all the ministers were present. The Vicar presided
and the meeting was opened by Rev. E. Williams, Baptist minister.
Prayers, praise, and solos followed for about two and a half hours.
The Rev. Robert Jones, Welsh Calvinistic Methodist minister,
having taken part, the Vicar said he could not express in words the
happiness he felt in seeing so many present; he had attended many

meetings during his career but he never felt such a thrill of emotion as he had on that occasion. The walls and hedges of dis-union had been swept away, they were now united, and they knew no distinction.'

Thirty years after the Welsh revival, Rhys Jones commented on some of the benefits. In particular he noted that 'sectionalism and suspicion' were ended, and he continued: 'Denominational walls, as high perhaps in Wales as in most countries, fell down as did Jericho's walls.' This was perhaps one advance of the 1904 revival in Wales over that of 1859; during the earlier revival the established church in Wales largely resisted the work of the Spirit, whereas in 1904 the barriers between church and chapel were broken down. R. B. Jones noted that 'Not only did Nonconformists of all hues blend together, but the wider gulf between Nonconformist and Conformist was also wonderfully bridged. Anglican clergy, as well as Free Church ministers, recognized the work as of God. Anglicans were seen in Nonconformist pulpits, and unordained revivalists welcomed in Anglican pulpits. What agitation and legislation could never have effected, to the Spirit of God was but the work of a moment.'[53]

It must be re-emphasized that unity like this is always an evangelical unity, and never an ecumenical unity where the true gospel is lost among the baggage of error and pretence.

Family relationships

Families are transformed in revival. In the eighteenth century Jonathan Edwards wrote of the joy that had been brought to whole families as salvation came to each member.[54]

In a very different age and culture, Festo Kivengere reported on the radical change to family life that revival in East Africa brought: 'It was an amazing thing to me to see what dignity and freedom of spirit the Lord had brought to the women of God. African men are often polygamous and traditionally they like to be treated as chiefs in their homes, with their wives as mere slaves. But here I saw a husband giving a place of honour to his wife, and watched her fill the place competently as a beloved equal in the sight of the Lord. I even saw a man kneel down before his wife and say, "I have been mean and hurtful to you, my dear. I am sorry. Please forgive me."...

Before dawn every morning, the families who loved Jesus would rise and wash, gather in a room and begin to sing praises to the Lord. Each morning, when I woke, I could hear the singing rise from one nearby home after another. Then I knew they were reading the Scripture Union portion for the day, and meditating on it together.'[55]

A minister reported from Ulster in 1859 that in one congregation, out of 209 families only two were not regularly observing family worship.[56]

The following year Thomas Phillips wrote from Wales that 'The general establishment of family worship is another blessed result of the present awakening.' In fact the young converts were told not to be content with public worship: they must worship God as families in their own homes.[57] In some homes where fathers were slow to start family worship, the children demanded it! This act of worship in the home almost became a test of true conversion. And it is certainly a mark of many revivals; Howel Harris is one among many to comment that 'Family worship was set up in many houses.'[58]

Inevitably such a new life and closeness in the families had other, more obvious results. One NSPCC inspector told a newspaper reporter how, in the mining valleys of Glamorgan, the revival of 1904 had such a great influence on the care of parents for their children that, because of the remarkable change in their homes he now no longer needed even to watch several families whom he had previously expected to have to prosecute.[59] In Swansea it was reported that adults were taking their parents from the workhouse to care for them at home.

To give examples from every revival would be tedious. These are merely samples. When God comes by his Spirit in revival then society is always aware of it, not only in the changed lives of the Christians and the more radical change in the lives of the converts, but also in the effect that all this has upon the community. Crime is reduced and the magistrates and police are among the first to notice a difference. This must be the case, and if it is not, then it is doubtful whether a true revival has happened at all. Nothing less than revival can halt the relentless march of drunkenness and violence in our society today.

But these examples, though typical, do not really demonstrate the larger value of revival in a national context. The great revivals in Britain of the eighteenth and nineteenth centuries radically altered our social and political history. They gave back a conscience to the nation. The national conscience had been lost by the restoration of Charles II in 1660 and a godless age of immorality had forfeited many of the benefits of the Reformation and the Commonwealth. Even the 'Glorious Revolution' of 1688, when William III sailed from Holland and snatched the crown from James, only settled the political and religious scene; it did little for the soul of the nation. When the eighteenth century opened it could be described simply by the phrase: 'Stomach well alive, soul extinct.' That is exactly where we are again today. And we must never forget that it was not the 'Glorious Revolution', but the 'Great Awakening' that changed the nation.

After revival

Error, excess and the unusual in revival

When Spurgeon once referred to revival as a time of 'glorious disorder', he used an expression that was bigger than he may have intended. Revival is not disorderly in the sense of everything always being out of hand and 'wild', but it is certainly disorderly in that God does not limit himself to a pattern or order called 'revival'. Reading about the revivals of the church can be very upsetting. We have already seen, and we must always maintain, that revival is an evangelical experience and is the glory of the evangelical church, whatever other denominational label a church may have; but that fact still gives God adequate scope for variety! No one comes to the subject of revival without prejudices. We all know the kind of experiences and behaviour we would like to see or expect to see when the Holy Spirit is powerfully at work, and it is tempting to choose those examples that fit *our* pattern, and to ignore the rest.

However, God is no man's servant and his Spirit moves where he wants to. If our pet theme is sanctification, we can find revivals where that became a doctrine of major importance; if we wish to prove that noise and uncontrolled emotion are a hallmark of revivals, we can find some to provide us with good examples. If it is 'gifts' we are after, we shall find a few revivals (not many) to suit our case; if we are looking for quiet, controlled and solemn meetings, they can be found as well. In revival God uses ignorant and theologically careless preachers, as well as men of great learning and precision; he uses men who encourage 'wild' responses and men who expect order and discipline. Whatever our experience or preference or our doctrinal emphasis, if we dig over the ground long enough we shall find a revival somewhere to support our cause.

For this reason I have tried to keep to the broad areas of common ground and have avoided the temptation to prove too much from too little. I am well aware that if I try to prove my preferences, someone will easily prove the opposite! There are revivals in the history of the church that have been, without question, a true work of the Spirit and yet I cannot find myself in agreement with all that was done or preached during the revival. Obviously Whitefield and Wesley could not both be right in the election versus free-will controversy — and my convictions lie wholly with Whitefield! Similarly, much as I rejoice in the experience and admire the courage of William Haslam of Baldhu in Cornwall, I wonder if he did not sometimes allow more unbridled Cornish emotion and noise than was always good for the honour of the gospel — a fact which he himself acknowledged when he admitted that his people between 1851 and 1854 had come to enjoy 'the gift of salvation more than the Giver himself'. I have no doubt he was wrong when, coming to see his deficiency in neglecting the doctrine of sanctification, he then made a separate experience of it.

But we dare not 'demolish' a revival simply because some aspects of it are not to our personal liking, doctrinal convictions, or denominational traditions. In looking at some of the strange and unusual things that happen in revival we must always keep one important principle in front of us: the Scripture is our guide; not culture, tradition, experience or personal preference. Where something occurs that is contrary to the Word of God, it is wrong, no matter how much God may seem to use it. Sometimes his use of it may be more apparent than real, and in any case, the fact that God may bless our failures and errors does not justify them.

Commenting on some of the problems encountered during the

revival in Borneo during 1973, an elder statesman in Sarawak wrote, 'In any revival there are usually two opposite reactions or attitudes of people, including the Christians. Some people totally reject all that takes place, and miss out on the fresh blessings and deeper things of God, and even miss out on salvation completely. On the other hand, some people blindly accept everything without discerning, and are deceived by Satan or are misled by the flesh and are in danger of straying away from the truth. While we know it is the genuine work of the Holy Spirit, we must also remember that Satan is very active in time of revival doing his counterfeit work and trying to deceive. There is also the human element such as emotionalism and hypocrisy.'[60]

Those are wise words because revival is a time of intense spiritual activity on both sides of the divide. If God is at work in power, so is the devil, who delights to counterfeit the good and holy work of the Creator. It is impossible to read of revival without, sooner or later, stumbling across some unusual, perhaps bizarre, or even frightening events. Everything from visions to faintings, from 'prophesying' to shrieking, has been recorded in the story of revival. It is the presence of these things that have led some to dismiss revival altogether as a dangerous hypnosis or an irrelevant side-show. True revival is neither, but it is hardly surprising that at times of great spiritual awakenings some will allow their emotion or their imagination to overtake a sound mind governed by the Word of God. In the excitement of the times some will allow themselves to be thrown off course and fall into error or excess.

In 2 Chronicles 30:18-20 we have an example of this in the time of Hezekiah: 'Although most of the many people who came from Ephraim, Manasseh, Issachar and Zebulun had not purified themselves, yet they ate the Passover, contrary to what was written. But Hezekiah prayed for them, saying, "May the Lord, who is good, pardon everyone who sets his heart on seeking God — the Lord, the God of his fathers — even if he is not clean according to the rules of the sanctuary." And the Lord heard Hezekiah and healed the people.'

This passage contains a very important corrective for us; because, whilst we are commanded by God to read his Word and not to do anything that is contrary to it, there are times in revival when in an excess of enthusiasm things are done that do go beyond Scripture. These people had come from Ephraim, Manasseh, Issachar and Zebulun. They had come down from the north and had been suddenly swept up in this great thing called revival, and they were not prepared for it. They were new converts to the covenant. God knew their hearts were sincere; they were not playing fast and loose with the Word. In fact they were not familiar with the Word of God and were not being deliberately disobedient. This is what makes them different from Uzzah who, in the time of David, disobediently touched the ark. He ought to have known better, but these people had been swept along on the great surge of revival and they had gone over the top, and outside the written law. It was sin, of course, but God forgave them because of what was happening.

By its very nature, revival brings in a large number of new converts in a short time, and it is not easy for them all to be taught the truth about God, because of the constant pressure of more people coming for counsel. New converts will watch what is happening and sometimes take it into their own heads to help forward the work of God. It is at this point that some of the errors and excesses creep in. Inevitably there will be things accompanying revival that form no part of the work of the Spirit of revival, but these should never be allowed to destroy the true work of God.

Writing of revival at Kilsyth and Cambuslang in 1742, James Robe admitted to the presence of 'imprudences, irregularities, and exceptional things', but, he says, these were condemned and opposed by the leaders, though sadly the enemies of revival exaggerated them to disgrace the work.[61]

A leader in the Shantung revival in China in 1932 admitted there were 'excesses and extravagances' because Satan is always present to destroy the work of God 'first by ridicule and second by duplicating it'.

We are never to think that such excesses are unimportant, or that they in themselves are evidence of revival. Some people are inclined to believe that the more excessive their behaviour is, the more authentic it must be, but hot air is not very nutritious! We must beware of copying the experiences of others, or even praying for the same experience. And we must never be intimidated into assuming that where there is a genuine work of the Holy Spirit, everything that happens must be right, or that even if certain things are wrong we ought not to criticize them for fear of touching holy things.

Sprague has left a wise comment on this from his wide experience of revival: 'You may be assured that the cause of revivals is far more likely to suffer by an attempt on the part of its friends to pass off everything for gold, than by giving to that which is really dross its proper name.'[62]

Physical responses

One of the most common experiences in revival has been the physical effects of a deep conviction of sin. We come across it in the ministry of John Wesley. During his meetings people would tremble, fall to the ground and faint. Others would cry out and scream.

One illustration of many is taken from Wesley's diary for the year 1739 during his ministry in Bristol: '*May 2nd.* John Haydon...a man of regular life and conversation...changed colour, fell off his chair, and began screaming terribly, and beating himself against the ground...Two or three men were holding him as best they could. He immediately fixed his eyes upon me, and cried, "Aye, this is he who I said was a deceiver of the people; but God has overtaken me. I said it was all a delusion; but this is no delusion." He then roared out, "O thou devil! Thou cursed devil! Yea thou legion of devils! Thou canst not stay!..." He then beat himself against the ground again, his breast heaving at the same time as in the pangs of death, and great drops of sweat trickling down his face...We all betook ourselves to prayer. His pangs ceased, and both body and soul were set at liberty.'[63]

This was not uncommon during the preaching of Wesley, and was even encouraged by the evangelist. However, Jonathan Edwards and George Whitefield were far less pleased with such outbursts and saw them as no certain sign of a genuine work of the Holy Spirit. Wesley himself later came to realize how easily a show of this kind could be put on, but there can be little doubt that the incident above was a true physical torment brought about by a very deep conviction of sin and the opposition of Satan.

At Kilsyth and Cambuslang the ministers noted that some, particularly among the girls and others who were for various reasons impressionable, fainted or threw fits; but the leaders were not impressed, and commented that 'The spirit of sal-ammoniac or hartshorn put to their noses was useful to revive them'![64]

After a period of serious spiritual decline in America the Spirit of God moved across Kentucky, North and South Carolina and Western Pennsylvania in 1800. Many of the meetings 'seemed as in bedlam, with emotionalized men and women weeping, groaning, shouting, jerking and dancing, or falling into trances and torpors. Such frenzies detracted from the revival in the eyes of many, especially the more conservative Presbyterians and Baptists, and were discredited among the better informed among the settlers.'[65] The genuineness of this revival cannot be doubted, but some of the responses were clearly exaggerated and unnecessary. Not only did these excesses divide churches and whole denominations, but the more extreme elements drew off into the Stonites (after Barton Stone) which slid into the sect known as the Shakers, a self-explanatory title!

On the other hand Asahel Nettleton, preaching in America in the first half of the nineteenth century, came across some who experienced 'horror of mind' which was so severe that they had to be taken away from the meeting until they found peace with God.[66]

Such experiences were commonplace in Ulster during the 1859 revival there. They were known as the 'strikings-down' and one illustration will cover many. At Berry Street Presbyterian Church a strong, powerful man set up a loud and bitter cry in the meeting and fell down. He was carried outside but was not unconscious; on the contrary his response to an enquiry was: 'Yes, awfully conscious.' The sheer horror of his sin had thrown him to the ground; this was a regular church-goer who was convicted of formalism and self-deception.[67]

The 'phenomenon' of a physical response to the conviction of sin and the presence of God has been reported as far away as Korea and India in times of revival. These physical responses have probably been the most debated part of the history of revivals; and generally the response to them depends upon whether the commentator is for or against the revival in the first place.

An interesting example of this is found in the columns of the *Wrexham Advertiser* during 1859. On 16 July the paper carried a report from Rev. W. McLlwaine of St George's Church, Belfast. He took great exception to the physical responses in Ulster during that year and described them in the most alarming way possible: 'After a good deal of actual examination, I have to state I believe that there is a dangerous physical malady abroad and that its seat is in the nervous system. It affects poor young girls who are working in

factories all day with very insufficient food, and these girls I have
seen myself suffering under the complaints I shall mention. I have
seen them in hysteria. I have known it to end in epilepsy. I have seen
them in catalepsy. I have known it to result in many cases in
madness. Will you find anything of it in the Bible? I deny it. I say
there is at present around us a dangerous amount of physical
disease. Now dear brethren let me affectionately appeal to you as
men, as brethren, and citizens. What do you think of the men, who
call themselves ministers of Christ that will collect these young
creatures in a crowded congregation, night after night, and speak to
them as the old divine of whom I have been reading? Every fibre of
their feelings is wrought up to excitement, and when they fall into
a swoon, not a drop of water is given them, and yet these men will
insist that this is the working of the Spirit of God. I have no words
to express my abhorrence of such conduct as this. I tell you it is
unworthy of any man, not to say a Christian minister…I have seen
whole roomfuls of these poor factory girls taken by it again and
again, and one of these poor creatures told me she had suffered from
it sixteen times. I ask you, were there sixteen convictions? They
were sixteen epileptic fits.'

On 20 August the same paper carried a report of a lecture
delivered by Rev. J. G. Short, who had recently spent some time in
Ulster. Clearly Mr Short saw things differently: 'I will now speak
to you of the physical manifestations by which this awakening has
been so largely characterized. Many have looked upon these with
wonder, and perplexity, and doubt. On this side of the channel they
are commonly regarded as the results of mere animal excitement.
This is a mistake. No one on the spot will ever dream of putting them
down to such a cause. I never saw meetings more free from all
display of mere feeling. A stranger going to any of these religious
gatherings that now fill evening after evening, almost all the
Protestant places of worship in Ulster, would feel at once there is no
rant here, no effort to get up any artificial feeling. An unwonted
solemnity and earnestness of feeling shows itself in the faces of the
people — but attempts to create any mere excitement there are
none…in a short time, perhaps half a dozen or more will be found
prostrate in the pews unable either to sit or stand. I have seen a
considerable number of these "stricken" cases. I have seen strong
men, as if smitten by an invisible hand, fall down nervous and
helpless, as I was near to them. I have seen some, their frame

trembling and convulsed as if the body shared in the anguish of the soul, as it travailed in the birth pangs of the new life...In every one of these "stricken" cases they cry for Jesus, and such a cry. I have heard many utter such words as "sweet Jesus", "lovely Jesus", in a very low tone of voice, but with a depth and tenderness of feeling that could not be described. I have seen them with hands uplifted as if beckoning to the Saviour, and then clasped over their breast as if clasping him to their hearts. The Saviour seemed as if visibly revealed, and as his love filled their souls, their faces looked as if they were literally transformed...I am quite sure, that with rare exceptions there is no consistent way of explaining them, except by confessing that they are the work of God.'

These two reports deserve quoting at length, because they clearly reveal the different responses to the same phenomena. Perhaps Mr McLlwaine chose only to observe the extreme cases, where the emotions of young girls were exploited; however, these physical experiences in revival are too common and too widespread to be dismissed either as all human or all satanic in origin. Even the cautious Scotsman Robert M'Cheyne reported from Dundee in 1839: 'I have seen persons so overcome [with love for Christ], that they could not walk or stand alone.'[68]

David seems to have felt the same crushing blow to his body when God dealt with him: 'Because of your wrath there is no health in my body; my bones have no soundness because of my sin. My guilt has overwhelmed me like a burden too heavy to bear' (Ps. 38:3-4). And the apostle John 'fell at his feet as though dead' (Rev. 1:17) when confronted by the risen Lord in all his glory. Similarly Saul of Tarsus crashed into the dust outside Damascus (Acts 9:4). We have a small view of God if we do not expect that when a man or woman sees himself or herself in the light of God's holiness there will never be an intense reaction. What must be noted is that in revival such a terrible experience of conviction is always followed by as great a joy in forgiveness.

It seems unnecessary to try to explain these things other than by the powerful effects of the work of the Holy Spirit on a bad conscience. To try to imitate such effects outside of revival is a dangerous delusion. They are not present in every revival and they should never be prayed for as a sign of reality; this was Wesley's mistake, and the more he prayed and expected them, the more they disrupted his meetings. There is a contagious psychology about phenomena like this: the more people expect them, the more they will appear, but that proves nothing apart from the frailty of the human mind.

There is a valuable corrective that comes from the experience of Duncan Campbell in 1949. There were times under the preaching of Campbell when people were thrown to the ground in physical prostration. Duncan Campbell observed that where people were looking for such physical manifestations they got them. And when they were not interested God said, 'Well, you don't need them,' and they did not have them. So Campbell himself admitted there was a certain psychological aspect to it. One day a man came to the evangelist and told him that he was praying for this physical prostration in order to be satisfied with Christ. Campbell gave him a wise answer. He said, 'You need only what makes you conscious you are a sinner. That is all.' The man was indignant. 'I am surprised', he said, 'that a man like you should give me that kind of advice. I want this special experience.' Campbell says the next time he saw this man he was being taken into a mental institution between two warders. When the evangelist saw him again some years later the man came to Campbell and said, 'Duncan Campbell, I am a wiser man today.'[69]

If we worry the Almighty enough he may stand aside and let us have the excess we want and then we shall regret having asked for it! Perhaps we can do no better than to agree with the Rev. J. G. Short, who at the close of his lecture on the physical responses of people in the revival in Ulster commented: 'I have heard some say: "We do not like these bodily prostrations — we like all beside." I do not think it is seemly to say to God what it is we like in his work, and what we dislike. Is God to give account of his doings?'[70]

Besides this, we may add that phenomena in revival need not be feared because they are passing things and will soon be gone. It is the lasting fruit that really matters. If the church majors on the phenomena it will soon bring revival to an end.

Emotion and commotion

Joseph Kemp described the effects of the revival at Charlotte Chapel in Edinburgh in 1905. The church was well and wisely led and yet when the flood came, 'There were irregularities, no doubt;

some commotion, yes. There was that which shot itself through all prescribed forms and shattered all conventionality. But such a movement with all its irregularities is to be preferred far above the dull, dreary, monotonous decorum of many churches.'[71]

Revivals are generally noisy times! It is a rare thing for deep emotion not to express itself in tears, of sorrow or joy, in singing and even, at times, in shouting. For those who are safe only in firmly controlled order, a time of 'glorious disorder' will prove a terrifying experience — especially as revival provides opportunity for the weak and unstable to take everything to excess. However, it is the experience of many in revival that, as Joseph Kemp himself saw it, 'The confusion never gets confused.'[72]

When Billy Bray, the converted Cornish miner, visited the church of William Haslam in Baldhu during 1853, revival was already in progress. Billy was known for his eccentric behaviour, and the congregation at Baldhu was known for its excessive noise in worship. It was inevitable that Billy would stir up the people and before long, comments Haslam, 'The people got what they called "happy", and shouted and praised God vociferously.' Haslam, who encouraged the people to respond in worship, tried in vain to bring them to order and only after some time could he quieten them down. William Haslam was sufficiently wise and discerning to comment: 'The power of God was great, though the demonstrations were very human.' A neighbouring minister, old William Aitken, himself a strong friend of revival, came over and preached a sermon 'on the difference between emotion and principle'![73]

Another significant point is that the degree of excitement and emotion in revival frequently depends upon the leaders and upon cultural characteristics. Wesley encouraged far more emotional outbursts in his meetings than Whitefield, so he got them! A revival in Norway in 1905, which came directly from the Spirit's fire in Wales the year previously, was never charged with sensationalism, although this charge was often levelled against the work in Wales. The wise and careful vicar at Rhos in North Wales, the Rev. T. Pritchard, defended Wales against the charge of mere emotionalism by reminding people: 'Sneers are made at our Celtic temperament, but God gave it, and God can use it for the glory of His Name.'[74] The same contrast can be seen by a comparison of revivals in Wales and Scotland. All of which goes to show that whilst emotion will always be part of revival, commotion need not be.

When William Haslam moved to Buckenham in Norfolk in 1863 he left behind the 'wild' scenes of Cornish praise in revival where the 'wrastlings in prayer' would embarrass his fellow churchmen. Someone had told him that the people of Norfolk were like turnips: 'They would not cry out, even though they were thrust through and through with the sword; and like turnip lanterns they would never take fire.' To a degree Haslam found this to be true, and though his preaching led to powerful times of revival, so that for seven years he preached to more than 1,000 each week in the Norwich Lecture Hall, the commotions of Cornwall were rare things in Norfolk.

Years later William Haslam answered the question which was often put to him, why he allowed such noise in his revival meetings: 'I lived amongst a people who were accustomed to outward demonstrations; and by descending to them in their ways I was enabled to lead many of them to higher things, and to teach them to rest not so much on their feelings, as on the facts and truth revealed in the Word of God. But theorize as we would, it was just a question, in many cases, of no work, or of decided manifestation. We could not help people being stricken down, neither could they help it themselves; often the most unlikely persons were overcome and became excited, and persons naturally quiet and retiring proved the most noisy and demonstrative. However, it was our joy to see permanent results afterwards, which more than reconciled us for any amount of inconvenience we had felt at the time...Most undeniable it is that many trying things happen in the excitement of a storm.'[75]

One thing is certain, noise and commotion are neither necessary to revival nor evidence of it. 3,000 miles away from Norfolk in East Anglia, and back in 1798, a revival took place in Norfolk, Connecticut. What was said of that revival is true of many: the people were 'by no means noisy or boisterous' — even though more than 150 professed conversion in the town! Similarly, in the same year at Granville in Massachusetts there were no 'outcries under conviction...nor rants of joy after receiving comfort'. A year later at Lenox, in the same state, the movement of God was free from any extravagance of gesture or outcry.[76]

In December 1859, when revival had spread from Wales to North Shields, the *Newcastle Chronicle* commented: 'It is only candid to say that whatever may have been the case elsewhere, there has been no rant or nonsense here. The fact that Mr Alderman

Mease and other prudent persons have taken a most active part being
a guarantee for order and decorum. Dr and Mrs Palmer have also
grown more cautious, and hushed down anything approaching
violent excitement.'

Women preachers

Just as God has used women on the mission-field for 150 years, so
they have been used in revival. Embarrassing to some it may be, but
it is a simple fact.

During 1905 1,200 people crowded into the Calvinistic Methodist Chapel in Coedpoeth and hundreds more had to be turned
away. According to the *North Wales Guardian* of Friday, 31 March,
'The principal speakers were the evangelists Miss Davies [Maude
Davies] and Miss Evans [Florrie Evans] of Newquay, who have
worked with Mr Evan Roberts. They sang, prayed, and addressed
the audience in English and Welsh alternatively.' On this occasion
the expected minister had been prevented from attending 'owing to
indisposition'. In the same edition, meetings at Rossett were reported, in which 'Mrs March, a well-known Liverpool lady...gave
an interesting address.' The young ladies Davies and Evans spoke
at many meetings, first in conjunction with Evan Roberts in the
south and later, as reported above, they travelled around North
Wales also.

The role of women as preachers during times of revival is not
common, but it is widespread, and instances come from various
parts of the world.

William Haslam's wife and Geraldine Hooper from Bath both
assisted Haslam in his work in the West Country and in East Anglia.
Haslam described the influence of Miss Hooper when she came to
the rectory at Buckenham in Norfolk in 1863: 'When it was known
that she would speak at the barn meeting in the evening, the people
came out in crowds, and the place was filled in every corner. Her
address was like kindling a fresh fire, and a very bright and warm
one it was. The people became wild with admiration, and their
eagerness to hear her was intense. Her fame spread so rapidly that
the Norwich papers took up the subject. The editor of one of these
papers began a series of tirades against Buckenham and the work.
Week by week fierce and long articles were published, which of

course did not stamp out the fire, but rather added fuel to it.'[77]

A Norwegian Evangelical Lutheran missionary, Marie Mon-sen, exercised an effective ministry in the Shantung province of China during the revival that commenced in 1932. Marie Monsen's testimony, messages and constant question to missionaries and nationals alike, 'Are you born again?' led the revival to be called 'the Born-again Revival'.

That people are converted through the preaching of women in revival is without question; what is questionable is whether they *ought* to be preaching and whether God's use of them justifies their actions. A rector's wife wrote to William Haslam to say that she and her husband had been praying for a revival in Norfolk for years but she added, 'If this is a revival, it has come in such a way that I cannot thank God for it!' This lady urged Haslam to submit the issue to the bishop, adding, 'Let us leave the question of women's preaching to his grave decision.' Haslam had no intention of doing so, but as a matter of fact there was a higher judgement than the bishop's and a clearer one for both William Haslam and the rector's wife; on this, as on every subject, Scripture must be our guide, whatever men or women may think. One thing is certain, and that is that we are unwise to dismiss a revival simply because there are some aspects that conflict with our understanding of Scripture.

Physical healings

With a few exceptions physical healings have never played a large part in revivals. They are almost unknown during the eighteenth-century Awakening. Evan Roberts held healing meetings in 1904, and three years later in Korea some churches held a prayer meeting for healing once a month.[78] John Sung of the Bethel Band, who was so greatly used in China and elsewhere, deliberately kept himself at a distance from the 'spiritual gifts' movement. And this has been true of many God has used in revival. Peterus Octavianus was greatly used by God in the Borneo revival in 1973; there were healings claimed from his ministry and he 'usually gave a fairly low-key opportunity at the end of a meeting for prayer for physical healing', but physical healing formed a very small part of the results claimed for the revival.[79] Today, parts of the Christian church major on physical healing under the idea that this is a necessary evidence of an outpouring of the Holy Spirit. It is a matter of simple historical fact that in the times of God's great work in the story of the church, physical healing is not significantly present. One exception would be the colossal claims made for the Indonesian revival during the 1960s.

The place of healing in the Korean revival earlier this century is revealed by one of the missionaries in an interesting comment when the churches held prayer meetings for healing: 'Before I attended this prayer meeting for the sick, it had been in my mind to tell the congregation assembled there that a man's salvation is more important than his cure. I intended to say to them, "Preach the Word! Forgiveness of sins is greater than healing of the body." I did not carry out my intention. What we in the West present as good theology, applying to biblical times, is actually carried out in practice today by these simple, devout people. As I have already mentioned, out of thirty prayer meetings there was only one for the sick, the rest being devoted to the worship of God and intercessions of every kind.'[80]

The following report comes from Madras during the years of the Second World War. I quote this because it is typical of the attitude of leaders even where God has given healing in revival: 'There were wonderful answers to prayer. The sick were prayed for and some were healed. A leper one day asked leave to give a five-minute testimony at a meeting. The week before he had sat huddled in a blanket in the corner of the church with two leprous sores on his leg. Long treatment had failed to heal him and he had been given up as hopeless. Then he asked to be anointed and prayed for, and thereupon had been completely restored with no trace of his disease. But the emphasis was never on healing the body but always on bringing sinners to repentance and faith. The preaching brought a constant challenge to our hearts for it set high standards of life. "As he which hath called you is holy, so be ye holy in all manner of conversation; because it is written, Be ye holy; for I am holy" (1 Peter 1:15-16). God sought in us hearts devoted to Him alone.'[81]

When revival came to the Shantung province of China in 1932 some remarkable instances of healing are recorded, but Dr Charles Culpepper, a missionary in China at the time, sets these in perspective: 'However, throughout the district, healing was not stressed. The emphasis was on repentance and confession of sin. The proof of the reality of the revival was seen in transformed lives...the revival…reminded me of the work in Samaria in apostolic days. Through the key of prayer of faith for sickness, doors were opened for the gospel.'[82]

Tongues, dreams and visions

It is an interesting fact that some issues that become significant for the churches when they are living without revival are insignificant when revival comes. The explanation is that in revival there are far more urgent and important matters to occupy the Christians. One simple example is that of 'speaking in tongues'. It is not necessary for us to discuss what this gift is, or even what part it should or should not play in the churches today, but this is a matter of fact: 'tongues' rarely accompany revival.

During the eighteenth-century Awakening under the preaching of men like Edwards, Whitefield and Wesley, tongues were virtually unknown, and yet there were in Wesley's meetings some strange and excessive emotional experiences.

One eyewitness of the Korean revival in 1907 specifically noted, 'The "gift of tongues" was not part of this revival,' and that particular writer was convinced that 'All the spiritual gifts mentioned in the New Testament are to be recognized.'[83]

'Tongues' were exercised a little during the revival in Borneo in 1973, but sadly they caused a division that took more than a year to heal.[84]

Kurt Koch, whose reports on the revival in Indonesia during the 1960s have been open to the charge of being extravagant and misleading, is for this very reason interesting on the subject of 'tongues'. When he spoke to the leaders of revival on Timor, Koch asked them what part tongues had played in the revival and he received this reply: 'Within a space of about two and a half years some two hundred thousand natives have become Christians. We have at the same time experienced thousands of cases of healing, together with many other miracles of faith, and yet we know of only one single instance of a person speaking in tongues, and even then the person doesn't use his gift in public.'[85]

Evan Roberts, whose leadership in the 1904 revival in Wales bore many characteristics of Pentecostal worship, actually discouraged 'tongues', not because he did not believe in the gift, but because he did not consider the church ready to discern the true from the false.

There are records of other strange phenomena in revivals.

At Beddgelert in 1817 people heard beautiful singing in the air; these were sane people who had no reason to make up stories.[86]

The same experience is reported from India when God came to the Khassi Hills in 1905. A group of Christians were on their way to the presbytery at Pariong and they stopped frequently on the road to pray. At one place, 'Some of them heard beautiful singing that no man could describe.' At first they thought it was another party on the road, but there was no one around.[87] Others during this revival claimed to see angels. In the Khassi Hills at this time visions were common, 'But they all tend to bring men to see their sin and to see Christ as their Saviour.'[88] There is no reason for us to be suspicious of these claims because they are paralleled in the New Testament, and the outcome in revival is always to draw people closer to Christ. Of course, there were 'spurious signs and prophecies', but the Khassi Christians soon learnt to sift the wheat from the chaff.

In 1921 Jock Troup saw a vision of a man at Fraserburgh calling on God to send the evangelist to that town. On the strength of this, Troup left the work he was doing at Yarmouth and went to Fraserburgh. Soon after he arrived he went to the town square where a crowd gathered and he started to preach. Because of the intense cold Jock Troup suggested they find a church in which they could continue the meeting. Being a stranger in the town he had no idea where the churches were and the crowd suggested the Baptist Church. They arrived at the church to be met by the minister and his elders, who had just concluded a special meeting at which it had been decided to send an invitation to Jock Troup to come and conduct an evangelistic mission. Amongst the group of elders Jock recognized the face of the man in his vision![89] Fraserburgh was the scene of some of the greatest work of God under the preaching of Jock Troup.

The *North Wales Guardian* for 20 January 1905 reported the following dream which made news during the Welsh revival: 'A North Wales correspondent writes: A remarkable fulfilment of a dream is reported to me. The coachman of a gentleman well known in Anglesey dreamed that his master came forward in a revival meeting and said, "I have come forward to show that I am not ashamed to confess Christ." He mentioned the dream to several persons next day, and that evening was astonished to see his master step forward at the revival meeting and say, "I have come forward to show that I am not ashamed to confess Christ." The incident created a profound sensation, especially amongst those to whom the coachman had previously related his dream. My informant, a Methodist minister, assures me he has personally verified the statements made above.'

During the revival at Baldhu in Cornwall between 1851 and 1854, William Haslam records: 'Every week, almost every day, we heard of some remarkable dream or striking vision.' He went on to relate a number of these, recognizing that some people would dismiss them as mere superstition. The examples he gives come from his own first-hand knowledge, and there is no good reason to doubt them, unless, of course, we deny the possibility of God giving such things today. Even then it would take considerable ingenuity to account for them in another way! Some of these dreams or visions were direct prophetic warnings to individuals which were actually fulfilled. Interestingly, they were given within the geographical area touched by revival and rarely strayed beyond; dreams came to Cornwall, but not to the 'Shires'.[90]

Significantly, almost all whom God has used in revival are quick to point out that these unusual things are merely incidental to the great work of God. One writer in *The Life of Faith* for January 1905 concluded: 'It is possible to be occupied too exclusively with the mere incidents of the movement — deeply impressive, thrilling, and important as they are.' R. B. Jones commented that the sensational provides 'copy' for the journalist, but the more vital things are of little interest to him.[91]

The reason for this caution is the danger of men taking over from God. Humphrey Jones is a sad example of this; his revival ministry came to an end after his claim to special revelations from God. The weakest part of the ministry of Evan Roberts was the freedom he gave to the meetings and the lack of preaching in them. Fortunately other men, like R. B. Jones, were well aware of the need for the converts to be taught from the Word of God and it was their ministry that saved the 1904 revival in Wales from greater losses once the fire had passed.

The danger of revival excitement getting into the wrong hands is clearly seen from the sad episode of James Davenport in the eighteenth century. Davenport was mentally unbalanced, but he gave the appearance of being a very spiritual man, and when Whitefield first met him in 1740 he too accepted this assessment. Davenport threw himself enthusiastically into the revival but saw himself as a great reformer with a special relationship to God. Soon he was claiming direct revelations and demanding that ministers should give account to him, denouncing those who refused. In 1741 even the students at Yale, including the godly David Brainerd, were for a while taken in by him, and by 1743 he had a considerable following. Fortunately Davenport came to his senses and published a full apology for his behaviour. But the damage had been done, and this kind of extremism always provides fuel for the fires of the opponents to revival.

John Wesley had similar problems with George Bell, ex-corporal of the Life Guards who led away a number of the Methodists, claiming that he had achieved perfection, had authority to represent God in London, had the power to heal the blind and raise the dead and, finally, knew that the end of the world was imminent. Bell's following was never large, for he was clearly a fool, but again, the cause of revival was hurt by men like this. A great danger to the cause of the gospel at any time, but particularly in revival, are those who, in the words of Jonathan Edwards, 'mistake fancy for faith, and imagination for revelation'.

On the other hand, we may well expect that in a time of increased activity by the Holy Spirit, when the minds of men and women are filled with eternity and absorbed with God, there will also be an increase in these unusual things. Revival is a time when spiritual forces are unleashed — on both sides — and we must expect the genuine and the counterfeit in spiritual phenomena. In his preface to *Yet Not I*, William Haslam referred to his previous volume of autobiography, *From Death Into Life*: 'Some people have considered the statements in my former volume as exaggerated, not to say "untrue"! I will only say that persons who have been in such scenes and have witnessed the mighty power of God, will think that they are somewhat guardedly and tamely put forth. Indeed, for fear of taxing the credulity of some of my readers too much, I have understated some things, and left many others unsaid.'

However, though some would wish it to the contrary, if we put all the recorded revivals together, we shall find that these 'phenomena', or unusual things, make up a very small part of the whole. Revival itself is unusual, and the great work of conviction, conversion and the creation of a holy life put all other things into the shade. When Duncan Campbell was asked for an explanation of supernatural manifestations, he replied that the main reason was assurance: God granted them to encourage weak and trembling faith to grasp the promises of life.[92] Campbell never encouraged such things, but did not despise what God allowed. That they are a feature of revivals we cannot, and need not deny, but their relatively small place should be recognized. In fact, considering that in revival men's minds are more in touch with eternity, and their spirits more sensitive to the Holy Spirit, it is not so much surprising that these phenomena exist, but that there are not more of them.

What was wrong among the men from Ephraim, Manasseh, Issachar and Zebulun was that they were behaving in a way that was contrary to 'what was written'. Every experience and teaching in revival must be checked by 'what is written', and every deviation from this should be clearly corrected. This is one reason why to allow revival to run on without any check from Scripture is a dangerous thing. Evan Roberts was so concerned not to meddle with the work of the Spirit that he allowed meetings largely to run themselves. The weakness of this is seen in the fact that a greater number of 'converts' appear to have fallen away in the few years following the 1904 revival than in any other revival for which we have such records. The centrality of preaching is a sound curb to excess and error and is, after all, one thing God has clearly committed to his church. We are never interfering in the work of the Spirit by insisting on a place for the sermon. One reason why the revivals experienced by Whitefield, Wesley and, a century later, by Charles Haddon Spurgeon continued so long was that preaching was at the centre. Perhaps there would have been more lasting benefit to Wales had Roberts not neglected God's plan for the building up of the church.

After revival

Revival opposed and tested

We may overlook the fact that when God comes in revival and sweeps thousands into the kingdom, sometimes within a few days, there are still many left outside. In fact, great though the numbers converted may be, there are almost always more left outside than are brought into the church. Not only this, but revival tends to harden men and create a greater opposition against the gospel than in the normal way. The reason for this is not hard to discover. In the normal way the unbelieving world can simply ignore the church and all that it stands for: after all, the church is hardly a threat to the life-style of the world, and its message seems to have little significance for daily life. That is the way the world sees it. But in revival God becomes a serious threat. Men are aware of eternal issues and the presence of God and the power of the gospel disturb their spiritual sleep. Thousands are affected, and even influenced by revival, who never experience salvation. In Rhos in 1904 strong men were afraid to go to work in case they got converted, and once at work they were afraid to come home again for the same

reason. Because men feel threatened, they will lash out in
opposition and ridicule.

Revival ridiculed

When Hezekiah sent his couriers to the north with the invitation to
come and worship in Jerusalem, it is recorded in 2 Chronicles 30:18
that 'many people' responded. But not all accepted the call; there
was a strong opposition: 'The couriers went from town to town in
Ephraim and Manasseh, as far as Zebulun, but the people scorned
and ridiculed them' (30:10). Paul met the same response 700 years
later, and Athens is just one example where 'some of them sneered'
(Acts 17:32).

In 1745 David Brainerd was among the North American Indians at Susquehannah and he described what happened when God
began to move by his Spirit among the Indians: 'I stood amazed at
the influence which seized the audience almost universally and
could compare it to nothing more aptly than the irresistible force of
a mighty torrent or swelling deluge, that with its insupportable
weight and pressures bears down and sweeps before it whatever
stands in its way. Almost all persons of all ages were bowed down
with concern together, and scarce one was able to withstand the
shock of this surprising operation. Old men and women who had
been drunken wretches for many years, and some little children, not
more than six or seven years of age, appeared in distress for their
souls, as well as persons of middle age...The most stubborn hearts
were now obliged to bow.'

That was among the Indian community. But Brainerd tells us
that the white settlers were almost universally unmoved: 'There
being a multitude of white persons present I made an address to
them at the close of my discourse to the Indians, but I could not so
much as keep them orderly, for scores of them kept walking and
gazing about and behaved more indecently than any Indians I ever
addressed. And a view of their abusive conduct so sunk my spirits
that I could scarce go on with my work.'[93]

Murray M'Cheyne recognized the same contrast in Dundee in
1839. The work of the Spirit in that town was so real and widespread
that 'The effects that have been produced upon the community are
very marked. It seems now to be allowed, even by the most ungodly,

that there is such a thing as conversion. Men cannot any longer deny it.' M'Cheyne went on to describe the change in the town with a greater awareness of the importance of the sabbath, and of the danger of sin. But, he adds, 'Multitudes of those who live within the sound of the Sabbath bell continue to live on in sin and misery.'[94] Following Cambuslang in 1742 the ministers noted that some of those who scoffed, or professed and then fell away, went further into sin than before.

We do not need to explain all this. We must just note that it happens. When revival comes, some are transformed whilst others ridicule. We cannot dismiss this in cultural or psychological terms because in the time of Brainerd God was working in revival in other parts of America amongst the white settlers. This kind of thing marks revival as supernatural. Revival is always bigger than our theories. It cannot be confined to geographical or social boundaries, though God may choose to do so. Dr Samuel Johnson went to many of the revival meetings addressed by George Whitefield in the eighteenth century and he greatly admired the evangelist. David Garrick, the great actor, heard Whitefield preach and longed that he could say, 'Oh!' like Whitefield could say it. But these two men were never converted as far as history records. In excess of 20,000 people would listen to Whitefield on Kennington Common. but not all were converted. Many came to scoff and went away scoffing and died scoffing.

Opposition to the gospel will be greater in the time of revival. Normally the world can ignore the church, but when revival comes it cannot. When the Spirit of God came in the sixteenth century, Christians were burnt at the stake. In the seventeenth century evangelical preachers were turned out of the churches. In the eighteenth century when a revival came there were physical attacks upon them. John Wesley was hounded out of town and beaten; Whitefield had filth and rubbish thrown at him. In the nineteenth century when a revival came the critics cut the Bible to pieces. In our century revival is met with verbal criticism or physical abuse, depending upon the part of the world.

Sadly, opposition often comes from those who should know better. Hezekiah's evangelists were ridiculed by those who professed to worship the same God. The apostles in the early church were first opposed by the Jews, who held the story of God's plan of salvation in their own Bible. The Jews were offended by the miracles and envious of the success of the gospel, so 'They were filled with jealousy and talked abusively against what Paul was saying' (Acts 13:45). Some of the most vicious opposition to revival has come from the professing church.

The revival that accompanied Evan Roberts was denounced by a Congregational minister, Peter Price, as 'a sham...a mockery, a blasphemous travesty of the real thing'. What made this all the more sad was the fact that Price's own church at Dowlais had been blessed with revival and the addition of hundreds of converts a few months previously in 1904. Price clearly objected to Roberts' style and had good cause to be concerned for some of the excesses that accompanied him. Unfortunately Price overplayed his opposition and could not see the hand of God in what he disagreed with. Dr Forbes Winslow, a psychiatrist, took a different line of attack against Roberts: 'I would have men like Evan Roberts locked up as common felons, and their meetings prohibited like those of social-ists and anarchists as being dangerous to the public.' Even though four doctors had signed a certificate of Roberts' physical and mental health, it was jibes like this, and the cruel attack by Peter Price, that almost broke the evangelist and by the spring of 1906 he began to retire from public life.[95]

When God moved among a group of Christians in Madras in 1940 the churches at first were supportive until they realized that the man God was using was Bakht Singh. Suddenly the ministers' conference came to a decision: 'We in the Indian Ministers' Conference have met and passed a resolution never again to make any place available to this Punjabi preacher. Our objection is that he is not an ordained minister, and therefore had no right to baptize anyone.'[96] Every church was closed to Bakht Singh.

The same had been the experience of Jock Troup in Fraserburgh in 1921. When the Baptist Church proved too small for the revival meetings an application was made for the use of other buildings, but it was refused on the ground that the preacher was not an ordained minister![97]

Whitefield went through a similar experience 200 years before in England. His greatest opposition came from the Church of England authorities and he was refused permission to preach in their buildings. It was this very opposition that forced him into field preaching. When Whitefield preached in America he experienced the same thing and recorded in his diary: 'Five churches have already been denied me, and some clergy, if possible, would oblige me to depart out of these coasts.'[98]

Again and again his diary reveals the opposition he received from clergymen in sermons and pamphlets and personal abuse. Dr Joseph Trapp was one of the most eminent Anglican clergymen in London and he wrote and preached powerfully against Whitefield. Trapp's chief concern was the shame and reproach of preaching and praying in the open air! On one occasion Whitefield and John Wesley sat up until one in the morning 'in conference with two clergymen of the Church of England, and some other strong opposers of the doctrine of the New Birth'. Whitefield concluded in his diary with a weary understatement: 'I am fully convinced there is a fundamental difference between us and them.'[99]

Even at Cambuslang, where, in 1742, God was so present to save hundreds, the Associate Presbytery found fault and issued a thirty-two page booklet in which some of the mildest attacks accused Whitefield of being a member of the idolatrous Church of England which made him, apparently, 'a limb of anti-Christ'.[100] James Robe, a minister involved in the revival at Cambuslang and Kilsyth, wrote of the 'lies, slanderous reports, and ridiculous stories' that were spread about to prejudice people against the work of God.[101]

Some who accepted Whitefield's gospel of the new birth, and who were convinced of his sincerity and honesty, nevertheless took issue with him on his style and forcefulness. Both Isaac Watts and Philip Doddridge fall into this category, though it has to be said that they modified their views as time progressed. Perhaps the maturing of Whitefield and the mellowing of Watts and Doddridge helped. But many of the Independents (or Congregationalists), who were themselves to experience great revival in the early part of the nineteenth century, strongly opposed Whitefield and the Awakening throughout his life.

Even more tragically, a work of the Spirit can be hindered by arguments among those whom God is using in revival. The sad but inevitable clash between Whitefield and Wesley on the subject of election did little to advance the work of God — a fact that both men came to appreciate more clearly. And the sharp difference between Daniel Rowland and Howel Harris on whether we can properly speak of God suffering and dying led to the withdrawal of Harris from the Welsh Calvinistic Methodists. One historian concludes:

'Inevitably therefore, that work suffered a serious eclipse without the guidance of a man of his calibre. For twelve long years Harris and Rowland went their separate ways, and Welsh Calvinistic Methodism went into temporary decline.'[102]

But if the gospel was a stumbling-block to the Jews, it was utter foolishness to the Gentiles (1 Cor. 1:23). There are always those who cannot understand what is happening and therefore oppose the work of God through blind ignorance. The apostles knew and expected vigorous opposition from the pagans. Often unbelievers will be forced to invent explanations for a work that defies normal understanding. Duncan Campbell was accused of hypnotizing people in the 1940s in the Scottish islands and 200 years earlier the cartoonist Hogarth viciously caricatured Whitefield in his powerful pictures of eighteenth-century life.

Before his own conversion, Festo Kivengere despised the work of God in Uganda: 'We "enlightened" young people were angry. We maintained that church people ought to confine their singing to church buildings and not spread it out onto public roads and into market-places. Women going to draw water were praising Jesus — how unsuitable!'[103] Festo's uncle complained bitterly because the revival seemed to be a 'new kind of religion' that invaded personal privacy and broke with tribal taboos. As an important chief he gave orders that his men could beat up these Christians, but still it did not change them.

Violent opposition to revival is nothing new. Whitefield reports often on the abuse of some in the crowds who were intent only to cause disorder and violence. At the fields of Mary Le Bone in London the rough opponents tried hard to push down the pulpit; another intended to stab Whitefield with a sword; others pelted the preacher with filth whilst trying to drown his voice with their own and yet another climbed a tree and 'shamefully exposed his nakedness' to the crowd. In the midst of scenes like this, when thousands of London's criminals and slum-dwellers mingled with the idle and rich, it is incredible that any heard the gospel at all. But clearly they did, and hundreds were converted.

John Wesley suffered as much, if not more, from the rough handling of the mobs and both Wesley and Whitefield knew Paul's experience of being stoned and beaten by the crowds.

Howel Harris in Wales described how, during a journey of three months preaching in Wales, 'I was almost murdered once, and twice in danger of my life, besides once being before the Magistrates in a Quarter Sessions.'

John Cennick, a companion of Harris, describes how, at Swindon in the 1740s, they took advantage of an ugly situation that must have been anything but amusing at the time: 'They then got the dust out of the highway and cover'd us all over, and then play'd an engine upon us which they fill'd out of the stinking ditches till we were just like men in the pillory, but as they play'd upon Brother Harris I spoke to the congregation, and when they turn'd their engine upon me, he preach'd and thus they continued till they had spoil'd the engine and then they threw whole buckets of water and mud over us.'[104]

Some, of course, are more open to be persuaded. Jonathan Edwards remarked that when news spread of the work of God in Northampton, New England, in the 1730s, 'Many scoffed at and ridiculed it; and some compared what we call conversion, to certain distempers. But it was very observable of many, who occasionally came amongst us from abroad with disregardful hearts, that what they saw here cured them of such a temper of mind.' In fact Edwards went on to remark that many who came to scoff went away converted.[105]

Every revival will be ridiculed and dismissed. Arthur Wallis has written, 'If we find a revival that is not spoken against, we had better look again to ensure that it is a revival.'[106] If they scoffed at our Master and his great works, it is certain they will scoff again when he is at work. When we are confronted with a work that appears to have the stamp of God upon it, we will be wise to exercise great caution before we oppose it just because it does not come out of the correct denominational stable.

Revival tested

Revival is always tested. This is brought out by the deliberate way in which God words 2 Chronicles 32:1: 'After all that Hezekiah had so faithfully done, Sennacherib king of Assyria came and invaded Judah. He laid siege to all the fortified cities...' The officers of Sennacherib challenged the work of God at every level. In their tirade around the walls of Jerusalem they challenged the faith of the people (2 Chron. 32:10), discredited the leaders (32:12), undermined popular morale (32:13), insulted God (32:17) and belittled his work (32:19). The challenge of the Assyrians (32:1-23), the king's illness (32:24) and the Babylonian envoys (32:31) were all sent to test the king and the people; only in the matter of the envoys did Hezekiah fail.

We may view the arrival of the Assyrian army as a God-sent test of the reality of the revival; on the other hand it could be viewed the other way. It may well be that the God-sent revival was intended to prepare the people for the severe test that was soon to follow. It is doubtful whether the persecution that followed the outpouring of the Spirit at Pentecost was intended simply to test the reality of apostolic faith. On the contrary, the experience of Acts 2 strengthened these frightened men and women for the trial that was soon to follow. It is remarkable how often times of revival are followed by a period of great persecution or the suffering of those who have experienced the power of God. It is as if God is preparing his people for what he knows is to follow. We may do well to keep this in mind when we so eagerly pray for revival. Revival is often a preparation for suffering that will follow, and the suffering itself becomes a test of the quality and reality of the revival.

Perhaps the outstanding example of this is the 1904 revival, which spread from Wales to all parts of the world during 1905. Within ten years, thousands of young men who had been converted in the revivals were fighting and dying in the choking mud of the Great War battlefields. How many of these were men who, but for the revival, would have had no hope of eternal life, only eternity will tell. Looking back on a revival in his church in Charleston, America in 1858, John Girardeau frequently referred to it as the mercy of God in gathering in his elect before the Civil War claimed the lives of hundreds of thousands of young men during the bitter conflict between 1860 and 1865. Interestingly there were a number of revivals, particularly among Confederate troops, during the American Civil War.[107]

When God came down so remarkably to the church in North Korea in 1907, the quality of the work of the Spirit was tested through three terrible waves of suffering: the first during the atrocities committed by the Japanese after the close of the Great War in 1919; the second in the persecutions following the government order compelling shrine worship in 1938, and more recently as a result of the Communist take-over of the north from 1948.

A revival that began in Japan during the late 1920s and early '30s was effectively destroyed by the compromise of many church leaders who were prepared, for the sake of their lives and freedom, to accept the government order to worship at Shinto shrines. This, together with the fervent nationalism of many Christians during the Japanese war effort and the horrific suffering of the Japanese people as the war came to a devastating close, effectively dealt a death-blow to what had been a hopeful indication of God's presence.

Revival came among the Lun Bawang people in Borneo just two years before the Japanese occupation in 1941, and again in 1973 before a government clamp-down refused to renew the visas of many missionaries. Revival came among students in China in 1946 and proved to be a preparation for the Communist take-over.

Revival came to East Africa in the 1930s and prepared the church for the eight years of terror under Iddi Ammin in the 1970s when more than half a million were brutally killed. It also prepared Kenya for the Mau Mau atrocities in the 1950s and the terrible inter-tribal wars in Rwanda and Burundi. Revival came to the Congo in 1953, preparing the church for the cruel Simba rebellion ten years later when many leaders, members and missionaries were massacred.

On the other hand, it was actually *during* the years of severe persecution that revival came to the church in Ethiopia. The more the Italians attempted to destroy the Wallamo church, the more the church grew: 'At one point the fifty leaders had been arrested and put in prison when the Italians realized that their efforts to stamp out the church were only increasing its strength and size. Each of the leaders received one hundred lashes, and one was given four hundred. None of them were able to lie on their backs for months, and three died...'[108] The suffering of some leaders, particularly men like Wandaro, who was beaten all day by a team of men, was intense; but the Spirit of God caused more and more to be converted until, when the missionaries returned at the end of the war, there were 10,000 Wallamo Christians to greet them. This is the story of the Acts of the Apostles all over again. The blood of the martyrs is the seed of the church.

The Waldensian revival, which spread across Europe during the twelfth and thirteenth centuries, was similar to that in Ethiopia 700 years later. The Roman inquisitors persecuted these Christians so rigorously that they could hardly build prisons fast enough to hold them, and the cost of feeding the prisoners became a heavy drain on resources. But in spite of all this, one estimate claims that by the year 1260 more than 800,000 had professed the evangelical faith of the Waldensians. A people of disciplined and holy lives, fervent in prayer and strongly attached to the preaching of the Word of God, the Waldensians spread all over Europe in spite of the severe persecution they met wherever they settled.

Revival sometimes flourishes in persecution and this was certainly the experience of the Christian church for the first 300 years of its life. In the strength of Pentecost and its benefits the church had to endure centuries of fierce persecution.

The threat of pride

The point at which Hezekiah failed was that at which others who have been used in revival have also failed: 'Hezekiah's heart was proud and…God left him to test him and to know everything that was in his heart' (2 Chron. 32:25, 31). In showing his armoury and storehouses to the Babylonian envoys, Hezekiah revealed his pride in his own achievements and his enjoyment of the praise and respect that he commanded in the world around. This must be the greatest danger to all who are used by God in revival. The world thinks well of the man who is clearly so 'successful', and the greatest battle Hezekiah ever had was not with his people, or with his enemies, but with himself. And that was the battle he lost. The greatest threat to revival lies within the hearts of its leaders.

It was pride that ruined the ministry of Humphrey Jones in Wales in 1859. Having been greatly used by God in America in 1858, Jones returned to his native Wales with a great passion to see his country set alight by the Holy Spirit. His early ministry was very fruitful and undoubtedly the revival in Wales began through his preaching, although many had been praying for it for years. During the early months of 1859 Jones found himself at Aberystwyth, where the work was hard and little was accomplished. Driven almost to distraction, he claimed divine 'revelations' which resulted in 'prophecies' to the church. These were quickly exposed as false and Jones was full of remorse. However, the damage was done and it was left to David Morgan to continue the work in Wales. Humphrey Jones never fully recovered, and although he preached again in Aberystwyth some four years later, he was often ill and in 1871 he returned to America, where he died in 1895. Similarly, Hezekiah never fully recovered from that one great error in boasting to the foreign envoys; whilst the fruits of revival continued, the best was past.

The sad story of Humphrey Jones is exceptional in the accounts of revival. God has chosen his men carefully, and few are on record as having given in to the terrible sin of robbing God of his glory and setting themselves up as oracles of the divine. Most who have been leaders in times of revival have been only too aware of this danger, and they have fought hard against it.

Asahel Nettleton was considered as great as George Whitefield in the nineteenth century story of revival in America. Crowds followed him around as a celebrity because of the power of his preaching, but he hated this and often took a strong stand against it. If ever he felt a congregation was relying upon him for the work of revival, Nettleton would simply disappear for a while and leave the people to themselves. This caused great concern on a number of occasions, but at least it drove home the importance of Nettleton's theology that revival belongs exclusively to God; he alone is the author of it all.

Similarly, the saintly Robert Murray M'Cheyne, in Dundee, trembled at the thought that he might rob God of his glory, and wept over his own sins as much as over the sins of others.

5.
Our response to revival

Towards the end of a decade of local church revival in the 1830s, the Methodist Conference declared, 'Some churches regard revivals of religion as gracious singularities in their history; we regard them as essential to our existence.' For this reason, whenever they considered the gospel was losing its impact on society, the Methodists of the early nineteenth century went to prayer for revival. This not only explains the continual 'outbursts' of revival across Britain, but also the steady growth of Wesleyan Methodism during the first half of the nineteenth century.

Whether we regard revivals as 'gracious singularities' or essential to our existence, or as something else, if we have read so far, we must be forming some sort of response to the subject of revival. It is the kind of issue that generally draws a reaction; it is not easy to remain coldly indifferent to the possibility of God coming among his people in such spiritual power and reality that the whole community seems to be 'saturated with God'!

Opposition

Some are definitely *opposed* to the whole idea of spiritual revival and will explain it away as mass religious hysteria or something similar. Generally this has to be the reaction of an unbelieving world that does not dare admit the spiritual reality of revivals for fear of conceding too much. We need not be surprised at this response because it is an understandable defence against a threat. However, there is a large part of the professing church that is opposed to revival as well. Generally this has to be the formal and 'liberal' part of 'Christianity', which discourages a total confidence in the Bible, has little to say on the necessity of the new birth and therefore does not press home the need for the lordship of Christ to invade every part of our life. After all, revival is exclusively an evangelical experience since it re-establishes those doctrines and experiences that are known to be evangelical. If a man is not an evangelical when he is drawn into embracing a revival, he will generally soon become one!

To those who are totally opposed to revival, or if not opposed, are simply prepared to dismiss it as a religious off-beat, I have nothing to say beyond Matthew 12:30-31: 'He who is not with me is against me, and he who does not gather with me scatters. And so I tell you, every sin and blasphemy will be forgiven men, but the blasphemy against the Spirit will not be forgiven.' This book did not set out to be an apology for revival or an explanation of it; I have tried to describe revival as it is, warts and all, and it can speak for itself. There were those who dismissed revival in the days of Hezekiah (2 Chron. 30:10) and the apostles (Acts 2:13; 17:32) and if God himself does not convince all men of the truth and urgency of his work, then I certainly cannot.

Cynicism

Others are not opposed but are *cynical*. The cynics in the world wonder if revival really does achieve all that is claimed for it, and the cynics in the church wonder if it is worth all the fuss. After all, they can confirm with some truth that revivals are often short-lived and the long-term results are not always easy to establish. Sometimes a church and community can be transformed in a few weeks, but within a few years the revival is all but forgotten. In addition some of the excesses or errors that accompany revival sow the seeds for disharmony or division for years to come.

This is an understandable response because it is partly true —

providing you pick and choose your examples. Elsewhere we have seen that some revivals have lasted for half a century or more, like those in the eighteenth century under Whitefield and Wesley. Others have brought with them benefits that are still enjoyed by Christians, often centuries later; for example, revival in the time of Wycliffe gave the people a taste for Scripture in their own language that has never been lost. Other revivals, like that in Wales in 1904-5, spread across the world giving new life to the mission-field far in excess of the sad story of revival soon lost in any particular Welsh town or village. The collective value of revivals in terms of godless lives changed for time and saved for eternity, godless communities 'cleaned up', missionaries sent out and God honoured in the worship of hundreds and even hundreds of thousands of new converts, cannot be disputed.

Some revivals have ended tragically because when the test came, men failed. Our response at the present time should be to lay the right foundations, so that when revival comes we will be better equipped to work with God rather than against him. We must not be blown about by every passing breeze of men's opinions. One value of reading the story of revivals is that we shall become aware of the dangers that threatened to wreck, and sometimes succeeded in wrecking, the work of God in the past.

However, we cannot always discover a reason why a particular revival came to an end, and it is quite wrong to assume that there must always be a reason other than the sovereign time-keeping of God.William Haslam admitted, 'As a fact, it is well known that revivals begin and continue for a time, and that they cease as mysteriously as they began.'[1] By March 1905 in Wales the press reported some decrease in attendance here and there; and by June, Christian leaders were seriously asking, 'Where now?' and how they should be caring for the new converts.[2] A gradual slowing down in any revival is inevitable and is no necessary criticism of revival itself. After all, the full force of Pentecost did not last for ever. By 1908 the awakening in Denmark had run its course but the leaders were quick to comment: 'We are not going backwards; a gracious congregational life prevails in so many parts of our beloved land.'[3]People now had a great hunger for the Word of God.

The brevity of some revivals is illustrated by the minutes of the Presbyterian Church Assembly in America during the 1830s. In 1832 the report glows with the benefits of revival; in one congregation alone 300 conversions were recorded. Everywhere the churches and societies were alive and growing. Controversy quenched the Spirit and by 1835 one sad paragraph bemoaning the lack of the Spirit contrasted to former times was the only reference to revival.[4]

Apart from human failure, there is a particular reason why revival rarely outlasts one generation: revival is not intended to be the normal life of the church. Preaching in 1929, Martyn Lloyd-Jones emphasized: 'There are not only the great experiences but also the ordinary, everyday experiences, and a church that is *always* praying for a continual revival is a church that has not understood her mission. The church is not meant always to be in a state of revival but is also to do ordinary, everyday work.'[5]

So revival is a 'great experience' and the church often needs it; as the Methodist Conference had expressed it a century earlier, it is 'essential to our existence'. Revival pulls the church out of its rut, awakens it from its sleep and sets inertia in motion. But if God did this always for his people they would never learn to fight battles in the desert. It would be the same as if God always kept his people from danger or illness; if no Christian ever lost his money, crashed his car, or broke his leg, we would become a careless and lazy people. Sometimes God does rescue us from harm, but not always; only in this way do we learn and grow. Revival is God's rescue of a church in danger, but when the rescue is over, we must learn to stand and fight in the 'ordinary, everyday experiences'. That explains why revivals are often short-lived. God expects every generation to seek him for themselves, and for this reason revivals rarely continue beyond one generation. Revival is God graciously giving his people all that they want for a while. He does this for his own glory and, like any good father, to show the children how much he loves them. But he cannot do it too often or for too long without weakening his people's strength for battle.

Doubt

There are Christians who are neither opposed nor cynical, but they are certainly *doubtful*. For some their doubt is whether we can expect God to bring revival; whether in fact the idea of revival belongs more to the Old Testament than the New, so that we should not be looking for such a thing today. The question is asked: 'Doesn't the New Testament expect Christian communities to go steadily forward and live consistently filled with the Spirit? Revival implies a period of spiritual coldness or backsliding from which we must be restored by the Holy Spirit. Is that a New Testament concept?' Our first answer must be to insist that an Old Testament experience of the church is there for our instruction and it remains relevant for the New Testament church unless it is specifically countermanded in the New or is seen to be no longer appropriate because of New Testament principles. The Acts of the Apostles covers only thirty years of the history of the early church and that may be too short a period to assess the work of the Spirit in the church over the next 1900 years.

On the other hand, the whole New Testament is the history of the church written small. Everything that would happen to the Christian church in later centuries is there in the New Testament.

The Acts of the Apostles opens with that great and unique flood of the Holy Spirit upon the church at Pentecost. That was not revival; it was bigger than revival. But from then on there were both the normal times of the church's life and the special occasions. When we read in Acts 4:31, 'After they prayed, the place where they were meeting was shaken. And they were all filled with the Holy Spirit and spoke the word of God boldly,' we are compelled to ask, 'If they were all filled with the Holy Spirit now, what were they like five minutes before?' Here was a fuller experience of the power and presence of God than the disciples had enjoyed earlier.

In the same way, Paul's command to be 'filled with the Spirit' (Eph. 5:18) implies an experience of receiving more and more of the evidence and power of the presence of God. Similarly Paul's cry for personal revival is found in Philippians 3:10: 'I want to know Christ and the power of his resurrection and the fellowship of sharing in his sufferings.' And this after walking the empire with the gospel and establishing churches all over!

As the New Testament story unfolds, churches get hold of wrong doctrines (Galatia), become careless and slovenly (Corinth), lose their fresh love for God (Ephesus) and slide into a sickly lukewarmness (Laodicea).

It is true that 'revival' and 'reformation' (and 'renewal' and 'restoration' for that matter!) are not, in the contemporary sense, New Testament words. But if reformation is the re-forming of an apostate church to the doctrine of the New Testament, then revival is the reviving of a sleeping church to the life of the New Testament. It cannot be wrong to pray for reformation and revival where they are needed. I can see no biblical reason why we may not confidently ask for and expect revival. Every generation of Christians believes itself to be living in a godless age, and most consider that things have rarely been so bad; in this we are no different today from our forefathers before any revival. In fact, unless we are aware of the badness of our age we are hardly likely to long for, or pray for, revival. Our values today, politically, economically, morally and religiously, are in collision with God's law. But so they were in the Middle Ages before Wycliffe, and in the eighteenth century before Whitefield, and in the nineteenth century before Spurgeon.

Our plea with God for revival cannot be based upon whether or not he wills it — that only God knows — but upon our desperate need; and we certainly stand for a good cause if that is our ground. Of course, it is hard to imagine modern man caught up in revival, and in some of our churches it is unthinkable that any 'glorious disorder' should take over from the set meal that has been served for years with faithful monotony; but the same has been true of many revivals in the past. Even when Hezekiah reopened the temple services he hardly expected the disorder of a double Feast of Unleavened Bread (2 Chron. 30:21). Whilst we may not know whether God will bring revival, we need never be in doubt whether we should ask him. The time is too urgent and the condition too serious to doubt.

I am also aware that some Christians are doubtful because of the changed times. Somehow the circumstances are very different today. Wycliffe brought the Bible to a religious people who needed no persuading that God was real; they simply needed the Scriptures to show them the kind of God he was. Wesley and Whitefield preached in a day when the public sermon was still respected, even by thousands who never went to hear one! Three godless young men were converted at Cambuslang in 1742 simply because after breakfast they decided to go and 'hear a sermon' before they continued their journey to enjoy themselves with the pleasures that Edinburgh had to offer. Today it would be a miracle in itself if three men on their way to the races spent time listening to a sermon!

During the 1860s when William Haslam was preaching in Lowestoft a man went from boat to boat to gather a congregation of fishermen to hear Haslam. By 1921 in the same fishing port it was not so easy, but even then many fishermen attended London Road Baptist Church during the herring season. Even Duncan Campbell admitted that when he preached in the Western Islands he preached to a people with an evangelical tradition and a history of revivals. In fact when Haslam preached in Scotland in the 1860s an Englishman preaching was a sufficient novelty to attract a crowd! From a human point of view it appeared that men only needed a loud voice to awaken them out of their sleep of death, but today our sleep is a drugged unconsciousness. Minds are captured by false philosophy, false religion and the comforts of this world. Every generation sees our nation slipping further away from the truth and more set in its opposition to the Word of God.

But all this is human reasoning. Our concern whether today's generation may be beyond the reach even of revival assumes that there is a limit to God's power — that there is a hardness of heart and confusion of mind into which even he cannot break. No Christian can allow himself to be sucked into this kind of thinking. Certainly the days are hard and the minds of men are far from God; certainly life is different today from that in any previous century. But there is one constant for the evangelical Christian, and that constant is God. When we abandon him we abandon hope. We dare not doubt God. If the days are harder, then all the more glory will belong to God when he brings revival.

Fear

The response of other Christians to the story of revival is to be *fearful*. They can see all the good reasons for praying for an outpouring of the Holy Spirit and may even join in a prayer meeting for revival, but their heart is not in it; secretly they may be hoping that no such thing will ever happen in their day! There are generally one or two reasons for this fear.

Revival is a time of deep searching by the Holy Spirit when sins of mind, attitude, or habit are found out by God. In revival we do not ask God to reveal our sin to us — he does! Even Christians who are not aware of sins now will become aware of terrible things in their lives when God searches them out. And that is scary! More than this, in revival Christians who are reading books and magazines, or watching programmes or films, that are slowly strangling their spiritual life will be forced to confess these things before God, if not before the church! The Christian cherishing a secret 'affair' or habit, or harbouring the gain of dishonest dealing, will be forced into the open. Bitterness, hatred and resentment will have to be dealt with. And so the list could go on. Revival is the work of the *Holy* Spirit; and holiness and revival are inseparable. When Evan Roberts prayed, 'Bend the Church and save the world,' this is what he meant. Only the Christian who is striving to be holy and whose conscience is touch-sensitive to sin need not fear revival.

Revival is also fearful to some simply because it is a time of unpredictable things. All of our churches and fellowships, whatever our label, have a programme; meetings are planned, activities arranged and speakers are booked for some way ahead. That is good. But revival makes changes! And some of us don't like change. There are Christians who live and worship with inglorious disorder all the time, and God will probably send them a revival of glorious order to teach them a lesson! But for most who fear revival it is the uncertainty that worries them. When Count Zinzendorf explained that, before the revival of 1727, '*We* had been the leaders and helpers,' but that afterwards, 'The Holy Spirit himself took full control of everything and everybody,'[6] he was not criticizing the way the leaders had gone about their work before revival. They had been 'shepherds, serving as overseers' (1 Peter 5:2), and they would be so again; but when revival came the leaders were aware of standing aside and watching God at work. God's Spirit will never work contrary to his own revealed Word, but there is such a rich diversity of his working revealed in Scripture that this gives him plenty of room to manœuvre! It is his sudden, unpredictable and overpowering work that seems to be a threat to some Christians.

Others are fearful because revival is often, though certainly not always, followed by a time of testing or persecution, as we have seen. This is an understandable fear of those living in times when revival seems so distant and even unreal. However, when revival comes there is such new life and certain confidence in God that Christians simply do not fear the future; after all, what can men do when God is on our side? Besides, the joy and privilege of revival far outweigh any suffering that may follow. For Christians who fear revival for this reason, their only refuge should be in the fact that

God's will for his people is always 'good, pleasing and perfect' (Rom. 12:2). We need never be afraid when God is in control.

Discouragement

Years ago a young Christian approached me after a series that had surveyed the stories of revivals. 'It's all very depressing', she suggested, 'because things just aren't like this today.' I understood her problem. Many Christians find the story of revival frankly *discouraging*. A time of revival is so different from the day of hard work for small returns; and the more we look at revival, the smaller our successes appear in comparison. You can work for a long time in the gathering darkness until you look up at a distant light, then suddenly everything around you is black. Revival is a distant light that may distract our attention just long enough to spoil our vision for working into the night.

But surely it is no bad thing to be reminded how much better we could work with a light on! The study of God's mighty works in the past is never meant to discourage us. We may find it disconcerting, but we should not be discouraged, least of all depressed. The church has a task to do *now*, and daydreaming about how God might intervene does not get it done. The story of revival should be an incentive to harder work, more earnest prayer and holier living. More rewards of 'Well done, good and faithful servant,' are earned in the normal days of the church's constant battle against sin and the devil than in the heady delights of revival. It is not hard to preach the gospel and witness to the neighbour when Christ is the topic of the community's conversation; but there is a particular courage needed when few are responding and the gospel is despised. To those who are discouraged, the story of revivals should prove a great incentive and encouragement to go on in hope: 'Like cold water to a weary soul is good news from a distant land' (Prov. 25:25).

Longing

The last response is the best: a *longing* for revival. Most Christians pray occasionally for revival; many will listen enthusiastically and talk excitedly of the great acts of God in revival; but there are some who will set themselves to get it from God, whatever the cost and however long it takes. What the church needs today is Christians, hundreds of thousands of them, who are longing for revival and are determined to have it. And these Christians will be identified by the way they prepare for revival.

The events of revival are what God expects to be present in the life of his church normally; but a revival is when these things are heightened and intensified to such a degree that they become something unusual and can only be described as supernormal. Or, to put it another way, God does not expect his church to be in continuous revival, but revival reveals those ingredients God expects always to be present. This is why it is a good thing to read and study what God's Word tells us about revival and also what God has done in revivals in the story of the church. In this way we begin to see something of what God expects us to be *now*. Whatever we find in a true revival we should be striving for now. By doing this we show God that we are serious about the business of wanting revival. There is no revival for those who do nothing and want nothing.

Of course, this is not the whole story, because there will be many caught up and swept into revival who beforehand could not care less about it. But we cannot expect revival if we do nothing, if we are careless and lazy. Whole churches can steadily slide into lukewarm apathy or proud disobedience; and this is very clear from the letters God sent to the churches in Asia Minor. The significant thing for us about these letters in Revelation is that God did not promise to revive them out of their disobedience or backsliding. On the contrary, he says to Ephesus, 'repent' (2:5), to Smyrna, 'be faithful' (2:10), to Pergamum, 'repent' (2:16), to Thyatira, 'hold on' (3:11) and to Laodicea, 'be earnest and repent' (3:19). Each time God places the answer in the hands of his people, whilst at the same time recognizing their helplessness without him. Always God places the responsibility upon us; he never encourages us to wait in lazy inactivity for him to take the initiative, even though it is in fact God who takes the initiative.

So we must go on doing those things that we know will please God; this is the way we prepare ourselves. We must work and witness *now*, however hard the way. We must sow in tears and in hope, and confidently expect that we shall 'reap with songs of joy'

(Ps. 126:5). And if we go on preparing ourselves, here and there we shall enjoy the outskirts of revival.

I must repeat what I said in the introduction: God expects his people to be doing constantly those things which he will take up in revival and use in a quite unexpected way; but we must never imagine that we can create a revival simply by imitating those elements that accompany it. And we dare not try to achieve by our plans and programmes what God alone, by his Holy Spirit, can do. Revival is God's sovereign work. It is his to give, but ours to long for, prepare for, pray for and perhaps to receive. He may wait, but we must work and worry God so that when he comes we are ready and he will not pass us by.

David Morgan, who was greatly used by God during the 1859 revival in Wales, felt he could see the approach of an outpouring of the Spirit and wrote in his diary during 1855: 'By reading the history of the Church we find that the great cause fluctuates up and down through the ages, but that, whenever the Lord drew near to save there was some considerable expectancy amongst the godly for His coming. As well as praying, we should be doing our utmost to revive the work. So did the godly of old: they prayed and they worked.'[7]

A year before the revival of 1859, a minister in Aberdare put forward suggestions for preparing for revival. These included 'a pure ministry — apostolic preaching...the awakening must start in the pulpit...the church must be in full sympathy...with the ministry...the particular use of the means of grace...earnest prayer'.[8]

In 1907 Dr A. C. Dixon was preaching at Charlotte Chapel in Edinburgh. The church was enjoying a time of revival under the leadership of its minister, Joseph Kemp, and had recently rebuilt to accommodate the rapidly increasing attendance. Dr Dixon warned the church of the danger of losing all that God had for them, but his warning is just as relevant for those who are praying for revival. Nothing will hinder the coming of the Spirit more easily than slack, indisciplined and ungodly living: 'Every Revival movement is a call for watchfulness, the present being no exception. If this work of grace is to be conserved, every member of the church must guard well his and her own behaviour. Do nothing that will grieve the Spirit of God. He is so sensitive, and may pass from us without our having received the full blessing He desires to give us. Let all evil be put away from us. Let our home life be consistent with our profession. Let us be on our guard in conversation. Utter no word of disparagement concerning any brother. Speak to God oftener about one another's faults, and there will be fewer faults to speak about. Do not neglect family and private prayer. Be in attendance at the church prayer meetings. Instantly obey the Spirit's promptings, and if He suggests to you to speak to souls about eternal matters, do it without questioning. He will give the grace and power.'[9]

When Martyn Lloyd-Jones had warned that 'The Church is not meant always to be in a state of revival but is also to do ordinary, everyday work,' he added a vitally significant sentence: 'But some remember this fact so well that they forget that the church is meant to have special occasions!' Some of us are so faithful in the 'ordinary, everyday work', and so faithfully good at it, that we have forgotten the 'special occasions'. It will not harm the church today to talk often and pray often about the 'special occasions' when God has visited his people; and we must be open to recognize where he has visited, and where he is visiting, even among those who do not stand in our church tradition. Revival is not God's mark of approval upon a church's detailed theology, or its method of government, or even its ecumenicity. Important as these things are, God wants lives that are clean.

Today we have two or three generations that know nothing of revival. We can never long and pray for that which we know nothing about. Rhys Jones looked back at the 1904 revival in Wales from the vantage-point of 1930, and he assessed its causes and results. Writing of its causes he came to this conclusion: 'If it be asked why the fire, when it came, fell on Wales? the answer may perhaps be found in much that was written at the time. Fire preferably falls where it is likely to catch and spread. Wales provided the necessary tinder...No fire can burn where fuel lacks. Let then the fuel be prepared. "Never let a generation grow up without that knowledge of Divine things which may contain the germ of national revival in years to come."'[10] 'No fire can burn where fuel lacks.' Is that part of the reason why we lack revival today? With all our excitement and activity, our programmes and our conferences, we have forgotten to read and talk about the 'special occasions'.

However, there is a vital conclusion that must never be forgotten. The description of revival in 2 Chronicles 29:36 was of something that 'God had brought about for his people'. With all our activity and preparing, with all our longing and praying, we dare not forget that revival is the sovereign work of an all-powerful God. The church cannot demand it, plan it, or control it; it is God's to give and to order.

Preaching in January 1860, Charles Haddon Spurgeon claimed that 'Divine omnipotence is the doctrine of a revival,' and he was right. Sixteen years later this great evangelical preacher of the Victorian age warned against the idea that the church could produce revival simply by putting in the correct ingredients. During a sermon preached in July 1876 Spurgeon made this point as plainly as anyone could: 'Christian men should never speak of "getting up a revival". Where are you going to get it up from? I do not know any place from which you can get it *up* except the place which it is better to have no connection with. We must bring revival down, if it is to be worth having. We must enquire of the Lord to do it for us. Too often the temptation is to enquire for an eminent revivalist, or ask whether a great preacher could be induced to come. Now, I do not object to inviting soul-winning preachers, or to any other plans of usefulness; but our main business is to enquire of the Lord, for after all, He alone can give the increase.'[11]

For this reason of 'divine omnipotence' we should never use the word 'revivalist' to describe a man. Spurgeon disliked it and so should every evangelical Christian. It carries too much the idea that somehow a man can make a revival; if we think that, we are beginning at the wrong end. As Spurgeon once commented, 'Instead, we ought to hold meetings for prayer.'

Nothing must be allowed to hinder our work in the 'ordinary times'. Our life of prayer, our striving for holiness, and our whole-hearted evangelism must all go on as if the future of the church of Christ depended upon them. At the same time we should long for our community to be 'saturated with God', we ought often to be talking of the great acts of God in revival and our prayers should continually remind God that we need a 'special occasion' for this generation.

When the prophet Micah looked around him he could find little to encourage him in the nation. An honest assessment convinced him that the forces of evil were gaining ground. In spite of this, or perhaps because of it, Micah set out his own position:

'As for me, I watch in hope for the Lord,
 I wait for God my Saviour;
 my God will hear me'

(Micah 7:7).

I was there

I was there

Rhos (North Wales) 1904

John Powell Parry was born in 1887 and was therefore seventeen years of age in 1904 when the revival came to Rhosllanerchrugog, a mining town three miles south of Wrexham in North Wales. The following account is taken from a recorded interview by Paul Cook of Hull with Powell Parry on 2 October 1974 in Plas Bennion, a small hamlet near Ruabon just south of Rhos. Powell Parry died on 27 June 1979 at the age of ninety-two.

In 1904 Rhosllanerchrugog was a Welsh-speaking mining town, with few English people living there. Almost every man worked down the pits and Powell Parry himself was working underground by the age of fourteen. Wages were poor and life was hard, the boys working a nine-and-a-half hours shift for three shillings (fifteen pence) a day; there was little social concern for the condition of the people and drink was a widespread social evil.

In spite of this, there was great respect for the Bible and ministers, so much so that the Bible was a subject of discussion even in the public houses. There were many preachers in the town who, though not well educated or men with degrees, nevertheless took their call to the ministry seriously; they stood firmly on the authority of Scripture, and 'modernism' was unknown among them. Churches and chapels were full and Sunday morning services were packed. The Christians were a serious people and whilst not expecting revival, they were concerned that the doctrine of the churches was pure. In the chapels two discerning elders would sit in the 'big pew', beneath the pulpit and facing the congregation, to discern any error in the preaching. Discipline and holy living were expected of the members and the town knew this; Christians were noticeably different and were generally respected.

The revival in Rhos started quite unexpectedly in the Welsh Baptist Chapel where Rhys Bevan Jones, from South Wales, had been invited to conduct a mission. The first knowledge that Powell Parry had about the revival came as he returned home early one morning at the close of the night shift. A young man told him that something wonderful was happening at Penuel Chapel, and as Powell came near to the church it was evident that something remarkable was going on: 'People were rejoicing, and it was bursting out of the walls and into the streets.'

Revival spread rapidly through the whole town until every church was affected. The Methodists, Congregationalists, Salvation Army, the Church of England and Baptists were all caught up in the great wave of revival so that 'denominationalism disappeared' and you could enter any church in the town and find crowds of people at prayer; there was a great harmony in the town.

This was a revival of praise and thanksgiving in which people learnt to enjoy God. There was a life and reality about everything that was done in the churches; people were involved with eternal issues and 'things' didn't seem to matter any more. In the Baptist Chapel R. B. Jones would sit at the front in the 'big pew' with his open Bible. He ensured that nothing took place contrary to Scripture, and preached every night from 8 to 18 November. Services ran without an order, but there was no confusion either; people would sing and pray and praise as the Spirit led them. Rhys Jones made sure that things never got out of hand, and in all the enthusiasm and joy, Powell noted that there was never any excess in the town. 'No one ever spoke of tongues or a second blessing; it was all peace and quiet and tranquillity.' It was very unlike some of the events that accompanied the revival that was going on in other parts of Wales at the same time, under Evan Roberts.

On Sundays the chapels were full by six in the morning. The pits worked an eleven day fortnight and every other Monday was an extra day off; this was known as the 'playing Monday'; in the revival the 'playing Monday' was given over entirely to worship.

Crowds could be heard simply walking along the streets singing and praising God, and when most of the Rhos silver band were converted they took to playing hymns in the open air. Mothers would be up at dawn, and when their husbands left for work they completed the housework early, saw the children off to school and then went to the chapel to worship. This was happening all over the town. Yet though the men spent hours in the chapels after a full day of work, no one appeared to be tired; 'there was life in the air' and people seemed to be physically as well as spiritually revived.

The effect of the revival on the unconverted was amazing. Hundreds were saved and it seemed as though the whole town was coming to church. People gave up drinking and smoking, and tobacco pouches and pipes were placed on the 'big pew' as a mark of the changed life. 'The terror of the Lord had fallen on the whole town', and within a few weeks many drunkards were afraid to come out of their homes or go into the public houses, which were being forced to close throughout 1905 because of a lack of customers. The famous football team, the Rhos Rangers, were afraid to go out and play; in fact, for a while the club closed because there were no spectators.

Fighting was a popular sport before the revival and William Price, a well-known fighter in the town, was converted. He had never been to chapel before, and after his conversion he was so full of joy that he reproached the Christians by asking, 'Why didn't you tell me, my friends, that it was like this?' Another fighter, Levi Jarvis, was the terror of the town. He was opposed to the work of God but at the same time was terrified of it. The terror had become terrified. He was afraid to go to work, and once there, was afraid to come home again in case he got converted. He could not sleep at night, and went off his food. Levi Jarvis knew that people were praying for him and this only made him more afraid; his wife feared that he would go out of his mind. One day R. B. Jones came to visit the home to reassure Levi's wife that they were praying. When

Jarvis learnt of this he swallowed his meal and fled to the mountains to get away from the revival. But God eventually saved him and the congregation watched the great fighter raise his hands in the air as a mark of his surrender to the Lord. Levi Jarvis the fighter became like a lamb. He was in his forties when he was saved and he had turned eighty when he died, but he never went back on his surrender to Christ. Powell knew him well and talked with him in his old age; Levi would often invite him with the words: 'Come on, let's talk about the revival.'

Life changed in the pits also, and men would meet for prayer before the day's work commenced. 'The Spirit was in the pits... It was as pleasant to go to work as it was to go to a place of worship.' There was no tension or disputes among the miners, and output was one hundred per cent. Everyone was talking about being saved, and men were even saved down the mines. Even those who were not saved were deeply affected.

Ponies were used to haul the coal trucks at that time, and two men were employed to look after them. There could be as many as ninety or more ponies in one pit, and it was long and hard work caring for the harness and feeding and grooming the ponies. After the revival came, a foreman found the man in charge of the ponies in a terrible state of mind, afraid that he would lose his job: the boys were each looking after his own pony and there was nothing for the man to do.

As the news of the revival spread, people travelled from all over Wales to see what was happening. Then they came from other parts of Britain and from the United States, Canada, Australia and elsewhere. Many of these visitors carried the revival away with them to distant parts of the world. Such was the presence of God that it could be felt by visitors as soon as they entered the town, and even beyond this. Powell Parry comments, 'The presence of God was everywhere.'

As an example of this awareness of the presence of God, he recalls the story of an event during the summer of 1905, when a Christian man arrived in Rhos with his two daughters from Barrow-in-Furness, in north-west Lancashire. He came to the 'big pew' in the Baptist Chapel and told his experience to the congregation, which included the teenage Powell Parry. This Lancastrian had read of the revival in his daily paper and one of his daughters had suggested they might go and visit the town to see for themselves what was happening. They caught the Sunday midnight slow train and arrived in Chester station at 6.00 a.m. Not knowing where to go from here, they enquired of a porter: 'How do we get to the place where the revival is?' They were told there would be a train at 8.00 a.m. to Wrexham and from there they could catch a local train to Rhos. 'But how will we know when we are near Wrexham?', they asked. 'Oh', replied the porter, 'You'll feel it in the train.' And they did! There was an unmistakable expectancy in the air. Two miles outside Rhos they enquired again and were told, 'Go down that road and you will feel it down there.' It was 9.00 a.m. on a 'playing Monday' when the visitor and his two daughters arrived at the chapel to find it already full of worshippers who had been there since 7.00 a.m.

There were no special meetings for young people; they all came to the adult meetings. Even children of six and eight years of age were talking about Jesus, even though they were not all converted, and teachers would weep as they overheard the children's conversations.

The effects of this revival continued right up until the Great War in 1914. Prayer meetings were changed and revitalized, and the 'experience meeting', where the Christians shared their testimony of God's goodness, proved a means of grace to many.

Powell Parry identified a number of factors that began to quench the work of the Spirit following the war. Modernism came into the pulpits as 'educated' men came from the colleges infected with a critical view of the Bible. A new generation, back from the war, wanted this 'modern preaching'. Powell said plainly of one such minister, 'He was a dud!' Modernism took the pulpit and emptied the chapels. At the same time social reform in the guise of 'practical Christianity', with its motto, 'Lift up the bottom dog, down with the idle rich,' took the spiritual life out of the churches. And, sadly, the Christians did not realize what was happening. In Powell's view, following the Second World War Welsh National-ism sealed the death of the revival.

But for those who experienced this great outpouring of the Spirit — and revivals do not often survive beyond one generation — there is a real sense in which revival is never lost. John Powell Parry could claim seventy years later, at the age of eighty-six: 'I still have it now.'

I was there

Lowestoft (Suffolk) 1921

The following account is drawn from an interview with pastor Robert Browne who, as a boy of fifteen years, was converted on the first evening of the revival in Lowestoft, Suffolk, in 1921. This remarkable work of God commenced in the London Road Baptist Church, where the pastor, H. P. E. Fergusson, had invited the Rev. Douglas Brown from Balham in London to conduct a week of mission meetings. Concerned at the lack of conversions, Mr Fergusson had called the church to prayer and for six months around sixty members met every Monday evening to pray only for revival. The effects of the revival spread throughout East Anglia and moved north to Great Yarmouth, where many of the Scottish fishermen carried the fire to their home fishing ports around Scotland. Douglas Brown had come into a new experience of God in February 1921 and on the last Sunday evening of that month ninety-six people came to faith in Christ in his London church. This account is limited to the experience of one boy in Lowestoft. The interview with Robert Browne took place on 22 March 1989 in Trowbridge.

*It is followed by additional comments from Henry Hannant, who
was born in 1901 and was a member of the church at the time of the
revival. This interview took place in Lowestoft on 30 March 1989.*

Robert Browne was born in 1905 and was brought up to attend the
Congregational Church at Oulton Broad where his parents were
members. At the age of fourteen he left the Congregational Church
and, though not a Christian, joined a Bible class at the London Road
Baptist Church in Lowestoft towards the end of 1920; there was a
good group of young people here and the church was well attended.
From October to Christmas, which was the fishing season, many
fishermen from Scotland joined the congregation because a fellow
Scot, H. P. Fergusson, was the minister. Services were typically
Baptist and the minister was decidedly evangelical. Prayer meetings were fairly well attended and some were obviously praying for
revival, though Robert Browne did not attend the prayer meeting
himself at this time.

He continues the story: 'The Sunday prior to the week's
mission, the Bible Class leader had urged the boys to attend the
meetings during the week to hear the Rev. Douglas Brown. My
friend, Alfred, and I went on the Tuesday evening. Nothing
happened on the Monday or the Tuesday. There were special prayer
meetings in the mornings and Bible readings in the afternoons; we
just went in the evening. At the end of the Wednesday evening
Douglas Brown had been preaching to a packed church and he
announced the closing hymn: "I hear thy welcome voice that calls
me Lord to thee..." with the chorus: "I am coming, Lord, to thee..."
I cannot recall what he had been preaching about, and there was
nothing emotional or sensational, but he gave an appeal for people
to come forward who were seeking Christ. Alfred and I went
forward and we were conscious that people were moving from all
over the large building. By the end of the hymn the aisles were full;
we were taken to the school-room, which was soon filled up.

'In describing the atmosphere of that meeting I can only speak
of a peculiar movement, something extraordinary. There was no
noise; it was very quiet and reverent. Both myself and Alfred were
counselled that night and I went home and told my parents. The next
day I attended the afternoon Bible reading which, because the
Baptist Church was too small for the crowds (though it could seat
700), was held at Christ Church where the Rev. John Hayes was

vicar. The meeting of the previous night had been "noised abroad" and hundreds were now attending. The Thursday evening meeting was back in the Baptist Church and I recall Mr Fergusson announcing, "There are so many people in the street outside wanting to get in, that I would like those of you who are Christians to leave your seats and go to the school-room to pray." He then walked up and down the aisles encouraging people to move to the school-room. Not untypically, we young people kept to our seats because we did not want to miss anything. That evening many more came to Christ.

'Douglas Brown was booked to return to London for the weekend, and many of the young people went to the station to see him off because they had become so enthused by what was happening. But before he left, Douglas Brown promised that, in the light of what had happened he would come back on Monday. He returned on Monday for another week of meetings, and this arrangement continued for four weeks. He admitted to having been unusually aided by God with both physical and mental strength, because he was preaching to his own congregation in London on Sunday and returning to Lowestoft for afternoon Bible readings and evening gospel meetings. The meetings moved to St John's parish church, which at that time was the largest building available in the town; it was well known to the fishermen for its tall spire that provided their landmark as they entered harbour. At this time all the evangelical churches were working together in the town, including two Anglican churches, the Baptist and the Sailors' Mission.

'Douglas Brown was in great demand all over East Anglia, and among the many services he preached at was one held in the parish church at Oulton. There hundreds knelt at the altar in a full commitment to Christ. Among those hundreds was myself, who, though only fifteen at the time, felt sure of my call to be a preacher. I was baptized soon afterwards, along with eighteen other young fellows, and one girl!

'Douglas Brown preached also for the evangelical vicar in Yarmouth, and here many of the fishermen were converted. Brown was a tall, handsome man with thick white hair. His strong personality came through when he was in the pulpit and his preaching was dramatic; some even accused him of over-much acting. The great burden of his message was the need for repentance and the greatness of the Saviour. Services were alive and there was a desire among the

Christians to bear witness. All over the town people would be asking each other, "Have you heard Douglas Brown?" I can recall being asked this question in Oulton by a friend of the family who was never converted and had little interest in spiritual things.

'Like so many revivals, this great work of God in Lowestoft did not last long. It seemed to fade out, but its influence certainly remained. There would be more than 150 at the Monday prayer meeting, and many young people joined it. I can hear now a young boy of ten years praying like an adult. Young people were winning friends to Christ and a number of them, after 1921, joined a village preaching plan. The church sent preachers to many villages around Lowestoft, and groups of young people would accompany them and give testimony; this was how many were introduced to preaching, including myself. The revival gave us a great desire to tell others the gospel. I worked in a factory at that time [1922]; it was a godless place, but I would read my Bible during the lunch breaks. After lunch on a Saturday, four or five of us would go to the Baptist church for prayer, then go to the home of one of the friends for tea and afterwards hold an open-air meeting. Every Saturday we would hold an open-air meeting somewhere in the town. We were all teenagers, fifteen and sixteen years old. We just said what we thought we would say; we had no rule or anything. I went so far as to go into a public house to preach the gospel! Of that little group, all went on in their faith. I went into the ministry and another, Francis Chaplin, spent thirty years as a missionary in Bolivia with the Bolivian Indian Mission.

'Almost seventy years after the events of that remarkable revival in Lowestoft, I can identify at least three marks of the revival: a coming together of spiritually-minded people, irrespective of their church labels; a renunciation of all that was offensive to God's law, and a sincere following of the Scriptures.'

Henry Hannant recalls that those who met in the school-room for prayer every Monday evening for the six months prior to the revival concerned themselves with nothing but prayer for revival. At these meetings there was a real atmosphere and a sense of the presence of the Lord. The effect of the Wednesday evening meeting was quite unexpected and when the sixty or seventy people walked down the two aisles in response to the invitation it was 'to the amazement of everyone'. He describes some of the meetings in the

Baptist Church when people sat on the window-sills and pulpit steps; and the same happened in St John's, where 800 people pushed into the large building.

The revival lasted only a month, but the results continued for years afterwards both in East Anglia and in Scotland. There are definite records of over 500 conversions, and the Baptist Church membership increased by thirty-eight in 1921, though, of course, others followed in later years as a result of their conversion during the revival. For a long time afterwards the church was alive and the prayer meetings doubled in attendance.

I was there

Lewis (Scotland) 1949

The following account is concerned with the revival in the Isle of Lewis between 1949 and 1952. Lewis is one of the Hebridean islands off the west coast of Scotland and it had experienced many revivals during the nineteenth century and earlier in the twentieth century. The record here is taken from the witness of those who were personally involved; their stories are recorded on a cassette issued by Ambassador Productions Ltd of Belfast, under the title Lewis — Land of Revival. *In 1949 Duncan Campbell visited the island to conduct a two-week evangelistic mission and in the event stayed for two years.*

In 1949 a new minister came to the parish of Barvis and decided to spend two nights a week in prayer. For three months he spent Tuesdays and Fridays in a barn with a few praying members. One evening they broke through in prayer and 'A power was let loose that shook the Hebrides.' Soon there was a hunger and a life in the congregation and 'a fantastic liveliness in the prayer meetings'. For the first two weeks of Duncan's mission no one was converted and then, on the last night, seven young people made a commitment to Christ. At the end of this service the benediction was pronounced and it was suggested that the congregation should go home; but when they went to the door of the church, a great crowd of people was gathering as if drawn by an unseen hand. Soon the church was packed, even the pulpit stairs were crowded and people were crying to God for mercy. The minister gave out the metrical Psalm 102: 'When Zion's bondage God turned back...', and one Christian present comments: 'We sang and we sang and we sang...You were aware of the Spirit of the Lord just there.' The minister eventually sent everyone home but announced that there would be another meeting in about an hour in the home of Mr McDougall. Crowds packed into this home and many were converted.

Throughout the revival Duncan Campbell preached with great power, demolishing the arguments of unbelievers as if he knew the condition of everyone present. Even those who resisted the Spirit were aware of the reality of it all. One young lady describes how she went to the meetings reluctantly; she recognized that the preacher and the singing were sincere, but at first she was not moved, even though 'The whole atmosphere was full of the presence of God.' Soon it became clear to her that the Christians had something she did not have, and she knew she would never be content until she found it. She began reading the Bible without anyone knowing, and often hid her Bible under a copy of *The People's Friend* so that people would think she was reading that instead. During one meeting Duncan Campbell stopped and said, 'You are sitting here with your Bible in one hand and *The People's Friend* in the other.' That shook her. The next night she went along with five friends and as they approached the church she announced to them: 'There are five of us here tonight and he will preach on the five foolish virgins.' She was not mocking and admits that she was secretly terrified that he would. That was Duncan's text that evening!

Duncan Campbell's method was to preach on sin, condemnation and hell during the services, but to reserve the way of salvation for the after-meetings attended only by those who were genuinely seeking the way of salvation. He did not preach the gospel to those who were uninterested until they were under conviction; then he showed them the loveliness of Christ and salvation. Coupled with this preaching was congregational singing of the unaccompanied metrical psalms in Gaelic which was 'very powerful'. One person involved in the revival comments: 'I have never heard, before or after, singing like I heard in the revival. The presence of God was often closer in the singing than at any other time. Many said the singing indicated the kind of meeting it would be.' Often people were converted during the singing. Everything became new and the things of the world did not seem to matter any more.

Whole families were transformed and sometimes would spend a full Saturday in prayer and praise. One man, who was only eleven years old at the time of the revival, recalls that his knowledge of Christianity was limited to what he had learnt at school; he had never been to Sunday School and only once to church. One morning he woke up to a quiet house as if someone was ill; he was told to be quiet because his father had been converted and wanted to read the Bible. He remembers his mother searching the shelves for the long-neglected Bible and unwrapping it from its old cloth. This was the first time the young boy had seen the Bible in his home. The whole home was changed and even the visitors to the house changed and Duncan Campbell himself stayed there. Listening to Campbell preaching, this young boy was aware of God searching him deeply: 'I managed to push it away, though many were saved around me. I was converted the following year.'

This revival cannot be explained in terms of mere emotionalism. A deep and lasting work was done in the lives of many, and in the same meeting that some were saved, others could go away challenged but resisting. Some never came to Christ although it was generally agreed they 'could never be the same again'.

The Spirit of God was moving through the island, often far away from the churches. Early in the revival one minister felt compelled to leave a meeting and go to a local dance-hall where many of the young people had gathered. He arrived just as there was a lull in the dancing and everyone was sitting down. When the minister, Mr McClelland, entered, the young man who was master of ceremonies was angry and ordered him out, demanding, 'Have you got a ticket to come in?' 'No', replied the minister, 'but I have a ticket to take me anywhere.' The MC was so angry he had to be restrained by his mother from hitting the minister! Instead he called for a dance, but no one moved. Mr McClelland invited the young girl who had just been singing to join him in a psalm, and they began to sing Psalm

139: 'Whither from thy Spirit shall I flee...?' Young people were in tears, and before the psalm was finished the MC was converted. He went to the minister, apologized and then rushed outside: 'It was just as if something hit me. I now know what it was, it was the power of God in that place. I went into the bus outside and wept my eyes out.'

The whole island was aware of God. 'It seemed as if the very air was electrified with the Spirit of God...There was an awesomeness of the presence of God,' so much so that many were terrified of being converted. Some refused to come to the meetings, but God met them in the fields; others sat near the door so that they could make a fast escape, but still they were converted. 'Revival can be a terrible thing,' comments one, 'to be face to face with God.' A young girl found herself in a home where all the talk was about those who had been converted: 'I got up and walked out because I was afraid I might get converted.'

One of the most wonderful things for many was the desire of the young people to attend church and read the Bible. Places of pleasure were closed because there were so few who wanted to attend. 'A whole generation was touched, many rejected and turned away, but they could never be the same again.' The revival affected every part of life and gave a new hunger for spiritual things. One man went home after a meeting but could not sleep: 'At 2.00 a.m. I asked God to take me as I am. Next morning everything was different; there seemed to be a change even in the rugged beauty of the village. All day I was longing for the meeting that evening.' Another comments: 'It didn't matter what you were doing, you were just longing for the prayer meeting.'

Those who witnessed the revival never had any doubt about its genuineness and the lasting value of its fruit. One claimed, 'The characteristic of revival that is not true of a campaign is that very few go back into the world.' In one church alone, three years later, most of the members were the fruit of the revival. Yet many found it impossible to describe what it was like to be in revival; it went beyond words. The power of the preaching and singing, the awesome presence of God, the packed congregations and prayer meetings, people crying for mercy or praising God for a new-found salvation — and all this to a degree unknown normally. One eye-witness comments: 'You cannot explain revival to those who have never experienced it. In revival God is completely in control, and the whole community is aware of that.' Another concluded: 'You were brought into touch with the powers of the world to come, and you will never be content with anything less.'

Duncan Campbell himself describes a prayer meeting in one village. There had been bitter opposition in the village, and although many attended the meetings from other areas, very few locals attended because of the opposition of the minister. A church leader suggested they should go to prayer, and thirty or so moved into the home of a friendly farmer. Prayer was hard, and about midnight Duncan Campbell turned to the local blacksmith, who had been silent so far, and said, 'I feel the time has come when you ought to pray.' The man prayed for about half an hour, 'because in revival time doesn't matter', and then drew his prayer to a close with a bold challenge: 'God, do you not know that your honour is at stake? You promised to pour floods on dry ground, and you are not doing it.' He paused for a while and then concluded: 'God, your honour is at stake, and I challenge you to keep your covenant engagements.' At that moment, Duncan Campbell recalls, 'That whole granite house shook like a leaf,' and whilst one elder thought of an earth tremor, Duncan was reminded of Acts 4:31: 'After they prayed, the place where they were meeting was shaken...'

Duncan Campbell pronounced the benediction and they went outside. It was about two o'clock in the morning and they found 'the whole village alive, ablaze with God'. Men and women were carrying chairs and asking if there was room in the church for them!

A few years later Duncan returned to that village and an elder pointed out to him a house, boarded up. 'That', the elder commented, 'was the drinking house and it has never been opened since the revival; last night fourteen men who frequented that building were praying in the church prayer meeting.' Duncan Campbell commented simply: 'Very remarkable things happen when God moves in revival.'

I was there

The Congo (Zaïre) 1953

The following report, compiled from a talk given at Hook Evangelical Church, Surbiton on 27 September 1989, concerns the experience of David Davies, who was a missionary with the World Evangelization Crusade in the Belgian Congo from 1937. David Davies was still in the Congo when revival came in 1953 and later he and his wife were under house arrest during the Simba rebellion in 1964. Returning from the field on their release, David and Anne now live in Swansea in South Wales.

'When God comes in revival power it is different from anything you can imagine. This is not a campaign, nor a mission; and it is not something whipped up either. Revival is when God comes down in his presence.

'I was the leading missionary in my station, and we had 130 churches in our area. They were busy churches with plenty of activity. We had many meetings, a medical work, and hundreds of children in the mission schools. But people were cooling off; they did not come to the prayer meeting and Bible study as they used to. Without a doubt salvation was there and people were converted, but something was missing. We were rather like Lazarus, out of the grave but with hands and feet wrapped around with a towel. One missionary put it simply: "We have a good shop window."

'Someone urged the missionaries to spend one whole day each month in prayer, and many took this up. As a result, a number of us became aware that we were not burning for God. Missionaries realized there were wrong relationships and they got right with each other; and then we got right with the national evangelists and pastors who asked to join us in prayer. But this was not revival.

'The revival actually began in the mission station at Lubutu, more than 500 miles from where I worked. It was the Saturday night Bible study and prayer meeting. For some time the study had been in the Acts of the Apostles and centred on the working of God in the early church. The missionaries were concerned that there was no freedom in prayer and the meeting was hard going. Then one pastor broke down and wept. This was a very unusual thing. He explained that he had a hardness of heart, and as he shared, so the conviction spread until there was sobbing, wailing, groaning and even shrieking, from all over the meeting. This was extreme to the missionaries present! Africans were on their faces crying and praying; the whole place seemed to be bedlam. I am reminded now that Charles Haddon Spurgeon once prayed, "Lord, send us a season of glorious disorder." That is exactly what the missionaries were faced with at Lubutu — "glorious disorder". The missionaries tried to quieten everything down, but they failed and the meeting went on until two o'clock in the morning.

'Letters began to arrive on other mission stations describing the happenings at Lubutu. My own brother heard about the revival and stood against it because it seemed to be excessive emotion. He had been praying for revival and told God that this was not what he wanted. Then, whilst he was in prayer, he saw a vision of warm blood being poured onto a large stone where it congealed. Shortly afterwards, at a meeting, he related this vision which seemed to speak of the revival fire being cooled on the stony heart of unbelief; at the same meeting an African lady recounted a dream she had had of sweeping away old ashes and it was at this point that the Spirit fell upon the meeting.

'Now it was my turn to doubt. I was receiving letters from my brother that troubled me because of the extreme language that he used to describe what was happening. But then, revival is always different because it is not organized by man. The revival had begun in Lubutu in January 1953; by May it had spread to my brother's station, 160 miles away, and by July it reached me at Wamba, a further 260 miles. And so it went on and on. The revival spread like a bush fire for hundreds of miles, and other missions were touched by it.

'My church had sent an evangelist down to Lubutu at the end of his training, and he was there when the revival came. On his first Sunday back with us he preached on Exodus 19:10-11: "And the Lord said to Moses, 'Go to the people and consecrate them today and tomorrow. Have them wash their clothes and be ready by the third day, because on that day the Lord will come down on Mount Sinai in the sight of all the people.'" It was a powerful message, but nothing happened so I gave out the last hymn and the benediction and then invited any who needed counsel to stay in their seat. As the congregation was leaving, a young teacher came and sat right at the front; he shook uncontrollably and was sobbing. A young cripple girl suddenly began screaming, "What shall I do? What shall I do? I'm going to hell!" People came running back into the church. The girl was known as a good Christian, but she was convicted of cheating a shopkeeper. The young man was guilty of jealousy, a little thing to many, but it terrified him.

'I was counselling those who were crying for help when an African ran in with the urgent message that my wife needed me at the house. I found the place full of people; the head man, a good Christian, was lying on the floor twisting and turning in agony, and crying over and over, "What shall I do? What shall I do?" After a while he confessed everything and declared with joy, "My heart is clean. I claim forgiveness through the death and blood of Jesus Christ my Lord." In a moment everyone present was claiming forgiveness with a radiant joy, and we all returned to the church for another meeting! The next day was a day for putting things right with one another. Suddenly God had come down and it was a visitation from heaven.

'At this time, God moved in powerful ways. I wrote a letter to an evangelist 200 miles away; all I intended to do was to tell him what was happening here at Wamba, but as soon as he read the letter he came under the power of God. He shared the letter with his church and the Spirit came upon them also. We were not in control; God was, and everything was in perfect order. I noticed that on the first day of the revival the leaders of the church were affected. On the second day it was the workmen who came under conviction; on the third day the women; on the fourth day the schoolboys, and on the fifth day the schoolgirls. We missionaries were like spectators, watching God at work.

'At this time it was a revival amongst God's people; very few unbelievers were saved for the first two or three months. God was cleansing the church first. Hearts were being searched, and this was one of the most cruel things. Some people had sins that had been hidden for years, and they had come to the conclusion that these sins did not matter. God was dealing with individuals painfully. A little boy was convicted of having stolen a razor blade before his conversion and he went to the godless shop-owner to make restitution: "Jesus has come into my heart," he offered as he passed over the cost of the blade, "and I'm on a different road now." The godless man was clearly frightened and urged the lad to continue on that road, "because it is the right one". On the other hand, a big, strapping evangelist was found wringing his hands, with tears dropping onto the floor. This man was a bright star in the mission; he had established churches and led many to Christ, but he had a great sin to confess and he could find no peace until he stood before the church and told it all. His words were like an electric shock and people dropped to the floor in repentance. By this time the whole town was talking about God.

'Sometimes conviction could be a terrible thing and those who resisted suffered most. An evangelist went into a coma for three days. Another woman went mad under conviction until she confessed her sin. This was the price for some of hiding sin and resisting God. We wondered at some of the strange things that happened during the revival, and only felt safe if we could find a scriptural parallel. Some Christians saw a strange light over the preachers, and we found such a light in the conversion of Saul of Tarsus. The terrible shaking and trembling experienced by some had parallels in the lives of Moses and David, and John who "fell as one dead" before the Saviour. Others seemed to be transfixed and could not open their hands; this too had a counterpart in the life of Jeroboam recorded in 1 Kings 13. The phenomena soon passed, but the lasting fruits of the revival were such things as holiness, tenderness, a love for the Bible and prayer and an exaltation of the person and work of Christ.

'The Christians all came to the meetings, which could go on for a long time. It was not unusual for a Bible Study to begin at 6.30 in the morning and still to be in progress at noon. People talked in whispers because they felt God near. One missionary wrote home, "We seem to be wrapped around by the presence of God." I have been in meetings where God was so real that you hardly dared to sit on a chair. I was reminded of Job 42:5: "My ears had heard of you, but now my eyes have seen you." The Word of God was powerful now, but this was not an altogether new thing amongst us. We had saturated our people in the Word of God for a long time and when the revival came the value of this was clearly seen. People who had left the schools years before could be working in a garden miles away from any Christian church, yet God came to them and brought verses to their memory.

'The reformation that resulted from this revival was wonderful. Many had stolen from the state, and the Christians and converts wanted to make restitution. So many things were being returned to the Belgian Office that an embarrassed official wrote to me, "Mr Davies, I've no time to handle all this. Tell them to come to your mission and fill a truck and you bring a load down." God is light and people could not live in fellowship with him if they were unholy.

'Hymns were written during the revival, some of them given directly by God. One workman, who had never composed anything before, was given four beautiful verses and the tune! And people prayed as never before. Simultaneous praying was a common thing in the revival, but it never seemed to be out of place or disorderly. The people also had a passion for evangelism. One Sunday it was announced in church that the following week the meeting would be held outside. And this went on every alternate Sunday for a long time. Even pagans wanted the Christians to go to their village to hold a service. People were saved by the hundreds and thousands as the church moved out.

'And did it last? I kept a diary for eighteen months, and at the end of that time the power of God was still there. Thirty years later the leaders of the churches are those who were blessed by the revival. But there is a new generation that needs its own revival because, "Another generation grew up, who knew neither the Lord nor what he had done for Israel" (Judges 2:10). But you cannot pray for revival to come to your church unless you are willing for it to come to you personally.'

I was there

East Java (Indonesia) 1972

The following report is taken from an interview at the home of Colin and Joan Waltham in Leigh-on-Sea, Essex, on 25 August 1989. It concerns their experience during the early 1970s whilst they were serving as missionaries at Madiun, the administrative capital of eastern Java in Indonesia.

Madiun lies at the riverhead on the floor of a large valley in eastern Java. Two mountain ranges, rising over 10,000 feet, tower over the hundreds of small villages where the people work a precarious living from the land. Desperately poor, they grow their sweet potatoes, cabbages and maize, and set their rice paddies as high up the hillside as possible. Fruit of all kinds is abundant and the woven bamboo huts of the villages are surrounded by coconut trees which form a main part of the local economy. Whether in the steaming jungles of the hillsides, or among the 125,000 people of Madiun, life is hard and luxuries are few. The 6,000,000 people in this 100-mile long valley live in fear and superstition.

Colin and Joan arrived in the administrative capital, which boasts a large sugar factory and little else, in time for Christmas 1970. Like most of

Indonesia, the population of Madiun is largely Moslem with a few Hindus, though traditional animism clings tightly to both. The Christian fellowship in the church where they served consisted of about sixty members, none of whom was more than seven years old in the faith and all of whom knew the meaning of suffering for the gospel. Many widows had struggled to bring up a family after their husbands had 'disappeared' in the aftermath of the attempted Communist *coup* in 1965; since then Moslem opposition to the Christians had only stiffened their resolve to be faithful to Christ. The church was firmly evangelical, simply taking God at his word, and keenly evangelistic, bringing the gospel regularly into surrounding villages.

Villages that could boast a market square were the focal point of life and commerce for the villages scattered around them. Village work formed the chief part of Colin's ministry, and although only five or six 'market villages' had a small group of Christians gathering regularly, the gospel was preached in thirty more. A table would be set up with tracts, Bibles and Christian books and, forbidden by law to preach directly, Colin, another missionary, and the young evangelists from Madiun would simply explain the books they had for sale! Opposition came from the people, the police, the Moslem leader, or the local chief, but often a crowd of fifty or 100 would give a noisy and sometimes abusive attention. Those interested would ask to be taught more; a few came to Christ, but not many.

Gradually Colin and Joan were identified with the people and accepted by them. The birth of their first child with the aid of a local midwife, together with Colin's insistence on ministering at the burial of a member of the church in spite of local opposition, all helped to endear them to the Christian fellowship. Their acceptance was increased even further when everything movable was stolen from their home whilst Colin was preaching on the text: 'Do not worry saying, "What shall we eat?" or, "What shall we drink?" or, "What shall we wear?" For the pagans run after all these things'!

The poverty of the area can be measured by the fact that in one village Colin was approached by the head man who remarked how wealthy the missionary was to own his own tooth-brush; in that place a communal brush hung on a piece of string in the centre of the village! The household rubbish tipped out from the home of Colin and Joan was searched through by their young girl helper;

when she had had her pickings the rickshaw drivers moved in and they were in turn followed by the beggars, until there was nothing left. In a very dry season when the crops failed people frequently starved.

By 1972 the church had outgrown their hired building and the people purchased a large roofless factory to rebuild. The sacrificial giving of these desperately poor people was remarkable. The Christians gave everything they had for their new building which would seat 300 people. If they had a spare shirt, or an extra chair, they sold it to buy bricks. A Chinese shopkeeper had been saving for ten years for a new shop, yet gave his savings to the church; a teacher gave all the money he had gathered to buy himself a motorcycle which would have saved him the eight-mile walk to school each day. When the bricks had been purchased, the members built with their own labour. They used to meet at five o'clock each morning to pray for more bricks, and when they had sufficient bricks they continued to pray for people to fill their new building. The people hurt themselves to build their meeting-place.

The Christians were not specifically praying for revival, but they so sincerely loved Christ that they lived in the light of his presence among them. With a simple faith that God always keeps his promise, they practised the presence of Christ and were 'at ease in Jesus'. During the summer of 1972 about thirty of the young people were gathered for a week of intensive Bible teaching. During a time of testimony and prayer they were suddenly broken, and with crying and confession many grievances and grudges were put right. It was the beginning of a new work of God among the people. The church building was ready by September and shortly after its opening the Spirit began to move among the whole congregation as he had among the young people. Evil attitudes and thoughts were confessed, cherished charms were thrown away, and Warcito, a blind lad, had his sight restored. Healing was not a significant part of this work but God moved in the lives of a few to restore them physically. Barriers seemed to fall away, and the church, normally a caring and loving people, though sensitive and easily offended, now experienced a depth of love and a reality of faith unknown before. Rivalry disappeared and all evangelized as one.

Over the next six months there was much evidence of the work of the Spirit spilling over into the community. A young girl stood up to give her testimony in a market village, an outrageous thing in a Moslem community, and yet some of the villagers professed faith in Christ. In the mountain village of Ngravyen someone left a copy of the tract *Four things God wants you to know*. Because it was the wet season Colin was unable to return until three months later, when he found forty believers waiting for him. An old man went to the village of Baturettno in the valley and led fifty to Christ. Startled by this, the church in Madiun sent Radjum, a mature evangelist, to verify the work in Baturettno. Even village chiefs began to ask for evangelists to come and preach to them. All down the valley people were aware of the work of God, and at least one witchdoctor was so impressed by the power of Christ that he began to use the sign of the cross in his efforts to heal and help people. Many were converted and when the churches in the valley required 2,000 members to register with the Indonesian government, they had no difficulty in mustering that number.

For two to three months there was incredible effectiveness in evangelism, but towards the middle of 1973 the work settled into a gradual and less spectacular growth. However, the lives of the Christians had become 'beautiful for Jesus' and they loved to worship and learn from Scripture; one blind lady regularly walked three miles to church, even though her Islamic neighbours often literally threw obstacles in her path to trip her up.

Colin and Joan found themselves in the middle of a work that was beyond their own power to control. 'It was like watching television,' they claim; God was working and they felt they had little to do with it. Sometimes Colin would go to a village to preach and nothing would happen, but when he came home he learned that the Spirit had been working in another village. God was not using the missionary to lead people to Christ, but the whole church was motivated to talk about the gospel. Colin found himself called upon to teach young believers everywhere. Rising at four in the morning and reaching home at midnight, he was trying to visit thirty-six villages in a month. Yet in spite of this programme, both Colin and Joan claim that in the revival, which they were too busy at the time to recognize as revival, 'We learnt to be lazy Christians; we learnt to wait and see what Jesus does before we do anything ourselves.' By the end of the revival there were groups of believers meeting in more than thirty villages.

There is something that can never be lost, even with the passing of time, from those who experience revival. Colin and Joan were given an awareness of what God can do, and a love for Christ, and from Christ, that they can never forget. God taught them lessons from the Indonesian Christians, who knew nothing of Western sophistication, but simply trusted that what God said he meant. There were no human methods, and numbers were not relevant. Colin is convinced that 'Since revival is totally in the sovereign plan of God, numbers don't count.' But for those who have lived through revival life can in some ways be very lonely afterwards. Very few, whether missionaries or ministers, can really understand what revival is, or how different Christian life and service are in revival times. In an age when our activity and methods count for so much, few can understand what it is like when God saturates his people.

List of revivals

The following are the main revivals referred to in this book. Note that the dates given are not necessarily the beginning, and are certainly not the end, of the revival. Often the Spirit was moving the people before this date; a specific date indicates the commencement of the main outpouring of the Spirit. The Christian church has seen very many more revivals in her history than those listed here.

Date	Location	Christian leader/ preacher
1150 onwards	Italy and Europe	Peter Waldo and Waldensians
1381 onwards	England and Scotland	Wycliffe's preachers
1500 onwards	England, Scotland, Wales, Czechoslovakia and Holland	Spread of Tyndale's New Testament and the Reformation. Jan Huss and Gerhard Groote.
21.6.1630	Scotland: the churchyard of Shotts in Lanarkshire	John Livingstone
13.8.1727	Germany: Herrnhut in Saxony	Ludwig von Zinzendorf
1730s-40s	America: New England Northampton etc.	Jonathan Edwards and others
1730 onwards	England, Wales, Scotland and America	George Whitefield, Howell Harris, Daniel Rowland, John Wesley and others
16.5.1742	Scotland: Kilsyth	James Robe and others
15.8.1742	Scotland: Cambuslang	George Whitefield and others

1742	Scotland: Baldernock	
1743	America: Susquehannah Indians	David Brainerd
1791	Wales: Bala	Thomas Charles
1794	England: Sheffield	John Moon and Alexander Mather
1798	America: Connecticut and Massachusetts	
1799	Cornwall: Penzance, Zennor, Walls, St Ives	
1800	America: Kentucky	
1805	Wales: Aberystwyth	
1812-44	America	Asahel Nettleton
1820-70	America	Charles Finney
1814	Cornwall: Redruth, Tuckingmill	
1817	Wales: Beddgelert	
1824-35	Scotland: Isle of Lewis	Andrew McLeod

1828	America: Savannah	Daniel Baker
1830s	England: Midlands	James Caughey
1832	America: Rhode Island	
1832	China	
23.7.1839	Scotland: Kilsyth	William Chalmers Burns
1839	Scotland: Dundee	William Chalmers Burns and Robert Murray M'Cheyne
1851-4	Cornwall: Baldhu	William Haslam
1858	America: Charleston	John Girardeau
1859-60	Wales	David Morgan and many others
	Scotland	Brownlow North and others
	Ireland	James McQuilkin and others
	England	Charles Spurgeon and others
1863-71	Norfolk: Buckenham	William Haslam
1880s	America	Dwight Moody
1903-4	Denmark	

1904-5	Wales	Rhys Bevan Jones, Evan Roberts and others
1904	South Africa: Fransch Hoek	
1905	India: Assam	
1905	Australia	
1905	Norway	Hans Hauge
1905	Edinburgh	Joseph Kemp
1906	India: Dohnavur	
1906	China	
1907	Korea: Pyongyang and then across the country	
1910	Malawi	
1921	Norfolk: Lowestoft and Great Yarmouth. Scotland: east coast fishing ports	Douglas Brown and Jock Troup
1930s onwards	East Africa, especially Uganda	
1931	Wales: Aberavon	Martyn Lloyd-Jones
1934-9	Scotland: Isle of Lewis	

1937-43	Ethiopia: Wallamo tribes	
1938	Borneo: Lun Bawang people	
1939-50	India: Madras	Bakht Singh
1949	Scotland: Isle of Lewis	Duncan Campbell
1953	Borneo	
1953	Congo (Zaïre)	
1960s-80s	China	
1960s-70s	Indonesia	Peterus Octavianus
1973	Borneo	

References

Introduction

1. Evans, *Howel Harris Evangelist*, p.34
2. Lacy, *Revivals in the Midst of the Years*, pp.112-14
3. Kemp, *Joseph W. Kemp*, pp.32-3
4. Orr, *The Flaming Tongue*, p.125
5. Woolsey, *Duncan Campbell*, pp.134-5
6. Baird, *Protestantism in Italy & the Waldenses*, p.274
7. Jones, *India Awake*, p.24
8. Davies, *The Moravian Revival of 1727*, p.7
9. Campbell, *The Lewis Awakening*, pp.14-15
10. Hayden, *Spurgeon on Revival*, p.59
11. Brown, *Revival Addresses*, p.77
12. Jones, *Rent Heavens*, p.55
13. As above, p.56
14. Orr, *The Eager Feet*, p.142
15. Wallis, *In the Day of Thy Power*, p.57
16. Blair & Hunt, *The Korean Pentecost*, pp.70-71
17. Paisley, *The Fifty Nine Revival*, p.38
18. Davies, *The Moravian Revival*, p.7
19. Lloyd-Jones, *Revival - Can we make it happen?*, p.63
20. Lees, *Drunk Before Dawn*, pp.182-3, 33

2. Before revival

1. Dallimore, *George Whitefield*, vol. 2, p.121
2. Evans, *When He is Come*, p.23
3. As above, p.24
4. Edwards, *A Narrative of Surprising Conversions*, p.9
5. Campbell, *The Lewis Awakening*, p.11
6. Jones, *India Awake*, p.2
7. Dallimore, *George Whitefield*, vol. 1, p.1148
8. As above, vol. 2, p.128
9. Paisley, *The Fifty Nine Revival*, p.77
10. Harris, *Extracts from the Welsh Press*, p.8
11. Evans, *When He is come*, p.90
12. Woolsey, *Duncan Campbell*, p.119
13. Ritchie, *Floods Upon the Dry Ground*, p.56
14. Orr, *The Eager Feet*, p.145
15. Told, *The Life of Silas Told*, p.67
16. Rajamani & Kinnear, *Monsoon Daybreak*, p.59
17. Harris, *Extracts From the Welsh Press*, p.2
18. Evans, *When He is Come*, p.31

19. Bonar, *Memoirs and Remains*, pp.151-7
20. Page, *David Brainerd*, pp.29-30
21. Edwards, *Select Works*, p.32
22. Evans, *Howel Harris*, pp.8-9
23. Lyall, *God Reigns in China*, p.33
24. Woolsey, *Duncan Campbell*, p.24
25. Brown, *Revival addresses*, p.8
26. Dallimore, *George Whitefield*, vol. 1, p.140; vol. 2, p.124
27. Evans, *When He is Come*, pp.69-70
28. Ritchie, *Floods Upon the Dry Ground*, p.107
29. Thornton, *God Sent Revival*, p.71
30. Brown, *Revival Addresses*, p.9
31. Evans, *Howel Harris*, p.65
32. Greenfield, *Power from on High*, p.26
33. Vulliamy, *John Wesley*, p.60
34. Page, *David Brainerd*, p.57
35. Harris, *Extracts from the Welsh Press*, p.27
36. Woolsey, *Duncan Campbell*, p.51
37. Brown, *Revival Addresses*, pp.80-83
38. Dallimore, *George Whitefield*, vol. 1, p.81
39. Goforth, *By My Spirit*, p.185
40. Edwards, *A Narrative of Surprising Conversions*, p.44
41. Moody Stuart, *Brownlow North*, pp.129, 213
42. Davies, *Fire on the Mountains*, p.245
43. Evans, *The Welsh Revival of 1904*, p.64
44. Brown, *Revival Addresses*, p.8
45. *Preaching and Revival*, p.45
46. Woolsey, *Duncan Campbell*, p.113
47. *Preaching and Revival*, p.93
48. Page, *David Brainerd*, p.58
49. Vulliamy, *John Wesley*, p.125
50. Dallimore, *George Whitefield*, vol. 1, pp.80-81
51. Evans, *When He is Come*, p.25
52. Evans, *The Welsh Revival of 1904*, p.57
53. Jones, *Rent Heavens*,
54. Greenfield, *Power from on High*, pp.29, 30
55. Hayden, *Spurgeon on Revival*, p.14
56. As above, p.41
57. Paisley, *The Fifty Nine Revival*, p.17
58. Greenfield, *Power From on High*, p.68
59. Evans, *When He is Come*, p.37
60. Evans, *When He is Come*, pp.36-8
61. Goforth, *By My Spirit*, p.29
62. Kemp, *Joseph W. Kemp*, p.32

63. Lees, *Drunk Before Dawn*, p.178
64. Jones, *India Awake*, p.64
65. Rajamani & Kinnear, *Monsoon Daybreak*, p.61
66. Ritchie, *Floods Upon the Dry Ground*, p.106
67. As above, p.14
68. Woolsey, *Duncan Campbell*, pp.113-14
69. See for example Orr, *The Eager Feet*, p.148
70. Jones, *Rent Heavens*, pp.31-2
71. Lyall, *God Reigns in China*, pp.160, 167
72. Thornton, *God Sent Revival*, p.60
73. Greenfield, *Power from on High*, p.68
74. Evans, *When He is Come*, p.38
75. *Narratives of Revivals of Religion*, p.12
76. Evans, *When He is Come*, pp.37-8
77. Orr, *The Eager Feet*, p.148
78. Thornton, *God Sent Revival*, pp.119-20
79. Kemp, *Joseph Kemp*, pp.29-30
80. Jones, *India Awake*, p.1
81. Orr, *The Flaming Tongue*, p.115 and article in *Evangelical Times*, Sept. 1986
82. Orr, *Evangelical Awakenings*, p.14
83. Blair & Hunt, *The Korean Pentecost*, p.75
84. Ritchie, *Floods Upon the Dry Ground*, p.54

3. During revival

1. Kemp, *Joseph W. Kemp*, p.32
2. Edwards, *A Narrative of Surprising Conversions*, pp.20-21
3. As above, p.21
4. Thornton, *God Sent Revival*, p.97
5. Bonar, *Memoirs and Remains*, p.503
6. Page, *David Brainerd*, p.85
7. Evans, *When He is Come*, p.71
8. *Narratives of Revivals of Religion - Kirk of Shotts*, pp.10ff
9. Davies, *Fire on the Mountains*, p.109
10. Paisley, *The Fifty Nine Revival*, pp.38-9
11. Edwards, *A Narrative of Surprising Conversions*, p.21
12. Jones, *India Awake*, p.18
13. Rajamani & Kinnear, *Monsoon Daybreak*, p.66
14. Bonar, *Memoirs and Remains*, p.503
15. Thornton, *God Sent Revival*, pp.68, 107
16. Woolsey, *Duncan Campbell*, p.127
17. Evans, *When He is Come*, p.15

18. As above, p.110
19. Jones, *Rent Heavens*, p.53
20. As above, p.55
21. Evans, *Howel Harris*, p.14
22. For example, *Whitefield's Journals* for 17, 20 February & 2 April 1739
23. *Whitefield's Journals*, pp.223, 274
24. Edwards, *A Narrative of Surprising Conversions*, p.14
25. Bonar, *Memoirs and Remains*, p.501
26. Rajamani & Kinnear, *Monsoon Daybreak*, p.68
27. Macaulay, *The Burning Bush in Carloway*, p.32
28. Lees, *Drunk Before Dawn*, pp.109, 198
29. Robe, *When the Wind Blows*, pp.157-61
30. Evans, *Howel Harris*, p.5
31. Davies, *The Moravian Revival*, p.6
32. Kemp, *Joseph W. Kemp*, p.30
33. Page, *David Brainerd*, p.105
34. Edwards, *A Narrative of Surprising Conversions*, p.14
35. Dallimore, *George Whitefield*, vol. 2, p.128
36. Greenfield, *Power from on High*, p.49
37. Edwards, *A Narrative of Surprising Conversions*, p.10
38. Evans, *The Welsh Revival of 1904*, p.166
39. Blair & Hunt, *The Korean Pentecost*, pp.72-3
40. Woolsey, *Duncan Campbell*, p.118
41. Orr, *Evangelical Awakenings in Eastern Asia*, p.35
42. Ritchie, *Floods upon the Dry Ground*, p.30
43. Lees, *Drunk Before Dawn*, p.189
44. Carvosso, *The Life of William Carvosso*, p.48
45. Thornton, *God Sent Revival*, pp.91-2
46. Page, *David Brainerd*, pp.80-82
47. *Preaching and Revival*, p.93
48. Dallimore, *George Whitefield*, vol. 2, p.123
49. Robe, *When the Wind Blows*, pp.108ff
50. Edwards, *A Narrative of Surprising Conversions*, p.25
51. Blair & Hunt, *The Korean Pentecost*, p.77
52. Lees, *Drunk Before Dawn*, p.194
53. Evans, *When He is Come*, p.109
54. Dallimore, *George Whitefield*, vol. 1 p.221
55. Bonar, *Memoirs and Remains*, p.498
56. Evans, *The Welsh Revival of 1904*, p.126
57. Ritchie, *Floods upon the Dry Ground*, p.54
58. Paisley, *The Fifty Nine Revival*, p.33
59. Blair & Hunt, *The Korean Pentecost*, p.15
60. Kemp, *Joseph W. Kemp*, p.34
61. Woolsey, *Duncan Campbell*, p.133

62. Lees, *Drunk Before Dawn*, p.63
63. Kemp, *Joseph W. Kemp*, pp.42-3
64. Bonar, *Memoirs and Remains*, p.116
65. Murray, *The First Forty Years*, p.220
66. Woolsey, *Duncan Campbell*, p.117
67. Lees, *Drunk Before Dawn*, p.194
68. Thornton, *God Sent Revival*, pp.67-8
69. Harris, *Extracts from the Welsh Press*
70. Kemp, *Joseph W. Kemp*, p.34
71. Bonar, *Memoirs and Remains*, pp.499, 500
72. Thornton, *God Sent Revival*, pp.67-8
73. Paisley, *The Fifty Nine Revival*, p.23
74. Evans, *When He is Come*, p.90
75. Dallimore, *George Whitefield*, vol. 2, p.128
76. Macaulay, *The Burning Bush in Carloway*, p.33
77. Jones, *Rent Heavens*, p.43
78. Evans, *When He is Come*, p.90
79. Davies, *The Moravian Revival*, p.7
80. Dallimore, *George Whitefield*, vol.2, p.128
81. Evans, *When He is Come*, p.55
82. Orr, *The Flaming Tongue*, p.111
83. Kemp, *Joseph W. Kemp*, p.32
84. Blair & Hunt, *Korean Pentecost*, p.71
85. Ritchie, *Floods Upon the Dry Ground*, pp.54, 106
86. Woolsey, *Duncan Campbell*, p.122
87. Campbell, *The Lewis Awakening*, p.24
88. As above, p.29
89. Lees, *Drunk Before Dawn*, p.191
90. Edwards, *A Narrative of Surprising Conversions*, p.14
91. Dallimore, *George Whitefield*, vol. 2, p.131
92. Evans, *When He is Come*, p.14
93. Bonar, *Memoirs and Remains*, p.94
94. Orr, *The Flaming Tongue*, p.134
95. Page, *David Brainerd*, p.106
96. Edwards, *A Narrative of Surprising Conversions*, p.14
97. Bonar, *Memoirs and Remains*, p.116
98. Paisley, *The Fifty Nine Revival*, p.23
99. Jones, *Rent Heavens*, pp.49-50
100. Kemp, *Joseph W. Kemp*, pp.29-30
101. Jones, *India Awake*, pp.21-2
102. Woolsey, *Duncan Campbell*, p.124
103. Ritchie, *Floods Upon the Dry Ground*, p.32
104. Lees, *Drunk Before Dawn*, p.193
105. Koch, *The Revival in Indonesia*, p.260

106. Rajamani & Kinnear, *Monsoon Daybreak*, p.69
107. For example, Jones, *Rent Heavens*, p.51
108. Evans, *The Welsh Revival of 1904*, p.59
109. As above, p.117
110. Paisley, *The Fifty Nine Revival*, pp.61-2
111. Ritchie, *Floods Upon the Dry Ground*, p.32
112. Rajamani & Kinnear, *Monsoon Daybreak*, p.68
113. Campbell, *The Lewis Awakening*, p.18
114. Paisley, *The Fifty Nine Revival*, p.184
115. Baird, *Protestantism in Italy*, p.272
116. Woolsey, *Duncan Campbell*, p.98
117. Page, *David Brainerd*, p.57
118. Evans, *The Welsh Revival of 1904*, p.70
119. Evans, *Howel Harris*, p.11
120. Bonar, *Memoirs and Remains*, p.503
121. *Narratives of Revivals of Religion, Kilsyth*, p.12
122. Jones, *Rent Heavens*, pp.82-3
123. Lees, *Drunk Before Dawn*, pp.148, 192
124. Jones, *India Awake*, p.18
125. Quoted by Orr, *Evangelical Awakenings in Eastern Asia*, p.35
126. Rajamani & Kinnear, *Monsoon Daybreak*, pp.102, 105-7
127. Kivengere, *Revolutionary Love*, p.41
128. Morod, *The Korean Revival*, pp.19-20
129. Sprague, *Lectures on Revival*, p.273
130. *Narratives of Revivals of Religion*, ch. 8, p.5
131. Bonar, *Memoirs and Remains*, p.500
132. Paisley, *The Fifty Nine Revival*, p.187
133. Morod, *The Korean Revival*, p.39
134. Davies, *Fire on the Mountains*, p.182
135. Lees, *Drunk Before Dawn*, p.154
136. Robe, *When the Wind Blows*, pp.44-5
137. Page, *David Brainerd*, p.81-2
138. Bonar, *Memoirs and Remains*, p.504
139. Evans, *When He is Come*, p.13
140. Paisley, *The Fifty Nine Revival*, p.68
141. Orr, *The Flaming Tongue*, p.18-19
142. Lees, *Drunk Before Dawn*, pp.195-6
143. Greenfield, *Power From on High*, p.31
144. Edwards, *A Narrative of Surprising Conversions*, p.151
145. Dallimore, *George Whitefield*, vol. 2, p.118
146. *Narratives of Revivals of Religion*, p.2
147. Evans, *When He is Come*, p.15
148. As above, p.104
149. Jones, *India awake*, p.34

150. Kemp, *Joseph W. Kemp*, p.31
151. Paisley, *The Fifty Nine Revival*, pp.60, 68, 92-3
152. Edwards, *A Narrative of Surprising Conversions*, p.10
153. Dallimore, *George Whitefield*, vol. 2, pp.180-81
154. Thornton, *God Sent Revival*, p.87
155. Evans, *When He is Come*, pp.38-9
156. Orr, *The Flaming Tongue*, pp.54, 119
157. Lees, *Drunk Before Dawn*, pp.185-9
158. Lyall, *God Reigns in China*, pp.170-71, 184
159. Jones, *India Awake*, p.159
160. Evans, *When He is Come*, p.104
161. Jones, *Rent Heavens*, p.42
162. Rajamani & Kinnear, *Monsoon Daybreak*, p.120

4. After revival

1. Edwards, *A Narrative of Surprising Conversions*, p.19
2. Lacy, *Revivals in the Midst of the Years*, p.42
3. Dallimore, *George Whitefield*, vol. 1, pp.295-6
4. As above, vol. 2, pp.122, 127
5. *Preaching and Revival*, p.90
6. Evans, *When He is Come*, p.97
7. Harris, *Extracts from the Welsh Press*, p.14
8. Paisley, *The Fifty Nine Revival*, p.137
9. Davies, *Fire on the Mountains*, p.109
10. Orr, *Evangelical Awakenings*, p.29
11. Lyall, *God Reigns in China*, pp.166-7, 169, 178, 179
12. *Preaching and Revival*, pp.95-7
13. As above, p.97
14. As above, p.99
15. Orr, *The Eager Feet*, pp.144-5
16. Ritchie, *Floods Upon the Dry Ground*, p.56
17. Lees, *Drunk Before Dawn*, p.182
18. Jones, *India Awake*, p.33
19. Kemp, *Joseph W. Kemp*, pp.31, 30
20. Jones, *The King's Champions*, p.60
21. Bonar, *Memoirs and Remains*, p.499
22. Evans, *When He is Come*, pp.97-9
23. As above, pp.98-9
24. Paisley, *The Fifty Nine Revival*, p.47
25. Page, *David Brainerd*, p.100
26. Robe, *When the Wind Blows*, p.175
27. Orr, *The Flaming Tongue*, p.17

28. Hayden, *Spurgeon on Revival*, p.40
29. Bonar, *Memoirs and Remains*, p.500
30. Edwards, *A Narrative of Surprising Conversions*, p.148
31. Dallimore, *George Whitefield*, vol. 2, p.136
32. Orr, *The Eager Feet*, p.63
33. Jones, *Rent Heavens*, p.62
34. Orr, *The Eager Feet*, p.145
35. Evans, *When He is Come*, p.101
36. Orr, *The Flaming Tongue*, p.17
37. Jones, *Rent Heavens*, p.64
38. *Wrexham & North Wales Guardian*, 10 March 1905
39. As above
40. Lees, *Drunk Before Dawn*, pp.63-4, 190-93
41. Kivengere, *Revolutionary Love*, p.13
42. Morod, *The Korean Revival*, p.19
43. *The North Wales Guardian*, 20 January 1905
44. Jones, *India Awake*, p.31
45. Kivengere, *Revolutionary Love*, pp.42-3
46. Jones, *Rent Heavens*, p.60
47. Rajamani & Kinnear, *Monsoon Daybreak*, p.76
48. Ritchie, *Floods Upon the Dry Ground*, p.58
49. Woolsey, *Duncan Campbell*, pp.142-3
50. Dallimore, *George Whitefield*, vol. 2, pp.131-132
51. Rajamani & Kinnear, *Monsoon Daybreak*, p.115
52. Orr, *The Eager Feet*, p.148
53. Jones, *Rent Heavens*, p.61
54. Edwards, *A Narrative of Surprising Conversions*, p.14
55. Kivengere, *Revolutionary Love*, p.55
56. Paisley, *The Fifty Nine Revival*, p.64
57. Evans, *When He is Come*, p.75
58. Evans, *Howell Harris*, p.13
59. Jones, *Rent Heavens*, p.66
60. Lees, *Drunk Before Dawn*, p.197
61. Robe, *When the Wind Blows*, p.138
62. Sprague, *Lectures on Revivals*, p.221
63. Dallimore, *George Whitefield*, vol. 1, p.322
64. Robe, *When the Wind Blows*, p.111
65. Lacy, *Revivals in the Midst of the Years*, pp.74-5
66. Thornton, *God Sent Revival*, p.60
67. Paisley, *The Fifty Nine Revival*, p.165
68. Bonar, *Memoirs and Remains*, p.501
69. Woolsey, *Duncan Campbell*, pp.108-9
70. *Wrexham Advertiser*, 20 August 1859
71. Kemp, *Joseph W. Kemp*, pp.30-31

72. As above, p.34
73. Haslam, *From Death Into Life*, p.142
74. *North Wales Guardian*, 27 January 1905
75. Haslam, *From Death Into Life*, pp.68-9
76. Orr, *The Eager Feet*, p.54
77. Haslam, *Yet Not I*, p.163
78. Morod, *The Korean Revival*, p.36
79. Lees, *Drunk Before Dawn*, p.183
80. Morod, *The Korean Revival*, p.39
81. Rajamani & Kinnear, *Monsoon Daybreak*, pp.69-70
82. Culpepper, *The Shantung Revival*, p.64
83. Morod, *The Korean Revival*, p.20
84. Lees, *Drunk Before Dawn*, p.196
85. Koch, *The Revival in Indonesia*, p.265
86. Evans, *When He is Come*, p.15
87. Jones, *India Awake*, p.22
88. As above, p.33
89. Ritchie, *Floods Upon the Dry Ground*, pp.57-60
90. Haslam, *From Death Into Life*, pp.88ff
91. Jones, *Rent Heavens*, p.40
92. Woolsey, *Duncan Campbell*, pp.108-9
93. Page, *David Brainerd*, pp.80-81, 87
94. Bonar, *Memoirs and Remains*, p.500
95. Evans, *The Welsh Revival of 1904*, pp.131-8
96. Rajamani & Kinnear, *Monsoon Daybreak*, pp.76-7
97. Ritchie, *Floods Upon the Dry Ground*, p.58
98. Dallimore, *George Whitefield*, vol. 1, p.219
99. As above, vol. 1, pp.226-7
100. As above, vol. 2, pp.131-2
101. Robe, *When the Wind Blows*, pp.137-8
102. Evans, *Howell Harris, Evangelist*, p.57
103. Kivengere, *Revolutionary Love*, p.10
104. Evans, *Howell Harris*, p.44
105. Edwards, *A Narrative of Surprising Conversions*, p.15
106. Wallis, *In the Day of Thy Power*, p.26
107. See evidence in Lacy, *Revivals in the Midst of the Years*, pp.115-45
108. Davies, *Fire on the Mountains*, p.115

5. Our response to revival

1. Haslam, *From Death Into Life*, p.71
2. See Harris, *Extracts from the Welsh Press*
3. Orr, *The Flaming Tongue*, p.55

4. Lacy, *Revival in the Midst of the Years*, pp.102-4
5. Murray, *The First Forty Years*, p.204
6. Davies, *The Moravian Revival*, p.7
7. Evans, *When He is Come*, p.25
8. As above, p.31
9. Kemp, *Joseph W. Kemp*, p.61
10. Jones, *Rent Heavens*, pp.87-8
11. Spurgeon, *Sermons on Revival*, p.39

Book list

Book list
This list contains only the titles referred to in the references and does not
represent the full range of books on the subject.

Baird & Collins, *Protestantism in Italy & the Waldenses,* 1847

Blair & Hunt, *The Korean Pentecost,* Banner of Truth, 1977

Bonar, *Memoirs & Remains of R. M. M'Cheyne,* Middleton, 1854

Brown, *Revival Addresses,* Morgan and Scott, 1922

Campbell, *The Lewis Awakening 1949-53,* Faith Mission, 1954

Carvosso, *The Life of William Carvosso,* Jennings & Pye, 2nd ed., 1835

Culpepper, *The Shantung Revival,* Southern Baptist Home Mission Board,
1971

Davies, *Fire on the Mountains,* Zondervan, 1966

Davies, *The Moravian Revival of 1727,* Evangelical Library, 1977

Dallimore, *George Whitefield,* 2 vols, Banner of Truth, 1970

Diesen, *The Free Church Movement,* Norway, 1957

Edwards, *A Narrative of Surprising Conversions,* Banner of Truth, 1965

Edwards, *Select Works of Jonathan Edwards,* Banner of Truth

Evans, *Howel Harris Evangelist,* University of Wales Press, 1974

Evans, *The Welsh Revival of 1904,* Evangelical Press, 1969

Evans, *When He is Come,* SMW, 1959

Gillies, *Historical Collections of Accounts of Revival,* Banner of Truth,
1981 (first pub. 1754)

Glasgow Revival Tract Society, *Narratives of Revivals of Religion,*
William Collins, 1839

Goforth, *By My Spirit,* Marshall, Morgan and Scott, 1929

Greenfield, *Power from on High,* World Wide Revival Prayer Movement,
1950

Harris, *Extracts from the Welsh Press,* published privately

Haslam, *From Death Into Life,* Morgan & Scott

Haslam, *Yet Not I,* Morgan & Scott

Hayden, *Spurgeon on Revival,* Zondervan, 1962

Houghton, *Amy Carmichael of Dohnavur,* 1955

Jones, *India Awake! Thy King has Come,* Sylhet, 1905

Jones, *Rent Heavens,* Pioneer Mission, 1931

Jones B. P., *The King's Champions,* 1968

Kemp, Winnie, *Joseph W. Kemp,* Marshall, Morgan & Scott, 1936

Kivengere, *Revolutionary Love,* CLC & Kingsway, 1985

Koch, *The Revival in Indonesia,* Evangelization Publishers, 1970

Lacy, *Revivals in the Midst of the Years,* John Knox Press, 1943

Lees, *Drunk Before Dawn,* OMF, 1979

Lloyd-Jones, *Revival — Can We Make it Happen?,* Marshall Pickering,
1986

Lyall, *God Reigns in China,* Hodder & Stoughton, 1985

Macaulay, *The Burning Bush in Carloway,* Carloway Free Church, Lewis

Morod, *The Korean Revival,* Hodder & Stoughton, 1969

Murray, *Jonathan Edwards,* Banner of Truth, 1987

Murray, *The First Forty Years,* Banner of Truth, 1982

Moody-Stuart, *Brownlow North,* Banner of Truth, 1961

Monod, *The Korean Revival,* Hodder & Stoughton, 1969

Orr, *Evangelical Awakenings in Eastern Asia,* Bethany Fell Inc., 1975

Orr, *The Eager Feet,* Moody Press, 1975

Orr, *The Flaming Tongue,* Moody Press, 1973

Orr, *The Second Evangelical Awakening,* Marshall, Morgan & Scott, 1949

Page, *David Brainerd,* Partridge & Co (modern - Edwards, *The life of David Brainerd,* Baker, 1978)

Paisley, *The 'Fifty Nine' Revival,* Martyrs' Memorial Free Presbyterian Church, 1958

Rajamani & Kinnear, *Monsoon Daybreak,* Open Books, 1971

Ritchie, *Floods Upon the Dry Ground,* 1980(?)

Robe, *When the Wind Blows,* Amassador Productions Ltd, 1985

Sprague, *Lectures on Revivals of Religion,* Banner of Truth, 1959 (first pub. 1832)

Spurgeon, *Sermons on Revival,* Kelvedon ed.

Thornbury, *God Sent Revival,* Evangelical Press, 1977

Told, *The Life of Silas Told,* Epworth, 1954

Vulliamy, *John Wesley,* Geoffrey Bles, 1931

Wallis, *In the Day of Thy Power,* CLC, 1956

Westminster Conference, *Preaching & Revival,* 1984

Whitefield, *Whitefield's Journals,* Banner of Truth, 1960

Woolsey, *Duncan Campbell,* Hodder & Stoughton, 1974

Index